C000235897

HARROW

PORTRAIT OF AN ENGLISH SCHOOL

HARROW

PORTRAIT OF AN ENGLISH SCHOOL

THIRD MILLENNIUM
PUBLISHING, LONDON

Copyright © 2004 Harrow School and
Third Millennium Publishing Limited

First published in 2004
by Third Millennium Publishing Limited,
an imprint of Third Millennium Information Limited

Farringdon House
105-107 Farringdon Road
London EC1R 3BU
United Kingdom
www.tmiltd.com

ISBN 1 903942 29 2

Edited by Robert Dudley
Copy-edited by Rosy Hayward of Honeychurch Associates
Designed by Helen Swansbourne
Printed and bound in Slovenia by Mladinska

Illustrations
FRONT COVER: Benjamin Busk against background of a panel
    in the Fourth Form Room
FRONTISPIECE: Dawn on the Hill, by Patrick Kaye
RIGHT: Vaughan Library
OVERLEAF: Late for school, by Patrick Lichfield

Contents

According to Harrow usage, superscript numbers following dates after authors indicate the term in which the author joined the school.

Foreword

ROBERT DUDLEY

WHEN I EMBARKED ON THE DAUNTING TASK of compiling a book intended as a portrait of Harrow over approximately the last 100 years, I had no idea what the outcome would be. I was anxious for pieces which would reflect the wide diversity of careers pursued by Old Harrovians – the outstanding achievements of many in sport, art, politics, the services, commerce and academia as well as the Church, the Turf and almost any field of human endeavour you care to mention! But I also wanted to give an authentic flavour of the life of the School, both as it was – in fact and in the memory of OHs – and as it is.

I knew there were many distinguished OHs. I did not know whether they would be willing to contribute to the book nor, if they were, whether their contributions would be thoughtful and serious or merely perfunctory. I was well aware that Harrow Beaks can write, but, again, I knew how busy they are and wondered how they would view being inveigled into such a project.

I should not have worried. I have been overwhelmed by the support and enthusiasm of OHs and of the Head Master and Harrow staff alike. We had a huge response to our request for pieces and in addition I approached a number of people whom I suspected might prefer to hide their light under a bushel and asked them to write. In the end we had much more material than we could use and I would like both to thank, and to apologise to those people, particularly those from whom I actually requested pieces, but for whose contributions we were simply unable to find enough space.

This is an illustrated book and many of the pictures in it have been provided either by the generosity of individual OHs or by Rita Gibbs at the Harrow Archive. The publishers and I are extremely grateful to both. The School and its buildings are visually of great interest, as is the School's day-to-day life in sport, learning and creative work. Again, my hope is that the book does justice to this.

In the end you will decide whether the Harrow which emerges from these pages is one that you recognise or not. I hope very much that it is. If it is not, I have no doubt you will let me know! If it is, a large measure of credit should go to Dale Vargas, Director of the Harrow Association, without whose unique knowledge of Harrow and Harrovians I would still be sitting scratching my head and trying to work out where to start.

It has been a huge privilege and pleasure for me to work on the book. I hope you enjoy reading it as much as I have enjoyed editing it.

LEFT: *The Old Schools*

Acknowledgements

In the course of compiling the book I received assistance from countless sources and I am extremely grateful to them all, but I owe the following special thanks for contributions of one kind or another:

Gen Sir John Akehurst, Ian Angus, Andrew Barrow, Peter Beckwith, Ian Beer, Sam Bellringer, Suzanne Benson, Jason Braham, Doug Collins, Liz Collinson, Nico Craven, Robin Fior, Duncan Fitzwilliams, Rita Gibbs, Stephen Green, Giles Havergal, The Head Master, Prof J. Hedley-Whyte, Alan Jaggs, Margaret Knight and all in the Vaughan Library, Hugh Lee, Martin Amherst Lock, Joanna Lumley, Ed Lyon, The Rt Rev Michael Mann, Simon Sebag-Montefiore, Tom Noad, Sir John Page, Angie Peppiatt, Barney Powell, Robert Powell, Kirsty Race, Jasper Rees, Hugh Saxton, David and Dorothy Stogdon, The Rev David Streeter, Martin Tyrrell, Dale Vargas, Sandy Wilson and Tim Wilson-Smith.

C.r Knight delin et Sculp.

A View of the Shooting for the Silver Arrow, at Harrow the Hill.

Names of the Archers, for 1769.	Num.r of Shoots.							Names of the Archers.	Num.r of Shoots.						
M.r Whitmore								M.r Leigh							
M.r Lemon								M.r Tunstal							
M.r Maclean								M.r Jones							
M.r Tighe								M.r Merry							
M.r Watkins								M.r Yatman							
M.r Poyntz								M.r Franks							

Printed for W.m Todd, in Adam & Eve Court, facing Poland Street Oxford Road & H. Webley Book-seller in Holbourn. also to be had at M.r Gardners Shop Harrow. Price 6.d plain

Present and past: twentieth-century reflections

CHRISTOPHER TYERMAN

I N 1907, THE OTHERWISE SOMEWHAT MALADROIT Head Master Joseph Wood (HM 1898–1910) neatly identified the source of much of the emotion inspired by Harrow School. Describing the Chapel on the fiftieth anniversary of its consecration, Wood remarked that 'every stone is eloquent with the memories of a personal past'. 'The Chapel,' he continued, 'is not a monument; it is a biography'. The same could be said of the School and the Hill in general. There Harrovians and Old Harrovians were young; servants lived and worked; Masters taught, socialised and reared their families. Inevitably, in an institution embracing a social as well as academic community, enclosed by geography, nature, precept and convenience, many have felt cherished, others rejected, some indifferent, their retrospective feelings consequently covering the range of emotions from fierce affection through loyalty to amusement, boredom, horror and disgust. Such sentiments depend not just on lived experience, but also on the potency of a particular form of memory, Byron's *Childish Recollections*. In common with all secondary schools, Harrow is special for its pupils primarily, as Wood suggested, because there they spent much of their adolescence. Short of trauma and war, few periods of life produce such vividness of recall. Schools such as Harrow exert a stronger pull because they act as homes and surrogate families, especially for the generations between the coming of the railways in the 1830s that set formal bounds, and the advent of the mobile phone. Terms were long, exeats short and rare, and physical horizons as restricted as they were visually enormous. Part of the function of a boarding school at least from the seventeenth century onwards was to create such a total society, complete in itself and its function.

The relation of Harrow's past and present operates as a dialogue between actual experience, wishful expectation or regret, and memory, mediated by the realities and myths of the institution itself. For the individual, only

later does the significance of schooldays come to be organised and gilded. The process was diagnosed by Arnold Lunn defending his novel, *The Harrovians* (1913), based on his school diaries: 'the trouble was that I had kept a careful record of the cynicism of Harrow youth rather than the sentiment of Old Harrovians'. For the institution, the past is similarly imagined in light of the present. Tradition can be of recent coinage or excoriated as irrelevant or harmful. It also defines and reassures, frequently through familiar ceremony – Songs, Speech Room, Chapel, even mealtimes (e.g. the food fight that follows clear rules of engagement). The force of memory and the power of the past are neither neutral nor

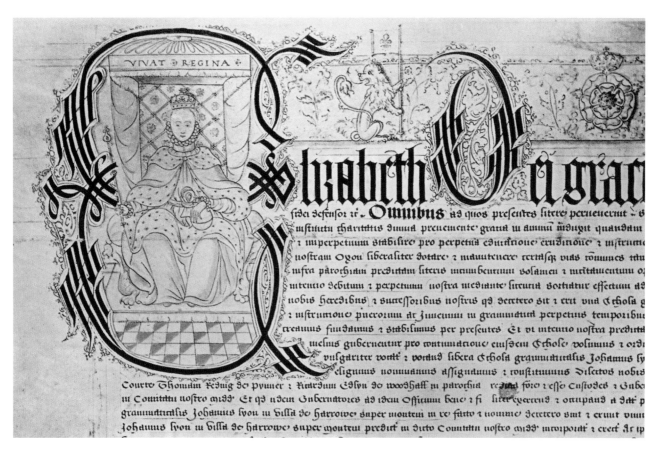

LEFT: *John Lyon's Charter from Queen Elizabeth I*

unimportant. A few years ago an obviously OH father was eagerly if loudly teaching a somewhat dubious and less than hearty Harrovian son how to kick a Harrow football ('It's the most marvellous fun and VERY important') on otherwise deserted, windswept fields one winter's afternoon. Memory had become expectation for both, moulding their shared experience, one past, the other future, both present.

It is easy to mock the sentimentality of OHs, yet without it the School would never have acquired the estate around the Hill in the thirty years before the First World War, nor have been able to rebuild itself in the thirty years from its Quatercentenary. There is more to the past at Harrow than wearing nineteenth-century evening dress on Sundays and misshapen *fin de siècle* boaters, or singing songs of myth and glory. The past can intrude on the present directly, not least by providing Harrow with the priceless marketing tool of brand recognition. Any portrait of Harrow without a frame of history becomes a story without a narrative, a picture without composition. Tradition may be an organic

growth; there have been OH subscription dinners at least since the early eighteenth century. But its cultivation has been conscious and careful, the price the present pays the past for its future. Yet the problem is to discover at any particular moment which element or interpretation of the past is still efficient in exerting its hold and which merely a dignified charade behind which the School can quietly (or loudly) change and adapt.

For much of the twentieth century the sense of tutelage to former times was compounded by the appearance that Harrow remained essentially as it had been reconstructed by Charles Vaughan, Montagu Butler and James Welldon between 1845 and 1898. As late as 1970, the physical environment was still dominated by what one OH of the previous century had described as 'terrible combinations of red and black brick'. Except for the War Memorial, the most telling contribution of the first half of the twentieth century as the CDT centre was to be of its second, almost all the main School buildings, at least in their exteriors, dated from the nineteenth century: Chapel, the front of the Old Schools, the New Schools, Science Schools, Museum Schools, Music Schools (old and new), Art Schools, Workshop, Gym, Speech Room, Vaughan Library. Domestic architecture, in Peterborough Road or Grove Hill, told the same story. No new House had been founded, let alone constructed, since the 1890s, with the exception of West Acre which had been rebuilt with studied drabness after its fire in 1908. Inside the Houses, the legacy of the nineteenth century federal school of over-mighty freehold hotelier House Masters secure in their fiefdoms, remained in manner if not, since the 1930s and 1940s, in financial or administrative fact. The enforced system of compulsory extra paid tuition known as 'Pupil Room', where most of the instruction actually occurred for much of the nineteenth century, had been abolished by Lionel Ford in 1913. Yet forty years later its shade survived in at least one House in a room known as 'Pupe'. Boys still ate all their meals in their Houses which retained highly distinctive characters only partly susceptible to the caprice of the current House Masters. Fagging and beating remained accepted into the 1970s, if in places increasingly in the breach, as did a whole vocabulary of School life and dress. The collar stud was not a fashion statement but an early morning opponent to be grappled into an uncooperative starched shirt. In School uniform, imposed piecemeal over half a century from the 1830s, the nineteenth century continued to exert itself. Sport was still god. Its liturgy would have been easily recognised and approved by its original archpriest, E.E. Bowen, who

RIGHT: Edward Bowen, Master 1839–1901, author of Forty Years On

BELOW: The Head Master's House

had died in 1901. Songs still spoke of Bowen's school, not Dr James's. To anyone walking the Hill in about 1970, Wood's remarks about its stones speaking of a personal past still held true, except that it was not always clear whose past they were talking about. There was a sense, encouraged by elders, some of whom had been colleagues of a master actually appointed in the nineteenth century, of there existing a timeless mystery to which they had secret access, into which, if good, new acolytes could be initiated.

Yet about the history of the School there persisted a cheerful naivety, an absence of inquiry compounded by the acceptance of a few mythical canons. To list some of the more egregious: John Lyon's foundation was unique in inviting fee-paying foreigners. The Founder had planned for what became known within a century of his death as a 'public school'. Lyon was a crypto-Catholic. Harrow was an Elizabethan school. It had developed separately and in distinction from Eton. It had been a royalist school during the Civil War and a notably Whig one a century later. The Hill was healthy. Harrow was a rich school. There was something disreputable about the Road Trust denying the School access to the profits of

Lyon's London estates. The Hill estate as it had developed by the twentieth century had been Lyon's original endowment. The boys wore black ties to commemorate the death of Queen Victoria (and would abandon the effort in 2001). Druries was the oldest House and Byron a member of it. Winston Churchill had led an undistinguished academic career at school. Association Football was somehow unHarrovian. All these and many more articles of faith were, in important ways, false. Although such fantasies tend to be harmless, they cloud the one theme of the School's history that may be of as much interest to misty-eyed *devotés* as to sceptical scholars. What made Harrow distinctive among the cluster of luxury schools that, within the propertied and prosperous classes, have maintained prominence since the eighteenth century?

Paradoxically, the chief distinctiveness, apart from certain indigenous rituals, lies not in the two dominant waking features of school life, games and work, still less in religion. In the nineteenth century, Harrow was sportingly and academically innovative. In games, the School came early to the cult of cricket, developed organised mass football that spawned ball-games enthusiasts such as C.W. Alcock, founder of the Football Association, and developed individual games, notably rackets, originally played against the Old Schools' walls with junior boys perched on the roof to recover lost balls. Only in the 1920s did it appear that Harrow needed to join the mainstream of similar schools and adopt Rugby Football. Academically, Harrow championed Science and Modern Languages before it became acceptable elsewhere. In its elevation of History as part of the Modern Side curriculum after 1869 Harrow produced one of its most distinguished teachers, G. Townsend Warner, and one of its most illustrious Old Boys, G.M. Trevelyan. In the twentieth century, changes in both games and the curriculum have closely matched other similar schools, sometimes ahead, sometimes behind, no longer a national force for educational experiment. What is true of games and academic work applies to Harrow's other great tradition, powerfully expressed in the dignity of the War Memorial. Since the Napoleonic Wars Harrow has been a military school, the armed forces for 150 years consistently attracting a higher proportion of school leavers than any other single profession. In religion,

Harrow followed the Low Church enthusiasm of the nineteenth century for much of the following century until abandoned for more beauty of holiness and a reversal of traditional hostility to Roman Catholicism. By contrast, the peculiarity of Harrow can be found in more prosaic aspects: how the School was funded, how it survived, and how life was organised.

The transformation of the local Free Grammar School of John Lyon at Harrow on the Hill, as it was originally styled, into a nationally recognised public school, rested on the twin seventeenth-century foundations of well-connected Governors and entrepreneurial Head Masters, notably the puritan William Hide (1628–61) and the Etonian swell William Horne (1669–85) who appropriately installed the Head Master's throne and pulpit in the schoolroom (now the Fourth Form Room). 'Foreigners', i.e. pupils not on the foundation of 40 free scholars, first appear around 1630, and by the 1680s the School had attracted a substantial proportion of lucrative boarders. In 1682 it was claimed there were 80 boarders to only 40 day boys. That was where the profits lay; so too the social cachet. Horne brought with him the first peers to be educated at Harrow. By 1700, another Etonian, Thomas Bryan (Head Master 1691–1730), was training future army and navy officers, gentlemen and MPs, as well as lawyers, doctors, parsons and schoolteachers. Shrewd Governors, who combined local propertied interest with metropolitan business or politics, supported Head Masters academically and socially able to benefit from the growing market for boarding schools. This led to their appointing exclusively Eton-educated Head Masters between 1669 and 1785, with the unfortunate interlude of the drunken spendthrift James Cox (1730–46), one of only three Heads appointed from within the existing teaching staff (Joseph Drury 1785–1805 and, in an exceptional time of war, Paul Boissier 1940–42 being the others). In appointing its Heads, if not much else, Harrow has historically proved a most open school, in marked contrast to its oldest competitors.

In 1690 Head Master William Bolton (1685–91) referred to Harrow as a 'Public School'. Originally this term described a school run by a board of Trustees, a corporate body in law, as opposed to a private school operated for the sole benefit of an individual schoolmaster. By Bolton's time it was beginning to attract overtones

RIGHT: *Druries seen from the Vaughan Library*

Harrow in the twenty-first century

The current School is different from that of five, 15 or 50 years ago. This is what Masters who have taught at Harrow for a long time tell me. It is a statement that can be made about every school (I hope). The school is larger – 800 boys now. Standards of physical comfort are higher: better quality and choice of food, good heating, carpets in every room. These days things are geared to the perceptions of mothers. New subjects have appeared on the curriculum such as Computing and Business, Japanese and Astronomy. Clever boys are not accelerated to a higher form as they once were, nor are the less academic relegated to a Fourth Form. Certain sports, such as rowing and hockey, have a higher profile. Boys eat in a central dining hall where once they ate in Houses. Although boys are still given leadership responsibility, this is carefully controlled; it is not possible for one pupil to punish another except with the specific agreement of the House Master. There are many more games and TV rooms in the boarding houses. Virtually all Harrovians go on to university. Music and the arts are possibly stronger than they have ever been. Many more boys take a mix of arts and science subjects in the Sixth Form. There are many more tours abroad. Most of our feeder prep schools are co-educational. Almost half of Harrow pupils have never experienced boarding before starting here. An increasing proportion of Masters are women. Careers advice is given a higher profile than ever before.

BARNABY LENON

Barnaby Lenon has been Head Master of Harrow since September 1999. He was an Assistant Master at Eton from 1979–94 and Head of Geography. He was then Deputy Head at Highgate from 1990–94 and Headmaster of Trinity School, Croydon, from 1994–99. He is the author of various geography books.

of exclusivity based on a growing awareness that a classical education could mark social status. As the professional requirement for Latin receded, its acquisition became the preserve and the badge of the leisured, cultivated and rich. Public schools became fashionable and Harrow, conveniently sited geographically, skilfully positioned itself institutionally to take advantage. By 1700 the three pillars of Harrow's future fortune, curriculum, class and money, were well entrenched. The special nature of the education defined a social elite that drew clients willing to pay high fees. The details of educational provision, the structure of society and the expectations of fee payers have all changed many times since then. However, this formula has remained essentially unchanged and central to Harrow's success over three and a half centuries, even if covered by shifting rhetoric of, variously, nineteenth-century religion or academic merit, Edwardian imperialism, uneasy twentieth-century egalitarian *noblesse oblige* or capitalist utilitarianism.

This could be argued for most of the old public schools. Yet Harrow's case differed from rivals such as Eton or Winchester. Because John Lyon bequeathed the income from his farms in Marylebone and St. John's Wood exclusively to the upkeep of the Harrow and Edgware Roads (as part of the deal by which he obtained a Royal Charter and large tax relief for his school), Harrow's endowment rested on a few farms in Middlesex and Hertfordshire. This gave rise to a fundamental paradox that has shaped Harrow as a poorly endowed school for the very rich, dependent on fees and fundraising to maintain itself as a luxury school. In all periods, this has imposed an acute sensitivity to the market and an eager search for donors, a process of fundraising for capital projects begun with vigour under George Butler and reaching crescendos between 1870 and 1914 and in the late twentieth and early twenty-first centuries. This mismatch of facilities and endowment explains the high fees and, historically, the extensive extra expenses. In the eighteenth and nineteenth centuries, before the consolidation of the curriculum begun by Head Masters Longley (1829–36) and Wordsworth (1836–44), the cost of extras (French, Maths, compulsory extra Classics teaching, music, dancing, drawing, fencing etc.) was greater than the basic tuition fee. Just as it took 80 years (the 1830s to the First World War) for the academic timetable

RIGHT: *First XV v Dulwich, 1999*

to become unified and comprehensive, so balkanised accounting lasted far into the second half of the twentieth century. Even the all-pervasive compulsory games attracted a separate element on the bill.

The inability of Lyon's Road Trust and, since 1991, its successor the John Lyon Charity to fund the School despite its massive reserves, forced the School to adopt another of its most characteristic features. From an early stage the School became a business not, as in certain other schools, as a matter of choice, but out of necessity for the institution and those who worked in it. Until the later nineteenth century (and some would argue far beyond), it was incumbent on all Masters to extend their earnings beyond what they were paid simply to teach. Until the structural reforms following the Public Schools Act of 1868, Head Masters, who paid the teaching salaries of the Assistant Masters, could corner all tuition fees and rely on the boarding income from what was called by George Butler, with pride, the Head Master's 'Barracks', stuffed full of paying boarders. In twenty years, 1785–1805, Joseph Drury, made, net, £80,000; to pack in as many boarders as possible he even moved out to a rented cottage (possibly with a Harrow Dame, or local reading teacher, Anne Batt).

A few of his colleagues, notably his brother-in-law Thomas Bromley and his brother Mark, were able to extract thousands from their own glorified dosshouses (The Abbey, now Druries, and the Old House). Harrow often appeared to be a family business, operated in turn by the Bryan-Cox family (1691–1746), the Heath-Drurys (1771–1863) and the Butler-Oxenhams (1805–1919). Others had to be more imaginative. One result was the creation of modern boarding houses, pioneered by Samuel Batten at The Grove (1819–30) and W.W. Phelps at The Park (1831–9). They realised there was a market for luxurious accommodation at a high price for comfort and good amenities, with a commensurately large profit. The other House Masters soon followed their profitable lead, including Head Masters after the rebuilding of their house from the 1840s following the disastrous fire in 1838. This historic decision to aim at the top of the market determined Harrow's destiny and became reflected in the costly struggle to maintain the most luxurious extra-curricular facilities possible. While Harrow had sporadically competed with Eton in social and academic reputation before, from the early nineteenth century it bound itself to shadow the royal foundation comprehensively.

The absence of dormitories, a product of this early nineteenth-century transformation, became a dominant and distinctive feature of Harrow, as well as an excellent selling device. Not only did these new style boarding houses turn good profits when the school was flourishing, they also, less expectedly, transformed the relationship of boy, House Master and House. Previously, boys had followed Masters when they moved property. Now, after Batten died in 1830 and Phelps left in 1839, their boys stayed in their House and it was the House Master who joined them, not the other way round. Thus a special *ésprit de corps* associated with a place rather than, as in Byron's time, a person, was created. With most House Masters also having to buy the freeholds on their Houses, as a sort of pension for their predecessor, all the ingredients of the federal school were in place. Even when this system broke down, as the School, fearful of suburban development and of indifferent or greedy House Masters selling out of the School, bought up the freeholds of the boys' Houses, many of the structures persisted. From the 1940s (Elmfield was the last freehold) House Masters ceased even to be tenant hoteliers managing their affairs and keeping their profits. But as financial control became increasingly centralised, the independent traditions of each House remained strong, robust enough even to have withstood to some degree the advent of central feeding in 1977 and further administrative standardisation and unified direction.

Parallel to this federal dimension, and most pervasive of all, has been the physical arrangement of the School. Many local grammar schools became public schools; Rugby, Shrewsbury, Uppingham, Oundle etc. Yet most either rebuilt themselves or moved themselves to meet the new material demands of the mid-nineteenth century public school revival. Harrow stayed and never built itself a quadrangle or a campus. Until the central feeding block opened in 1977 boys and Beaks ate as well as lived scattered across the Hill. This bred independence among the staff as well as the boys. The well-attested raffishly bickering quality of Harrow lay not just in the inmates' backgrounds but in the diversity of experience within the School, which historically Head Masters found exasperating if not worse. Yet it also provided opportunities. A school more dominated by ancient statutes or collegiate foundations may have found it difficult to open a House for Jewish pupils, as Butler did in 1881, or a Muslim one, as proposed by Welldon in 1890. Harrow has never been a campus school, a shock to some newcomers to the staff, although central feeding inevitably homogenised aspects of daily social life. Yet during the School's worst financial crisis, in 1938, when the School was running an overdraft of £100,000 with falling rolls, schemes were proposed either to move to a centralised green field site or to rebuild the School on the Hill on a campus model. If either had happened, the whole nature of the School would have changed far more radically than anything seen in the last thirty years. To distil the distinctiveness of Harrow, contemplation of what might have happened in 1938 is a good place to begin. The accident of history lent Harrow a diversity that, for better or worse, has informed its character.

Yet Harrow, as well as its history, requires to be seen in perspective. Let Joseph Wood have the last word as he did the first. Invited to attend the visit of George V and Queen Mary to Speech Day in 1912, a celebration of the School and its imperial mission, Wood, who had retired only two years before, declined. He preferred to play golf.

Dr Christopher Tyerman DPhil FRHistS (Newlands 1966³) was Head of History from 1990–2000 and author of A History of Harrow School *(2000). He has held various History fellowships and is now a lecturer at New College and Hertford College, Oxford.*

LEFT: *The Queen planting a tree outside Druries in 1971*

19

A Governor's tale

MICHAEL CONNELL

HERE IS NO POINT IN AGREEING TO SERVE AS A Governor of Harrow School unless you love the place and you enjoy an exciting life. Harrow possesses the ability to inspire the enthusiast and to reward the committed; it can also frustrate and from time to time infuriate its proudest supporters.

My time as a Governor spanned 19 years (1983–2002). For the last five of those years I was Chairman of a Board of (usually) 22 members. By Royal Charter, five of those Governors are the subject of specific nominations (The Lord Chancellor, the Royal Society, The Senior Common Room and the Universities of Oxford and Cambridge). The rest are invited to fulfil roles which are seen to be important in the various tasks which the Governing Body must carry out. In addition to governing Harrow School, the Governors oversee the John Lyon School; they assess the education provided at the International School in Bangkok and contribute to its governance; they run the John Lyon Charity (the Road Trust) and they work closely with the Harrow Association, the Harrow Development Trust and the Harrow Club. These are all major undertakings and the responsibility for the day-to-day running of them rests primarily with the two Head Masters, the Bursar, the Clerk to the Governors and the Directors of the Development Trust. The Governors decide on policy issues and control the School's assets and income, but they are not so concerned with day to day matters. The Head Masters run the Schools. They appoint the Beaks. They direct the boys. The Bursar administers the finances guided by the General Purposes and Finance Committee; the Clerk tries to ensure that all is properly conducted within the Charter and the law; and the Development Director seeks to raise funds for new projects. All this takes a little while to understand.

The Governing Body meets three times a year in full session. Usually there is an informal meeting at 4.30pm on a Friday afternoon, when a presentation may be made to the Governors by, say, a Head of Department or a House Master or someone else who is advising the School in connection with a new project. At this meeting the Head Master reports to the Governors on matters of importance in the School's life, including highlights and low points. The discussions on all these matters are (to borrow a phrase from the lawyers) full and frank.

Unfortunately, on the first occasion that I attended such a meeting, I arrived late because a jury in Birmingham had taken a long time in reaching their verdict and my departure from Court was delayed. I arrived at Harrow at 5.45pm for a meeting which had started at 4.30pm. In apologising to the Chairman I said that "on occasions the wheels of Justice move exceeding slow" – which provoked from a very senior Governor and a senior Judge the repost "Not in my Court".

After the informal meeting the Governors move in to the Shepherd Churchill Room for dinner with various

LEFT: *The Red House at The John Lyon School*

guests, usually a selection of Beaks and their spouses or the School Monitors. These occasions are primarily social, and fairly relaxed, but the opportunity may be taken on either side to discuss particular matters which are topical in the progress of the School at that time.

The conviviality of these occasions is appreciated very much by the Governors and, I believe, by their guests. Usually these dinner parties end at about 11 to 11.30pm, and most of the Governors spend the night in one or other of the Houses on the Hill, as the guest of the families who occupy them. This is convenient and provides another opportunity to gather information on topical matters as well as to meet some of those closely connected with the running of the School. The Governors inevitably vary in their habits and their acceptability as guests. A senior Governor when I first joined the Board was a short sleeper. He liked to re-read his papers over an early morning cup of tea, which he often requested for 5am. In consequence he was not the most popular visitor, although he was a keen supporter of the School.

On the Saturday morning the Governors meet in more formal circumstances at 9am; save on Governors' Speech Day when the meeting follows after *Contio Latina*. This Saturday morning meeting is structured around a detailed agenda, which will itemise the various important issues of the moment. All the main committees will report back to the Governing Body (for example the Finance and General Purposes Committee, the John Lyon Committee of Management, the Road Trust or the Development Trust) such reports being communicated by the relevant Chairman or Chairwoman. The sub-committees will usually have made a recommendation (for example to proceed with a new project, to support a Budget, to approve specialist advice or not, as the case may be). The discussions, although more formal than those at the Friday evening meetings, can still be vigorous and even controversial, but only on a few occasions has it been necessary for the Chairman to take a vote on a particular issue. In the event of an equal division of views, the Chairman will have the casting vote. On one occasion early in my career as a Governor I can remember a difference of opinion between two Governors on an important matter. They were seated at opposite ends of the meeting table, and the progress of their exchange of views reminded this observer of watching the Wimbledon final; serve, return, volley, pass, smash, baseline recovery, etc.. All the skill of the Chairman of the day was needed to conclude the point and move on.

The Saturday meeting usually ends at about 12.45pm and a quick lunch is always available in the Shepherd Churchill Room for those Governors who wish to stay.

In some cases several Governors may join the crowd in support of a school cricket or rugby match in the afternoon before setting off for home. These weekend meetings were always challenging affairs (especially for the Chairman). There were heavy papers to digest before the meeting, detailed discussions during the meeting and consequent exchanges of view over the Friday night dinner or the Saturday lunch. There are papers to sign, questions to be asked, views to be expressed, and decisions to be made which may guide the future of the School for many years.

Let me illustrate. In the late 1980s the School contemplated the construction of the School Theatre on the site below the Rackets Court and behind West Street

BELOW:
Speeches, c. 1890

RIGHT:
Luka Gakic,
Contionator
2003

erected and many others were refurbished; the International School in Bangkok was debated and eventually created; the terms of the Road Trust were adjusted more to modern reality; the Development Trust was born; IT came to the Hill and Harrow School continued to educate its sons to a high standard. This was achieved thanks to a dedicated and talented team of Masters and some excellent facilities, set in surroundings where history and progress live side by side and continue to inspire and to enable. I served as a Governor with about fifty men and women who in every case dedicated hours of precious time for no personal benefit; and who were all faced with the delicate task of making decisions designed to benefit the two schools in their control. As each will confirm, the office is no sinecure; but close involvement in a vibrant institution which promotes the education of the young provides its own reward.

Sir Michael Connell QC (Rendalls 1953[2]) was a Justice in the Family Division of the High Court and was Chairman of the Governors from 1997–2002.

FAR RIGHT: *The*
School Chest
which contained
the Governors'
Muniments

which is adjacent to the Church Fields. This particular site was rather neglected and it seemed to many that the redevelopment proposed, which included some new housing, could only improve the area. There were, however, objections both from local planners and some local residents. A public planning enquiry was convened. The inspector recommended approval on conditions which the School was content to meet. Some local residents continued to object vociferously, using the correspondence columns of *The Times* to supplement the banners and posters distributed up and down West Street. When construction got underway, emotions continued to run high. One or two posters described the Governors as murderers; there was a demonstration by opponents on Speech Day and many Governors found their mail full of vitriol. Now, some ten years on, it is difficult to understand how a project which has produced such an excellent and well-used theatre building, as well as some decent new homes, can have given rise to such strenuous disagreement.

During my time as a Governor two Head Masters were appointed, many new buildings were

John Lyon's Charity

ANDREW STEBBINGS

MYTHS ABOUT THE 'ROAD TRUST' ABOUND. Some are harmless, for example that the Governors have owned the 'Roads' or some of the property along them: others less so. In particular, despite weighty legal opinion to the contrary over the centuries, the draughtsmen of nineteenth-century Acts of Parliament perpetuated, if they did not actually create, a belief that surplus income could be applied for the benefit of the School, by 'reserving the rights of Harrow School'; there was no basis for any such assumption.

The Royal Charter recited that John Lyon had 'purposed in his mind liberally to endow and maintain common ways between Edgware and London'. In 1578 and 1582 he gave to the Keepers and Governors of the School a farm in what is now St John's Wood, comprising approximately 48 acres as the endowment of a separate trust for the purpose of repairing and maintaining two roads from the City of London, one to Harrow and the other to Edgware or Kenton, where he also owned land, for that purpose and 'to no other'. At that time the land was undeveloped farmland of poor quality and may have been more desirable for its gravel deposits than for the income it produced. In his 1590 Statutes John Lyon directed the Governors 'to appoint two honest men yearly, one to oversee and look unto the filling of the gravel and the other to the laying of the same; and the two overseer to have for their pains yearly thirty shillings apiece'.

Although the Governors were Trustees of both the School and the Road Trust, they were required to keep the funds separate and only to apply the income from the Marylebone and Paddington Estates to the upkeep of the roads, which are now known as Harrow Road and Edgware Road, converging at Tyburn, down Oxford Street to the St Giles Pound and the gates of the City. However, they did not always strictly comply with the terms of the Trust. In 1752 the statutory Trustees appointed

to oversee the maintenance of Edgware Road brought an action against the Governors claiming that they had failed to apply the income from the Estate to the maintenance of their road. The action was inconclusive because the Governors were able to claim that they had spent the money on the other road, the Harrow Road, although it seems probable that they had not spent anything like all of the income on the maintenance of

ABOVE: *Chapel window depicting John Lyon (left) and Mistress Lyon*

either of the roads as it was not the first occasion on which they had been challenged.

Indeed in the next half century, as little as £120 was paid over to the Trustees of both roads whereas, the income from the land amounted to around £70 a year. This is despite the fact that in 1774 the part of Edgware Road between Edgware and Kilburn was described as 'ruinous'. The balance of the funds seems to have been applied to the School.

By 1800 so few payments were being made that the Trustees charged with the maintenance of the roads were not even aware that they were supposed to be receiving funds from the Governors. Unfortunately for the Governors a chance discovery by one of those Trustees led to an investigation. An Act of Parliament in 1801 made it clear that the income was indeed to be applied to the maintenance of the roads and further Acts followed in 1803, 1804, 1819 and 1826. The result of these was that the Governors had to keep proper accounts, which were to be produced to the Trustees responsible for the maintenance of the roads, and the net income was to be paid over to the Governor of the Bank of England for distribution to the road Trustees. Although no special provision was made, the idea that the School could benefit from the trust once the roads were in a perfect state of maintenance (which clearly was never going to happen) was allowed to subsist. Thereafter all of the income was applied for the maintenance of the roads, latterly being given to the relevant local authorities whose duty it was to maintain the roads under The Metropolis (Kilburn and Harrow) Roads Act 1872.

By the late eighteenth century it was realised that the Governors would make more money by selling building leases rather than letting the land for agriculture. Originally, however, the Governors had no power to grant building leases and this power was given by an Act of Parliament in 1803. Development really got under way following the conclusion of the Napoleonic wars and by the early 1820s the first roads had been laid out. In 1827 a new boulevard running down the centre of the Estate was laid out to be called Hamilton Terrace after the Hamilton family, Earls and Marquises of Abercorn, who had close ties with Harrow School. Development continued throughout the 1830s and 40s with properties being built in a variety of styles. In 1846 a new church,

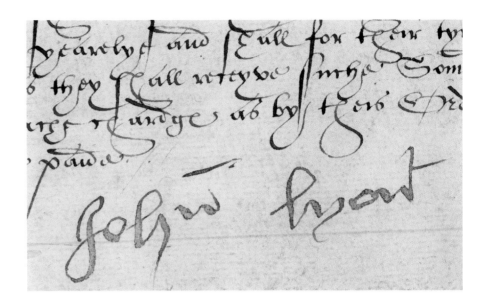

ABOVE: *John Lyon's signature on the Statutes of the School*

St Mark's, was built within the Estate and by the 1860s development was almost complete. By the late nineteenth century St John's Wood had become famous as the home of artists and one of the Estate's most famous residents was Sir Edward Landseer. Successive Chief Rabbis have lived in Hamilton Terrace for the last 100 years. On a less salubrious note, it was noted that in the 1880s and 90s nearly two-thirds of the houses at the southern end of the Estate were occupied by women living alone.

One difficulty for the Governors was that they were unable to accept premiums for the grant of new leases. This meant that rents were relatively high and in times of economic depression it was sometimes difficult to find tenants.

The St John's Wood Estate remained relatively intact until the extension of the Leasehold Reform Act in 1972 raising the rateable value limits. In the 1980s, in expectation of the further extension of the enfranchisement rights, the Governors adopted a policy of allowing voluntary sales where this encouraged the conversion of properties back to single houses to improve the quality of the Estate. The funds received from the sale of property were invested in the stock market, steadily increasing the income of the Charity.

In 1965 the Charity Commission approached the Governors and the trustees of other similar London Charities in an attempt to set up a Common Good Fund, under the new Charities Act 1960. The Governors declined the approach, still hoping that the schools might eventually

The Arms of Harrow School

Mr G. Woods Wollaston (Newlands 1888³), Norroy King of Arms, wrote the following account of the origin of the Arms granted to the School in The Harrovian *of November 1929.*

We are apt to accept without question familiar objects in our daily life and it is probable that the majority of Harrovians, present and past, have never stopped to enquire, or even to wonder, how Harrow became possessed of those Arms and Heraldic devices which adorn the School notepaper, decorate the School prizes, and in many other ways proclaim Harrow to the world at large. Presumably they were the arms of the Founder; or, if not, perhaps they were granted by the Charter of Queen Elizabeth, or by some document from the Heralds' College, preserved with other muniments of the School in a repository known only to the Governors. Anyway, they were the School Arms.

The facts were otherwise. John Lyon had no arms; the Charter of Foundation is silent on the subject; and the records of the Heralds' College and the muniments of the School were alike devoid of any evidence supporting a claim to Armorial Bearings.

We live in an age in which few things, from mummies to memoirs, are allowed to sleep in peaceful obscurity and, outside Harrow, it had long been known that the Arms used by the School lacked proper authority. This is perhaps hardly surprising, for the School itself has never been consistent in its use of arms. The Governors may, perhaps, be pardoned for having adopted, as a device on their seal, a lion rampant. It was, at least, allusive to the name of our Founder. They did not place it on a shield, or represent it as Arms, but merely as a device. The School went further. Somewhere about 100 years ago (it is difficult to assign a precise date), a lion began to ramp proudly, as a Coat of Arms, on School buildings and elsewhere in Harrow. But he was not very certain of his own identity or of his proper environment, for he appeared variously as a white lion on a blue ground, a blue lion on a white ground, a

gold lion on a blue ground, a red lion on a white ground, and finally (a violation of all Heraldic rules) a blue lion on a red ground. Most of these various Coats can be seen at Harrow today.

The facts were brought to the notice of the Governors in 1922, but they were then unwilling to face the necessity of any

alteration in the Coat which – as they alleged – the School had hitherto used. Some alteration was, as they recognised, inevitable; for a lion rampant, pure and simple, with whatever tinctures, could not be granted by the Heraldic authorities, with the due regard which they were bound to pay to the rights of other persons who already bore that

device with authority. It is probable that the matter would have remained long in abeyance, had not the School itself changed the whole situation by assuming a new Coat of Arms. Consciously or unconsciously, the School authorities adopted as a badge for the School Rugby XV a shield charged with a lion rampant and, above the lion (also on the shield) the well known crossed arrows and laurel wreath.

Here was a brand new Coat of Arms, and one with such a 'difference' as the Heraldic authorities could accept. Representations were again made to the Governors, and it was suggested that this Coat of Arms (with a slight modification of the position of the crossed arrows, to give more scope to the lion) should be the design for a properly authorised grant. To this the Governors assented. An application to the Earl Marshal was signed by the Chairman of the Governors and by Letters Patent under the hands and seals of Garter, Clarenceux, and Norroy Kings of Arms, dated 3 October 1929 (the anniversary of the death of John Lyon). Armorial Bearings had at last been granted to the School.

The Letters Patent fall into two sections dealing separately with the Arms and the Badge. While a small alteration, as stated above, was necessary in the former, the badge of the Crossed Arrows could fortunately be granted unchanged. Harrow is the only leading Public School that is entitled to bear a Badge.

The Heraldic description, or 'blazon', of the Arms and Badge, as given in the grant, is as follows:

ARMS – 'Azure a lion rampant in dexter chief two arrows in saltire points downward tied in the centre with a bow and enfiled with a wreath of laurel all argent.'

BADGE – 'Two arrows in saltire points downward tied in the centre with a bow and enfiled with a wreath of laurel all argent.'

RIGHT: *The High Street from outside The Park, 1905*

benefit. Such a notion, however, was largely dispelled by the researches of Sir John Hobson in the 1960s and by the late 1970s it was finally shown to be without basis. In the early 1980s under the guidance of two Governors, Tom Blackwell and Nicholas Owen, discussions began with the Charity Commission to vary the terms of the trust in order to permit the money to be applied by the Governors for other charitable purposes, on the grounds that the maintenance of the roads was now publicly funded. Both roads were by then designated as metropolitan roads funded by central government and it is almost certain that the Local Authorities to whom the income was being paid were using it for other purposes. Protracted negotiations began with the Local Authorities who naturally did not want to lose the income, which was increasing rapidly from £150,000 in 1980 to £1 million in 1990. The negotiations were concluded when the Local Authorities were threatened with a reference to the Attorney General for misapplication of the Charity's money and the Governors agreed to consult them on its application in each borough. In 1991, a Statutory Instrument was laid before Parliament to introduce a scheme whereby the income of the Charity would be applied by the Governors for charitable purposes in boroughs in North West London. At the same time the name was changed from Harrow School Road Trust to John Lyon's Charity, thereby helping to break down the erroneous perception that Harrow School owned and benefited from the Estate.

The Charity's objectives are 'to enhance the conditions of life and improve the life chances of children and young adults through education'. The beneficiaries are the inhabitants of the boroughs of Barnet, Brent, Camden, Ealing, Hammersmith and Fulham, Harrow, The Royal Borough of Kensington and Chelsea and the Cities of London and Westminster, the boroughs served by the two roads. A committee set up by the Governors oversees the work of the Charity, scrutinises applications for grants, and recommends the distribution of its income which has increased to over £3 million. Since 1992 the Charity has spent over £18 million on a wide range of projects and activities benefiting young people, including youth clubs and youth services, arts organisations, child care and parental support, sports schemes and academic bursaries and scholarships. Over 100 state primary and secondary and independent schools have benefited, including both Harrow and The John Lyon School, in support of the Charity's objectives.

Andrew Stebbings (Rendalls 1964[3]) is a Partner in Pemberton Greenish, Solicitors. He has been Clerk to the Governors since 1983.

The architecture of the Hill

CHRISTOPHER MARSDEN-SMEDLEY

H UMAN SETTLEMENTS USUALLY HAVE A particular reason for their siting. It might be a plentiful supply of well water, a curve in a river, or a defensible position. Harrow Hill, rising out of a wide alluvial plain, would have been eminently defensible.

The topography of the Hill is dumb-bell in shape with two summits, one the site of the church, the other in the High Street near The Park. Between the two, the ridge curves and slims to its narrowest where West Street meets the High Street. The topography informs the character of the Hill. The early settlers on the Hill were probably Saxons. They would have worshipped their heathen gods on the site of St Mary's Church.

From the Hill there are distant views, formerly of fields, now largely of Metroland, with the City towers, St Paul's and the Houses of Parliament visible on a clear day in the south east. Less dramatic, but no less expansive, are the views to the west. From the School (or Bill) Yard both views can be seen from one spot, thus giving cause to Howson's words: 'In the windy yard at Bill'. From all directions the School and other buildings are seen at varying levels, culminating in the spire of St Mary's.

A Church was consecrated here in 1094. The earliest part of what we now see is the tower, dating from the twelfth century. Various additions were built in succeeding centuries. The spire was struck by lightning in 1765 and rebuilt in timber and lead. Another hazard appeared in the 1940s when lighting was fixed to the top of the spire, to warn pilots approaching Northolt of the spire's presence. The walls of the Church are largely of flint with freestone dressings, features picked up in many of the School's buildings. There are interesting tombs and headstones in the churchyard, in particular the Peachey stone. This is now covered by an iron superstructure, thus depriving latter-day poets of emulating their great predecessor, Byron, who wrote some famous lines on this spot. 'Byron lay, lazily lay,

hidden from lesson and game away, dreaming poetry all alone, up-a-top of the Peachey stone.' Church Hill leads steeply up to the churchyard. Although the Church is out of sight behind the Old Schools, the vista is closed by an attractive lych-gate. The roof is of ornamental tiles supported on a timber structure and low brick walls. On the left is the old Vicarage. The vista is framed by the Old Schools and the War Memorial.

The Old Schools incorporate the original School building. Although there is evidence of a school at Harrow as early as the fourteenth century, the date of origin is normally assumed to be 1571. It was in that year, or the year following, that John Lyon was granted a Charter to 'found create and forever establish anew … a Grammar School…'. Lyon was childless and work on the new building did not start until after his wife's death in 1608. It was ready for occupation in 1615. It housed accommodation for the Master and also the original Fourth Form Room, with its seventeenth-century panelling carved with the names of hundreds of early Harrovians. The walls were of red brick with sand-coloured freestone dressings. Three massive brick chimneys gave high relief to the west facade.

The School outgrew its first building and in 1819 Head Master George Butler decided to double its size. A Speech Room (now The Old Speech Room Gallery),

ABOVE: *View from The Park*, c. *1830*

with a grand flight of steps up to a *piano nobile* entrance was added, giving a symmetrical facade to the south. Large oriel windows were formed in the south and east walls (including one in the Old Fourth Form Room) and the gables were capped with Flemish style 'crow-steps'. The architect was C.R. Cockerell. His work at Harrow came early in his career and much credit should be given to George Butler and the Governors for their choice. Cockerell went on to win the RIBA Gold Medal and to become President of the RIBA. He is best known for the Ashmolean Museum in Oxford.

The resulting enlarged School building is a vast improvement on its predecessor. The roof is capped with a central clock tower and weathervane, the clock numerals and hands in gold leaf on a Harrow blue face — a fitting climax to a majestic design. How fortunate that these happy later additions to the gaunt original building came when listed building officers had yet to be born.

In the harsh winter of 1948 I remember sitting for an exam in the Old Speech Room. My desk must have been near the oriel window. A snowflake found its way between the glass of the leaded light and the surrounding lead and landed on my exam paper. The temperature was such that the snowflake seemed in no hurry to melt. The exam subject and the result I forget. The snowflake I remember. The Old Speech Room was converted into a museum in the 1970s. Heating and air conditioning were then installed; very necessary from my personal experience.

The vista up to the Old Schools was further enhanced in the 1920s. Before that, access to the Bill Yard was limited to steps to Church Hill in the east and the long flight down to the gymnasium in the west. Land to the south of the Bill Yard was occupied by Custos's garden, various small shops and houses and a pub. When these were all removed, a grand flight of steps, on the axis of the Old Schools entrance led up by easy stages from the High Street. Level terraces, with planting, lawns and clipped yew trees were formed on either side of the steps. The walls of the Bill Yard are of the same red brick, the columns topped with Portland stone capitals and classical urns. Between the columns are wrought iron railings with ornamental gates to the south and east. The vista from the High Street, up these steps to the Bill Yard and Old Schools, is dramatic. At roughly the same time much demolition was taking place on the other side of Church Hill. Dame Armstrong's and Church Hill, former boys' Houses, were removed to clear the site for the War Memorial.

The building of the War Memorial and its associated works had a fundamental effect on the character of the Hill. The building does not stand on its own. It serves as a frontispiece, or grand processional way, from the High Street to the Speech Room. There are more grand steps down from Church Hill to the forecourt. In the centre of this forecourt is a bronze cross of Lorraine, alleged to have been formed from a French cannon. The walls against Church Hill and the High Street are of flint with Portland stone dressings. A niche in the west wall seems

to be expecting a statue of some eminent Old Harrovian. The architect for the War Memorial was Sir Herbert Baker, best known for the Bank of England, South Africa House and parts of New Delhi. One enters the building through the shrine. On the left is a stone sarcophagus. The walls are carved with the names of the 644 Old Harrovians who lost their lives in the First World War. Passing through the shrine one enters a large space with steps at intervals leading up towards the level of the Speech Room. On the floor of this space is a wreath in stone, commemorating the dead of the Second World War. Against the walls are busts of eminent Old Harrovians. On the left is a double staircase leading up to the Masters' Common Room, the Old Harrovian Room and the Alex Fitch Room. The collection of watercolours that used to hang on this staircase is now housed in the Old Speech Room Gallery. In their place is a collection of photo-portraits and short biographies of distinguished Old Harrovians: 'Giants of Old'.

The Old Harrovian Room is used for medium-size meetings or lectures. Now, with increased numbers of teaching staff, it serves as an overflow from the Masters' Room. Beyond is another shrine, this time to Alex Fitch, who was killed in France in 1918 aged 19. The fireplace, panelling and furniture date from the sixteenth century. The building is arranged on two grand storeys. Gables facing on to the High Street are placed at either end of the building, aligned to follow the slight change of direction of the High Street. At the centre of the High Street front is an oriel window over three arched windows at ground floor. Another oriel on the south front lights the Alex Fitch Room. These features pick up the earlier examples in the Old Schools. The foundation stone was laid in 1921 by Randall Davidson, Archbishop of Canterbury, an Old Harrovian.

There is a gap between the War Memorial and Speech Room large enough for Masters to assemble in fine weather before entering Speech Room. Internally Speech Room is an amphitheatre, with steep stepped seating. This allows for excellent acoustics. The Head Master, when officiating at morning assembly can have eye contact with every boy in the School, striking fear into the hearts of miscreants – or inspiration if need be. The ceiling is of timber boarding, the central part flat. Beyond is an ingenious arrangement of vaulting supported on

BELOW: *The Old Schools after the enlargement to the design of C.R. Cockerell*

pointed arches on 14 paired columns, which follow the semicircular shape of the building. The columns and arches are richly decorated in red, blue and gold. The exterior is of red brick and polychrome dressings. Unlike the War Memorial, the East front is straight, following the line of the High Street. The principal windows to the auditorium are grand in scale, with semicircular heads and an intricate design of arches and roundels. The two towers over the main entrances were finished later, to slightly different designs. The foundation stone was laid by the Duke of Abercorn in 1874.

There is a statue of Queen Elizabeth I in a niche in the southern tower. She holds an orb and sceptre, finished in gold leaf. Her fierce expression reminds one of Bowen's lines:

Draw it shorter and prose it less;
Speeches are things we chiefly bless
When once we have got them over.

ABOVE: *The interior of Speech Room*

The statue was presented by Lord Frederick Hamilton and his family in 1925. The following verse was then added to the well-known song:

> Queen Elizabeth stands outside
> With sceptre and orb in all her pride,
> Viewing her realm of England wide,
> From Cheviot Hills to Dover.

Once again the Head Master and Governors selected an architect at the top of his profession. This was William Burges, one of the greatest architects of the Victorian era. But his designs were often extravagant and paid scant attention to the funds available. This may have been the reason for his falling out with his clients. Perhaps this was the case at Harrow. There was a lengthy delay. At the Tercentenary Meeting in 1871, Head Master Montague Butler proposed, among other developments, a new Speech Room. Three years were to elapse before the foundation stone was laid, and a further three before the opening in 1877. The two entrance towers were not completed until 1925. The final design was something of

a compromise, not a characteristic for which Burges was renowned.

Retracing our steps and crossing the High Street, we pass the New Schools and come to the Chapel. In early days the School had worshipped in St Mary's Church. Head Master George Butler had considered the building of a School Chapel, but it was his successor, Dr Christopher Wordsworth, who was to initiate the first Chapel. He appointed C.R. Cockerell, who had been so successful with the enlargement of the Old Schools. But he was not so successful with the Chapel. It was built in a debased neo-Jacobean style, of brick with stone dressings and a tower in the south-west corner. There was a very small apse at the east end. The floor sloped from west to east following the contours of the ground. It was soon too small, and if one reason for thinking again was not enough many described it as a 'red brick monstrosity'.

Under Dr Vaughan the numbers in the school increased rapidly and a new Chapel, large enough to contain the whole School, was planned. Thus Cockerell's

RIGHT: *Speech Room by William Burges, completed in 1877*

FAR RIGHT: *The War Memorial Building, designed by Sir Herbert Baker, completed in 1926*

short-lived and unloved Chapel was demolished. Once again an eminent architect was employed, this time Sir George Gilbert Scott. The design incorporated a nave, chancel with a larger apsidal end and two aisles. The south aisle was added a little later as a memorial to those killed in the Crimean War. The floor this time was level, allowing for a crypt Chapel and vestry at the east end. These were completed by Head Master Ford as a memorial to those killed in the First World War (before the grander War Memorial was conceived). Externally the walls are of flint with Portland stone dressings. The roof is of ornamental plain tiles with an ironwork design along the ridge. The roof is crowned by a delicate spire, sheeted in copper, with crockets along each of the ribs. This spire, though smaller than that of St Mary's, contributes greatly to the silhouette of the Hill. Internally the Chapel is lofty and dignified and the apsidal end is particularly beautiful. The walls are covered in memorial plaques. The chancel was re-ordered and oak choir stalls were added in 2003, a happy 21st century addition in keeping with the High Victorian interior. The Chapel came into use in 1855.

On the north side of the Chapel are the New Schools, built in 1855, with additions on the east side in 1924. The building is of brick, with gables and parapets to give interest to a reticent design. On the south side is the Vaughan Library. Between the Chapel and both these buildings are glimpses of distant London.

The library was built in memory of Dr Vaughan. The architect, once again, was Sir George Gilbert Scott. It is built of red brick with sand-coloured stone dressings and polychrome surrounds to doors and windows. There is a blind arcade of arches on Purbeck marble columns at lower level, under a *piano nobile* of pointed headed windows. There is a rose window at high level in the central gable. The tiled roof is very steep. The external features of the library are similar in character to those of Speech Room, built some years later. The foundation stone was laid in 1861.

A wide terrace was formed below the Library, the Chapel and New Schools, from which there is an uninterrupted view to the east. Wide steps lead down to gardens and what must be one of the greatest challenges to the mowers of lawns. Further steps lead down to more form rooms. The first block of form rooms provides a

ABOVE: *Moretons, rebuilt in 1828*

visual stop to the northern end of the terrace. One access is from the terrace, the other from the further side in Peterborough Hill. Further down the slope is the Butler Centre, a memorial to Head Master Montague Butler. Another great Victorian architect was employed. This was Basil Champneys, best known for his design for Mansfield College, Oxford. It is built of red brick with brick mouldings and dressings. A grand external staircase, with square terracotta balusters, leads to the upper storeys. The design is redolent of the chateaux of the Loire. The view from the terrace of the Butler centre, partially obscured by the magnificent cedar tree, is sublime. The same tree happily obscures the Maths and Physics Schools, a venture into flat-roofed 1970s architecture.

Further down the Hill, and approached from Football Lane, is the Music School. The architect was Edward Prior, a pupil of the better known Norman Shaw. It was opened in 1891, before which music was taught in the small building at the top of the lane, now housing the Museum of Harrow Life. The influence of John Farmer was strong and the need for a larger, better music school was urgent. The new building provides a concert hall, practice rooms and a band room. The acoustics are excellent. To the north of Speech Room is the Art School. The first part was completed in 1896, with an additional wing in 1913. The exterior shows Jacobean influence with Dutch gables and another fine oriel window, not unlike those in the Old Schools and the War Memorial. There is a wall plaque to Charles I, commemorating the time during the Civil War when he paused to water his horse and have his last view of London, before continuing on his journey from Oxford to the north.

The present Head Master's House, next to the Vaughan Library, dates from 1840. Its predecessor had been destroyed by fire. There were various additions in the nineteenth and twentieth centuries. The High Street front is a successful composition, with a grand neo-Gothic porch, arched first floor windows and gables. Opposite The Head Master's is Druries. In earlier times the entrance was through a tunnel. This was swept away to form the grand approach to the Old Schools. Druries was thus exposed to view. Initially the neo-Gothic, somewhat haphazard composition met with fierce criticism. But after the Second World War, that reviver of taste, John Betjeman, described it as his favourite building; and incidentally Harrow as his favourite school. (He himself

was an Old Marlburian.) The Grove suffered a serious fire in 1833 and was largely rebuilt. Most of the front facade predates the fire and is a sublime composition, the best Georgian building on the Hill. Of the other Houses, The Park and Moretons are late Georgian, with additions, the remainder Victorian. The Knoll was rebuilt in 1982 on a site in Football Lane. The original building has been converted for use as staff accommodation.

The twist and turn of the High Street, following the contours on which it is formed, is echoed by the buildings which bound it. The School buildings, the shops and other houses, are seldom in straight alignment. The pavement level rises and falls, usually at variance with the road level. The steep slope of West Street, meeting the High Street at a crazy angle, curves away at a gentle angle, and so do the houses that bound it. All of these varying facets contribute to the character of the Hill, so that its spirit and ethos is so much greater than the sum of its parts.

Christopher Marsden-Smedley (The Park 1944²) was Senior Partner in the Nealon Tanner Partnership, Architects.

RIGHT: *The Museum Schools and Butler Centre, designed by Basil Champneys, 1886*

Harrow religion

NICHOLAS CRANFIELD

ABOVE: *St Mary's Church*, c. 1840

O N ASCENSION DAY 1928, THE PRIME MINISTER of England, Mr Stanley Baldwin, stood in Westminster Abbey, as did Ramsay MacDonald, as one of the pall-bearers of the recently deceased former Archbishop of Canterbury. Such a singular honour, of a serving Prime Minister for a past Primate, would be unthinkable now and it is perhaps a measure of how values and status constantly change that both men were Old Harrovians. Whether Baldwin reflected on this as he stood in the sunlit Abbey alongside the coffin of the 82-year-old prelate is not known. What is rather more obvious is that in the twenty-first century it is just as unlikely that a future PM will have been educated on the Hill as a Metropolitan of All England.

Baldwin, by 1928 already in his third administration, had worked closely with Dr Randall Davidson, most notably in the often difficult matter of episcopal appointments. Davidson, the older man by a generation, had from a young age been critical of Harrow religion. In the year of Baldwin's own birth, the future Lambeth Archbishop wrote to his father of one of the sermons given by the scholar who would become his own future House Master: 'We had a very learned sermon from Westcott this morning, which might possibly have been intelligible had one been thoroughly well up in the ecclesiastical histories of Rome, Greece, and Syria for the first five centuries AD' (17 February 1867). The sentiment will be widely shared by generations of Harrovians since. Davidson also resisted confirmation as some sort of rite of passage connected with the onset of puberty. He did not choose to become a communicant member of the Church of England until he had turned seventeen.

Both men were the product not only of the public school system at the apogee of its Victorian imperialist ideals but also of that unique English disease, public school religion, which, then and now, has done so much to inoculate generations of boys in many schools against the concept of God and the quest for a spiritual inner Being.

For to many, the term 'public school religion' is not one of approbation, suggesting as it does rather a degree of constrained formalism, most commonly manifested in compulsory Chapel attendance (at Harrow until 1973) and in 'House Prayers'. Both practices were unlikely to engage with the real spiritual needs of the community (whether of boys or Beaks) as they were given over to a military-like demand for attendance at fixed times, and often with fixed seating to make it easier to keep both registers and discipline.

But what may appear to us to have been abusive, and essentially counter-productive, was never the intention of the Victorian progenitors of the idea. Many of them would have grown up with a similar prescriptive turn-out to Sunday worship in churches which retained fixed seating and family pews, as well as designated seating by hierarchy; the squire in his box pew and the better seating reserved for the well-to-do. All Saints' Ascot Heath, a modest red brick church of 1864 where I served my title, had kneeling rails for pews on one side of the church and none on the other; the indigent could kneel on a

RIGHT: *East Window and Chancel of the Chapel, before installation of the new choir stalls*

bare board while the more wealthy would have cushioned hassocks set in place for them.

At Harrow it was Christopher Wordsworth who finally determined on a specific place of worship that would allow the School to worship as a community entire of itself, which was not realistic in the parish church, as had been the practice since the fourteenth century. This also gave the Head Master a forum in which he could put into practice his High Church style. At Rugby there had been a chapel since the year before the battle of Waterloo and Thomas Arnold saw it as offering an opportunity for the dedicated instruction of the future governing classes. Wordsworth shared in his opinion (there is correspondence between the two men about the building of a chapel for Harrow) and immediately upon appointment he set about raising funds for a chapel.

The Statutes of 1591 that John Lyon drafted for the School, for which he had obtained a Royal Charter in 1572 from Elizabeth I two years after the newly Protestant nation had been placed under papal interdict, show that he provided thirty sermons a year in the parish church, much in the style of the later Puritan lectureships, for the edification of the boys. This was the only express intention to address the specific needs of the boys themselves, as their religious upbringing was still centred on the parish church. The boys were also expected to have use of John Calvin's *Catechism* and also of the *Catechism* of Dean Alexander Nowell (which today is, in a revised form, still in the *Book of Common Prayer*), the twin pillars by which generations across the Nation learned their faith by rote.

In this John Lyon was acting in a way that was a commonplace amongst contemporaries. Born and raised a catholic in the catholic England of Henry VIII, John Lyon saw in his own lifetime the vicissitudes of religious change, and even if the farm at Preston was neither a hotbed of the old orthodoxy nor of the new conformity it is likely that he retained friendships across a range of pieties; certainly the evidence of the catechisms would suggest Protestant leanings but the nearest he came to establishing closed scholarships at Cambridge was at Caius College, which was noted for its continuing catholic sympathies.

As the School was part of the local community, and in origin had grown up from within the parish long before it became a Free School in 1615, worship in the parish church would have been a commonplace where boys and staff took their place within the wider community of the Body of Christ, unlike foundations such as at Eton where the royal benefactor provided a chapel as part of the foundation.

It was only at the start of the Victorian era that some change became almost inevitable when the Head Master and the parish priest were at loggerheads in the matter of religious practice. Christopher Wordsworth became Head Master in the year before the accession of Queen Victoria, at a time when the place in society of the Church of England was becoming more openly debated. Catholic Emancipation in 1829 and the debates over the Irish Church Temporalities Act of 1833, that sparked John Keble's notorious Assize sermon in the University Church in Oxford on 'National Apostasy', called into question the very nature of an Established Church. Wordsworth's invitation to Keble to become an examiner for leaving scholarships in his first year as Head Master as well as his determination to build a chapel where he, as Head Master, would oversee worship, brought much dissension and argument, not just with the local Vicar of St Mary's but also with Governors.

He was finally able to build an unlovesome chapel in 1839, but it was to prove as temporary as its builder and, although religion was not the sole cause of Wordsworth's downfall as Head Master, much of it brought about by a jealous and slighted Vicar, it did at least offer him a pay-off. The OH Prime Minister of the day, Sir Robert Peel, offered Wordsworth a Canonry at Westminster in 1844, rescuing the School from an acrimonious debate that was costing money in lost revenues at a time when the economic prospects for the wider society were much in doubt.

The new Chapel had allowed the Head Master an arena within which to foster the Christian attitudes of the boys committed to his care. The tradition of clerical Head Masters might seem quaint to us in our day. (At Harrow it survived until 1926. Oxbridge colleges retained ordained clergymen as Heads of House until the 1960s.) But it had enjoyed long years of practice as a virtual guarantee of a certain educational standard as much as of religious orthodoxy. With the emergent demand for a graduate qualification for all clerics in the early Stuart

ABOVE:
*Dedication
Service for the
new choir stalls,
14 September
2003*

period, school-mastering offered ministers an alternative (and often more lucrative) career to that provided by a living with a benefice. In both, Christian instruction would be assumed as the *raison d'être* even where it was not always practised; in 1605 Bishop Vaughan in his Articles of Visitation for the diocese of London asked, 'whether are your schoole-masters negligent in instructing their schollers in the catechisme, and grounds of religion, and in bringing them to the church to heare divine service and sermons?'

Wordsworth's hopes were, therefore, to go beyond the intentions of placing the boys in the church on the Hill to hear 'divine service and sermons' and were more fully realised under his successor, Charles Vaughan (Head Master 1845–59). The burgeoning School had rapidly outgrown the small red-brick Chapel and a new building, by Sir Giles Gilbert Scott, was erected between 1854 and 1857. By 1857 Vaughan had finally broken links with the parish church (one wonders which party felt easier) and the School kept away from worshipping at St Mary's.

Generations of living Harrovians might find it difficult to think that the Chapel is only this year celebrating its sesquicentenary, even though much of the internal decoration is more recent. The reredos and mosaic panels

of the choir were designed by Sir Arthur Blomfield in 1899 and the Memorial Crypt Chapel of 1918 by the distinguished Sir Charles Nicholson (who elsewhere sympathetically completed the earlier plans of William Burges for Speech Room). In its own way the Chapel now is more fitting to the sort of worship of which Wordsworth had been suspected.

This Victorian inheritance, that largely shaped the School's religious practice well into the twentieth century, has cast a long shadow. Tyerman's recent history of the School begins to see changes only after the chaplaincy of Martyn Hughes in the 1970s, when Chapel attendance for the whole school was no longer compulsory on a daily basis (Mondays had long since been taken over by a general Assembly in 'Speecher'). But such changes were more the result of a shift in the Nation's own attitudes to public and private prayer than of any personal pieties, or lack of, in successive Head Masters and also are reflected in the whole matter of curricular change.

For whereas war often brings a nation to its knees, and the Church of England had both harnessed and exploited such events throughout the first half of the twentieth century, introducing for instance the practice of an early service on Sundays as a pattern known to returning soldiers from the First World War, the rise of a modern world has privatised religion as yet one more optional good for sale. In the private sector of education parental choice is bound to be in the mind of any Head Master. In some cases that choice has helped put an end to the anti-Semitism innately harboured in the School until the 1970s by allowing for a wider recognition of faith groups other than presumed Christians.

Since the lifetime of John Lyon the Church of England has ceased to be the voice of the Nation. In many places, in common with other churches since the rise of Non-Conformity and the emancipation of Catholicism, it has become sectarian, now offering worship for a chosen, self-justifying membership. This shift at first was kept at arms' length from schools of a Christian (for which read Anglican) foundation but is inevitable within the constraints of a Church that has a rigorous territorial policy (the Parish) but nonetheless claims to be broadly tolerant across a wide spectrum of opinion (the Evangelical Revival and the Oxford Movement in the nineteenth century vividly show as much).

Religion at Harrow today

Perhaps we are bucking the trend but religion at Harrow at the start of this century IS taken seriously and, to the extent that these things can be measured (they can't), is a success.

We believe that the spiritual dimension of his life is a central part of a boy's education. Every school week starts with a prayer in Speech Room. Every school year ends with a service of thanksgiving. All pupils are required to attend Chapel three times a week with the exception of non-Christians who are expected to attend an alternative form of reflection.

The Christian life of the school is strong. Nobody these days is forced to be confirmed, so the 120 boys who are confirmed at Harrow each year have chosen this course for themselves. We have three full-time Chaplains – including a Catholic priest. There are 130 pupils from Catholic families at Harrow and many of them chose us because they know we will take their religion seriously: their sons will be required to attend weekly Catechism and Mass as part of our vibrant Catholic community in the school. Anglicans have the option of attending the Eucharist daily. The School Christian Union, Flambards, is prospering. A very successful recent innovation has been the taking of Morning Prayer services by groups of boys on a House basis: they do it well, and their efforts are respected by other boys. New choir stalls have been recently built in the chancel to accommodate a choir of up to 70 boys, and the new ecumenical Service Book contains modern and traditional liturgies from both the Anglican and Roman Catholic traditions.

The Chaplains make an essential contribution to the pastoral life of the school community and they are available to boys and adults alike, irrespective of their faith allegiance. Baptisms, weddings and funerals frequently take place in the Chapel.

There are about 90 boys at Harrow who follow a faith other than Christianity. Wherever possible we make arrangements for them too. For example, Jewish pupils have occasional meetings with a rabbi and they mark the main Jewish festivals with a service and meal at the School.

Religious Studies is a popular subject. All boys take the GCSE and numbers opting for it at A level are high: one of the biggest RS departments in any English school.

Our Chapel stands at the centre of the School and the centre of School life. It is not easy to persuade teenage boys to take an interest in matters spiritual, but we try and we believe we have some success.

BARNABY LENON

Despite the claims and demands of the 1988 Education Act, few schools can now offer a worshipping tradition that is exclusively Anglican while being inclusive of all its members. As chaplain to a fourteenth-century foundation private school in South-East London I well know that the Act is more honoured in the breach. Beaks at Harrow long ago started to stay away, and more recent exceptions on grounds of conscience have rightly been made to allow non-Anglicans, and indeed persons of other faiths, to be absent or to attend their own prayers with a visiting minister.

John Lyon envisaged that his series of benefit sermons would educate the boys in his school. Victorians believed that compulsory Chapel attendance would achieve much the same goal. Nowadays learning about the Christian religion is, for some, only an option to be taken in the form room.

In 1971 I was one of only two boys in the School who undertook 'O' Level Divinity out of hours with the tutelage of the Chaplain in his own private time. (Fifteen years later I was ordained and my *confrère* has since written *Four Weddings and a Funeral*!) Even though every boy in School now undertakes RE at GCSE, it is difficult to see how a subject taught in form can inform the ethos of a school if the practice of faith is no longer a central part of that understanding of Christianity.

Since the Nation as a whole is no longer conversant with the Bible (whether in the Authorised Version of 1611 or its more accurate recent translations) and the Prayer Book (whether the *Book of Common Prayer* or *Common Worship*), church-going has become an option for a paid-up membership that is, in turn, reflected in schools of a Christian foundation. This has several immediate consequences of which the loss of community-singing, the recognition of whole tracts of English literature and an understanding of the variety of the Western musical tradition are only a part.

It will fall to successive Head Masters and Governors to seek for the proper place of the Chapel in the life of the School and so to determine the flavour of 'Harrow Religion'.

The Rev. Dr Nicholas Cranfield (Elmfield 1969²) was a Fellow of Selwyn College, Cambridge, from 1992–99 and is now Vicar of All Saints, Blackheath.

The Vaughan Library

PETER HUNTER

Every school ought to have an attractive and comfortable library where a boy can delve for himself amongst good, old books, free from his mates and his masters. It is a great help to self-education. I shall never forget the happy and profitable hours I spent in the Vaughan.
Sir George Trevelyan, *The Grove*, 1851

NOT LONG AFTER DR CHARLES VAUGHAN announced his retirement, a meeting was held to decide what would be a suitable memorial of his reign as Head Master between 1845 and 1859. The new Head Master, Dr Henry Montagu Butler, suggested a library to be named after his predecessor, which would replace the small Monitors' Library at that time housed

in the Old Schools. This had been founded by Dr Sumner (Head Master 1760–71), but was the exclusive domain of the Monitors, who were given a personal key: this explains the origins of the ceremony at which each Monitor, even today, receives a key to the Vaughan as a symbol of his office.

Dr Butler's vision and energy were largely responsible for the success of the project. He encountered early difficulties, such as in the acquisition of the site, which was partly occupied as a house and stables by Mr John Bliss, landlord of the Crown and Anchor Inn, known popularly by the boys as 'the abode of Bliss'. Out of his own pocket Butler gave inducements to the tenants to vacate the premises, including a sum of £100 to Mr Bliss

RIGHT: *The Vaughan Library by George Gilbert Scott. Lord Palmerston laid the Foundation Stone on 4 July 1861*

who was heart-broken to leave the home he had so long inhabited, though his son was delighted with the prospects which his superior new house offered. The Charity Commissioners had to give permission for the Governors to hold the site and to erect a new building, and insisted that the Head Master meet the running costs out of the School fees.

The architect chosen was George Gilbert Scott, RA, a pupil of Pugin, whose designs can still be seen in the tiled pavement that leads from the street to the main entrance of the Vaughan. Scott had recently been awarded the design for the new Foreign Office and would soon undertake the Albert Memorial in Kensington Gore.

In June 1861 Dr Butler wrote to a friend:

'The long expected work of demolition here at last has begun. When Scott came down on Saturday I told him the open space with its view of Hampstead would be so beautiful, that everybody would cry shame upon him for venturing to profane it with a building, however well.'

The view from the window has inspired generations of Harrovians. The Rt. Hon. George Russell, writing in his 1913 autobiography noted:

'I should be shamefully ungrateful to a place of peculiar enjoyment if I forbore to mention the library at Harrow … Its delicious bow window looking towards Hampstead was my favourite resort. I used to read there for hours at a stretch.'

Although the view today is made even more beautiful by the terrace gardens in the foreground (created after the topsoil was moved from the Speech Room site in 1871), the back of the Vaughan was, for its first decade, a less attractive prospect. Lord Frederic Hamilton recalled the 'uncompromisingly ugly vegetable garden and rows of utilitarian cabbages and potatoes [which] filled the area then known as the *slopes*'.

On Speech Day, Thursday 4 July 1861, the Old Harrovian Prime Minister, Lord Palmerston, then aged seventy-nine, rode out from London on his white horse and, under an umbrella held over his head by the Head Master, laid the foundation stone (in the cavity of which are buried coins of the realm) just opposite the south door of the Chapel, riding back straight away to take part in a parliamentary debate.

At the celebration luncheon, Dr Butler explained his

vision of the Vaughan, not just as a place to house a book collection, but also as 'a temple in which all memorials of deep interest to Harrow would eventually be deposited'. He looked forward to its holding portraits and busts of famous Harrow men and he was delighted that the first treasure would be a portrait of the Prime Minister, painted by Old Harrovian Francis Grant (soon to be knighted and elected President of the Royal Academy), to which many OHs subscribed. Other portraits hung in the Vaughan at this time included that of Lord Byron by W.E. West (now in the Old Speech Room Gallery) which his mistress Teresa Guiccioli said was 'such a frightful caricature that it ought to be destroyed'. George Richmond's image of a saintly-looking

BELOW: Extract from an essay by Winston Churchill, 1889

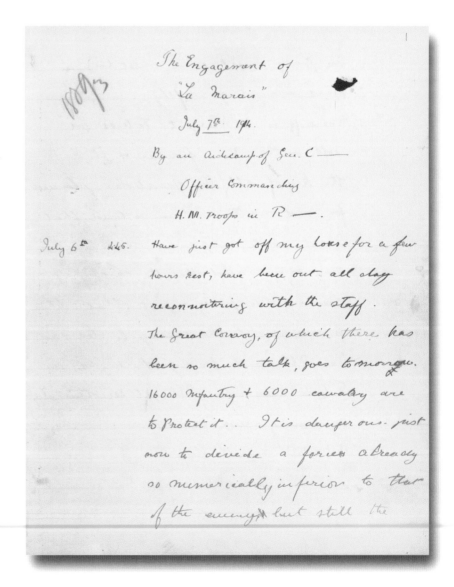

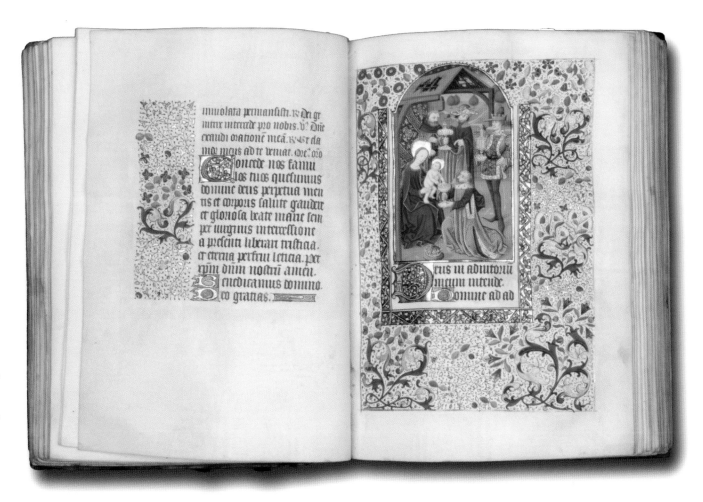

Vaughan was also given pride of place. Sir Matthew Ridley was so delighted with his son's progress at the School (M.W. Ridley, later 1st Viscount Ridley,) that, as a token of his appreciation, he presented the new library with a massive clock which is mounted on the south wall. The marble table given to the Monitors' Library by Captain L.R. Keene, which had come from the Temple of Peace in Rome, was placed in the bow window.

Dr Butler had great admiration for the foreman of the building works, Titus Lander, and wrote to his friend the Reverend F.G. Vesey to help him raise money to send Lander to Europe to see the great cathedrals such as Chartres, as a token of his respect for a man who 'keeps all the men in capital order and harmony'.

For a century the Vaughan was the School's principal repository for its various treasures and collections. Whilst the Butler Museum came to hold Harrow's ethnographical and natural history items, it was the Vaughan that displayed Marie Antoinette's work box, the Silver Arrow archery costume, the Sheridan manuscripts, the 'Doria throne' and the world-famous Byron Collection, the most interesting items in which were bequeathed by H.

Panmure Gordon in 1902. Can a school have too much Byroniana? Perhaps it could, as Dr Wood (Head Master 1898–1910) instructed the Librarian B.P. Lascelles to reject the offer of a bust of the poet on the grounds that Harrow already had sufficient mementoes of that 'noble but not first-rate poet'. (Lascelles, nearly seven feet tall, could remove books from the highest shelves without a ladder and had the disconcerting habit of looking *over* the door of his form room before entering). Sir John Mortimer recalled how he 'fell in love with Byron at school. We were not exact contemporaries, but his Turkish dagger and slippers were in a glass case in the library at Harrow. I tried to write poetry by the grave where he lay to write'.

The Vaughan gave inspiration, perhaps, to another OH author, Sir Terence Rattigan. In his day there was on the shelves a copy of Robert Browning's translation of the *Agamemnon* of Aeschylus. Was it that book, or the graphic representation in the stained glass windows of Clytemnestra standing over the murdered body of her husband, that inspired him to write his drama of school life *The Browning Version*?

'Crocker-Harris: Then why do you invent words that are simply not there?

Taplow: I thought they sounded better, sir. More exciting. After all, she did kill her husband, sir. (With relish) She's just been revealed with his dead body and Cassandra's weltering in gore.

Crocker-Harris: I am delighted at this evidence, Taplow, of your interest in the rather more lurid aspects of dramaturgy, but I feel I must remind you that you are supposed to be construing Greek, not collaborating with Aeschylus.'

The stained glass windows repay more careful observation. On entering the Library, visitors pass six small lancets in the porch representing the great academic disciplines: on the north wall Mathematica, Theologia and Historia, and on the south wall Rhetorica, Philosophia and Poetica. These were designed by A.C. Bell and date from 1863. In the main library the bay window overlooking the Terrace contains three cinquefoils: a lion rampant to represent John Lyon, the Founder; the Arms of Queen Elizabeth I, who granted the Charter in 1572, and the Arms of Dr Vaughan, after whom the Library is named.

Dr Butler was energetic in his pursuit of funds for the windows, persuading members of his own family to subscribe to eight of the roundels which could be purchased for £1 for quatrefoils or 25 shillings for cinquefoils. The south wall contains two large windows: that on the left, consisting of two cusped lights, shows representations from Tragedy and was given as a memorial to Douglas Anderson who had died two years after leaving Harrow. The three panels on the left show scenes from Sophocles' *Oedipus at Colonus*, Aeschylus' *Agamemnon* and Euripides' *Alcestis*; the panels on the right are all from Shakespeare: *King Lear*, *Macbeth* and *Othello*. Dr Butler appealed to OHs who had obtained scholarships to underwrite the cost of installing a similar window representing Comedy. The left-hand panel shows scenes from Aristophanes: *The Knights*, *The Clouds* and *The Frogs*. The right-hand panel has two scenes from Shakespeare: *The Tempest* and *A Midsummer Night's Dream*, with the central picture showing a scene from *The Critic* by Richard Brinsley Sheridan. On the west wall are scenes from *The Merchant of Venice* and *King John*, placed as a memorial to Georgina Butler, wife of the Head Master who oversaw the building of the Vaughan. The windows were designed by John Clement Bell and constructed by Messrs Clayton and Bell.

During the second half of the twentieth century the library's multiple role as book collection, art gallery and study hall put increasing pressure on the limited space available; additionally, the Vaughan was being used as a venue for Governors' and Masters' meetings and various School societies. In 1967 the Governors created improvements in the light of comments made in the School's recent inspection: a large cabinet was installed for the more attractive display of artefacts, and the northern half of the room was subdivided into study corrals. Though functional, these were poorly lit and somewhat claustrophobic and had the unfortunate effect of breaking up the openness of Scott's original conception. It was a priority of the 1998 refurbishment that these should be dismantled.

The role of art gallery was removed by the welcome opening in the 1970s of The Old Speech Room Gallery.

Portraits of Head Masters were moved to the Old Harrovian Room whilst distinguished Old Harrovians were hung in Speech Room. The creation of an environmentally controlled store room in the Old Speech Room Gallery meant that the Vaughan's best literary treasures could be better looked after and displayed more appropriately in the gallery's library showcases. Here today can be seen a small collection of medieval manuscripts and incunabula; a French fifteenth-century Book of Hours; a collection of books published by the Aldine Press, mainly in the sixteenth century; a 'Great Bible' of 1539 (the first translation in English), as ordered to be placed in every church by Henry VIII;

BELOW: *Interior of the Vaughan Library, 2004*

and a first edition of the 1611 Authorised Version. The Vaughan also owns three bibles which contain curious translations or misprints: two 'Breeches Bibles' of 1599 and 1607 (where Adam and Eve sew *breeches* of fig leaves to cover their nakedness) and a sumptuously bound 'Vinegar Bible' of 1717, once in the Blenheim Palace collection, where the running title at Luke xx reads 'The parable of the vinegar' (for vineyard). More modern treasures include a manuscript of part of Trollope's *Framley Parsonage* and Winston Churchill's essay, written as a schoolboy, about an imagined Russian invasion of Afghanistan.

As with the original construction of the building, the refurbishment also had its difficulties. Objections from the local planners put paid to Andrew Reed's original ideas for glass-fronted galleries and a new glass door in the entrance porch. Other objections seemed less rational – to the idea, for example, that boys who were standing on the new galleries and looking out of the windows might be visible to passing motorists! One planning official favoured two diagonal staircases connecting the main chamber with the form rooms below, in preference to Reed's discreet and elegant solution of a single central spiral. The 'new' library was now effectively on four levels, as the galleries added valuable shelf space upstairs, whilst the lower floor benefited from the addition of a new mezzanine level.

The work started in the summer of 1998, but the planning and preparation had begun some years earlier, the first major project being to transfer the card catalogue, then housed in large wooden cabinets, to computer. Prior to this, 25,000 books had to be reclassified (exchanging the old shelf number (eg 21F) for a Dewey decimal number) and bar-coded. This monumental task was undertaken by library and voluntary staff. The equally Herculean job of computerising the catalogue was farmed out to a professional firm who completed the work quickly, but with many inaccuracies. Which other library, for example, could boast a copy of that celebrated novel *Withering Heights?*

The second serious setback was the initial shortage of funds: the project had therefore to be undertaken in two stages. The library service continued upstairs whilst the workmen moved in below; then librarians and contractors swapped over. Conditions were far from ideal, but relationships between personnel were very amicable throughout. Echoes of Titus Lander?

As part of the refurbishment, the ceiling was repaired (falling pigeon feathers had been an occupational hazard) and the roof was stripped, with new custom-made tiles for the garden side where a stunning impact was created with the juxtaposition of fresh reds and dark blues. Stonework was cleaned outside and inside to reveal delicate pinks and creams under the ubiquitous grey. New stone finials were copied from nineteenth-century steel engravings. New lighting was installed, the price of the chandeliers in the main chamber almost matching the original £12,000 cost of the whole building; Scott's heating system, which had run below the bottom shelf of the wall cases, was removed and replaced with under-floor pipes beneath a reproduction Victorian grille.

The collection itself now required attention: most departmental libraries were married with Vaughan stock and approximately 15,000 volumes were moved out to a reserve collection store. The book purchase budget was increased and expanded to include CDs, videos and DVDs. Opening hours were extended and, both inevitably but gratifyingly, the number of users rose significantly. Before refurbishment, fewer than 4,000 user visits would be recorded in a term; in the academic year 2001/02 there were 73,000 users counted.

At the start of the twenty-first century this much loved landmark has found a new lease of life. It was built with the generous support of OHs and friends of the School; and it was refurbished and brought to its present splendid condition with the equally generous support of a new generation of OHs and friends, of whom His Late Majesty King Hussein, Sir Michael Connell and Mr John Hignett were the principal benefactors.

In 1939 Philip Bryant, brother of the popular historian Sir Arthur Bryant, wrote a guide to Harrow in which he paid special tribute to the Vaughan:

'The Vaughan has been to many Harrovians the most blessed abode in Harrow … The atmosphere of the Vaughan is a strange combination of privacy and good fellowship … Here one is in the heart of Harrow'.

Peter Hunter was Vaughan Librarian from 1989–99 and has been House Master of The Park since 2001.

Old Speech Room Gallery

CAROLYN LEDER

THE OLD SPEECH ROOM GALLERY, DESIGNED BY Alan Irvine, opened in the Old Schools building in 1976. This provided a distinguished gallery in which to preserve, display and interpret the School's collections. The majority of treasures, which make a vital contribution to the cultural life of the School, were given or bequeathed by Old Harrovians. Harrow is indeed fortunate to have a museum of this calibre within the School, so that boys are afforded a rare opportunity for such artefacts to play a role in their formal education. In addition, the 'OSRG Arts Society' allows them to take part in the running of the museum itself, and serves as the fulcrum for a regular programme of external visits to museums and exhibitions in London.

The gallery contains a number of discrete collections, encompassing antiquities and fine art as well as the notable Byron collection and rare books from the Vaughan Library.

In 1864 Sir John Gardner Wilkinson, one of the first British Egyptologists, presented Harrow School with a large and celebrated collection of Egyptian, Greek, Etruscan and Roman antiquities, so that they could be used for educational purposes. He regarded his *alma mater* with affection and considered that such a collection would have interested him in his school days. He later explained, 'many advantages are to be gained by having in our youth an opportunity of examining objects illustrative of classical authors, as well as those connected with science and art. At that period of life our minds are more open to receive impressions, & a strong interest is often awakened when we are predisposed to such inquiries.' As he had hoped, his gift has inspired many young men, including a notable series of classical scholars that includes Sir Arthur Evans.

Sir John Gardner Wilkinson's Egyptian objects, which he acquired on his travels through Egypt, still form the core of Harrow's unique collection. They reflect his interest in the religious beliefs and everyday life of ancient Egypt and helped provide the basis for his most famous book *The Manners and Customs of the Ancient Egyptians*, which won him a knighthood in 1839. The display of nearly 300 items in the gallery is arranged thematically to illustrate the travels of Sir John Gardner Wilkinson and a variety of aspects of life and death in ancient Egypt such as Death and Mummification, the Pharaohs, Daily Life, Religion and Magic. By preserving the body of the deceased and placing it in a suitably furnished tomb the Egyptians believed that they could ensure survival in the afterworld. The process of mummification is thought to have taken about seventy days and the mummy was often provided with an elaborate cartonnage funerary mask.

Gardner Wilkinson began to collect Greek vases in 1833 on his return from Egypt. Many of the vases he gave to Harrow, as in most museums, were created for drinking parties, or symposia. These all-male events, literally a 'coming together' of men who fought in the same units, to talk, drink and listen to music and poetry, were governed by formalized rules, that included the playing of the game kottabos (flicking wine from a drinking cup at a target). The women who attended were not wives, but courtesans. Wine and water were mixed in a krater, the central vessel of the symposium. The magnificent Red-Figure krater, is attributed on stylistic grounds to the early classical artist, the Cleveland Painter. Like many vases at Harrow the krater is decorated with an episode from Greek mythology: the battle between Kaineus and the Centaurs. In this dramatic representation, three wild, unruly centaurs

RIGHT: *Attic Red-Figure Column Krater by the Cleveland Painter, c. 470–460 BC*

47

(part man and part horse) attack Kaineus, a hero of the neighbouring Lapith tribe. At first the centaur's crude weapons of boulders and trees had no effect on the invulnerable Kaineus. In the end they recognised that the only way to defeat their opponent was to pound him into the ground, so that Kaineus is shown partially buried. He gains some measure of revenge by stabbing the central centaur in the chest. With a fine sense of irony, the shield of Kaineus is emblazoned with the emblem of a centaur bearing a branch. Artists working in the Red-Figure technique, in which the figures remain the natural colour of the vase, painted the interior markings with a brush, allowing for a fluid technique that permitted the exploration of foreshortening, as in the centaur seen from the back.

The acclaimed collection of watercolours, given by C.J. Hegan in 1935, is being shown in a systematic series of themed exhibitions, as the pictures are researched and catalogued. The roster of great names from the pantheon of English watercolour painting make the collection one of Harrow's outstanding treasures. Girtin's 'An Old Farmstead', de Wint's magisterial 'Distant View of Lincoln Cathedral' and David Roberts' 'The Convent of St Catherine, Mount Sinai' afford some indication of its depth and variety. John Sell Cotman was one of the most original and gifted English landscape painters. His austere sense of design and simple, flat washes of colour were in advance of his time. His response to Normandy, one of the key artistic experiences of his career, was immediate and passionate. His watercolour of 'Mont St Michel'

1818, captures his description of the 'solitary grandeur of the awe-striking Mont St Michel'. But Cotman also reacted with apprehension, writing of the total darkness of the interior and his treacherous journeys through the quicksands, when 'all round shook like custard meat'. The remains of a boat in the sand act as a symbolic *memento mori*.

Turner's range and virtuosity is unsurpassed in English art. He was the leading landscape painter of the nineteenth century, who aimed to confirm landscape as a serious art form, which could set forth something of significance about human destiny. The son of a London barber, he travelled restlessly in search of subject matter, both in Britain and on the Continent. Unprepossessing in appearance, taciturn and secretive, he amassed a considerable fortune from his engraving projects, and in one of his few recorded epigrams, is said to have remarked of painting that it was a 'rum thing'. His 'The Waterfall in the Gorge of Pre St Didier' (1836) was traditionally thought to represent the Reichenbach Falls, where Sherlock Holmes appeared to plunge over the falls locked in mortal combat with Professor Moriarty. But it has now been securely identified as a Val d'Aosta scene from his tour of the Alps in 1836. The waterfall is one of the most spectacular sights in the Alps, pervading the gorge with spray and sound when in full flow. Standing on the terrace at the foot of the cataract, Turner made this study at about midday, before the sunlight reached the water. The growth of Romanticism had led to a passion for the sublime and landscapes which invoked a frisson of terror in the spectator. Here he presented the overwhelming strength and scale of the forces of nature, with a dizzying verticality that excludes all but a fragment of sky.

Sculptures range in date from a spirited Roman marble torso to Thomas Woolner's poignant Pre-Raphaelite statuette of Elaine, who dies for love of Sir Lancelot. The gallery contains busts of Old Harrovians such as Sheridan, Byron and Spencer Perceval, who enjoys the unenviable distinction of being the only British Prime Minister to be assassinated. The day of the tragedy, Joseph Nollekens, the leading portrait sculptor of his day, was summoned to Perceval's rooms at the Treasury to make a death mask. His resulting sculpture is paradoxically lifelike, with sensitive modelling of the lean, shrewd face

Victor Pasmore CH CBE RA

1908–1998 (Bradbys, 1923[1])

Victor Pasmore played a key role in the development of modern British art. He recalled his school days for his Old Speech Room Gallery exhibition in 1990: 'There is one place at Harrow which I remember both with pleasure and gratitude – the Art School … But apart from academic exercises of copying, Maurice [Clarke] took a few of us on Saturday afternoons in the summer term outdoor sketching from nature in the country and local villages, trips which sometimes ended with tea, strawberries and cucumber sandwiches en route. Harrow was my only art school; so although I learnt nothing that I can remember in the form rooms there I did discover Art.'

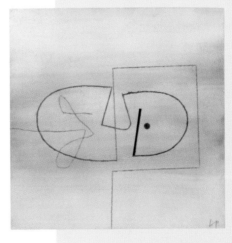

The death of his father forced him to take a local government post in the LCC. At the same time he experimented with abstraction and became a member of the London avant-garde. In 1937 he established the famous Euston Road School with Claude Rogers and William Coldstream, becoming a full-time painter the following year. From 1938–1947, Pasmore painted traditional works and naturalistic landscapes, often wonderfully evocative views of the Thames. His final move to abstraction in 1948 was described by Herbert Read as 'the most revolutionary event in post-war British art'.

In his writing, Pasmore did much to provide a theoretical underpinning for abstract art. As he explained, 'true painting, in any form, always develops a concrete existence of its own, independent of what it represents.' As Director of Painting at King's College, Newcastle-upon-Tyne, he did much to stimulate new thinking in art education towards courses based on the abstract principles of composition. He also designed part of Peterlee New Town, County Durham. In 1966 he acquired a house and studio in Malta and Mediterranean light and colour are often reflected in his subsequent work.

Pasmore's 'Linear Image: The Ambiguous World, No 1' 1975 displays his virtuosity and variety in the use of line, which is here allied to the earth colours which have been a consistent theme within his oeuvre. Even at his most abstract, Pasmore's images carry associative meanings and celebrate the power of the imagination in a mechanistic universe. His titles for pictures frequently contribute a layer of poetic allusion to his work.

CAROLYN LEDER

of the barrister turned politician. Eschewing the blind eyeball, Perceval's eyeballs are deeply incised, with a dot of marble at the centre to add animation.

Romney painted his fine, early portrait of John Sayer when the youth was Head of School in 1770. He is portrayed in the School Archery Dress of pink satin tunic, white lace collar and blue sash which dated from the institution of the annual Silver Arrow competition in the reign of Charles II. The artist has given Sayer a suitable, swashbuckling Van Dyckian pose, with out-thrust elbow and hand bent at the wrist. Riotous behaviour led the Head Master to abolish the competition in 1772. Sayer was the first Harrovian to become a Fellow of Gonville and Caius College, Cambridge, but on his marriage he left to pursue an active career as a London barrister. He later endowed two Sayer Scholarships for Harrovians coming up to Caius, 'for the promotion of classical learning and taste'.

The growing collection of Modern British pictures includes David Jones's numinous 'Tree at Harrow' c.1950 and significant works by Old Harrovians such as Sir Winston Churchill, Spencer Gore (our most recent acquisition), Sir Cecil Beaton (an amusing portrait of artist Marie Laurencin), Victor Pasmore and Richard Shirley Smith.

The son of the first Wimbledon Singles Champion, Spencer Gore was educated at Harrow where he was the first winner of the Yates Thompson Drawing Prize and excelled at cricket. The introduction of modern art to England owes much to Gore who produced some of the most dazzlingly original Post-Impressionist pictures in English art. His relatively early Landscape c.1908–9 may have been painted on the South Downs on a visit to his aunt at Woolbeding. It has a strong, geometric structure, decorative interest and loosely painted small pointillist brushstrokes on a light ground.

Sir Winston Churchill's 'A Distant View of Venice' 1929 is an excellent example of his robust and energetic style. Churchill was above all a colourist. He captured the essence of Venetian colour in the city, the clouds and the boats with their reflections in the water. The bravura brushwork gives texture to the surface of the canvas, from the impasto in the sky to the long, fluid strokes in the lagoon. His enthusiasm was inexhaustible. In his essay *Painting as a Pastime*, he wrote: 'When I get to heaven I mean to spend a considerable portion of my first million years in painting, and so get to the bottom of the subject.'

Richard Shirley Smith is one of this country's most distinguished wood engravers, book illustrators and artists. 'Archaeological Fragments' 1986 is a quintessential example of his style in which he draws on a variety of sources for a virtuoso display of painterly technique. Sources range from the statue of a Roman matron, seen in Turkey, to one of the Boycott Pavilions by the architect James Gibbs. The painting finds its counterpart in a witty 'collage frame' of diverse elements which include, with pleasing pertinence, the Crossed Arrows of Harrow School.

'Art should speak to us across the centuries' (W.H. Auden). This axiom is a guiding principle for the Old Speech Room Gallery from the interpretation of the antiquities and fine art in the permanent collection, to temporary exhibitions and museological projects for the boys. The gallery has an active exhibition programme, with free admission to the public and several major shows each year. These comprise a mixture of works on loan as well as treasures from the School's collections. The boys of the Old Speech Room Gallery Arts Society participate in a wide range of activities, including the mounting of exhibitions. Taking advantage of the School's proximity to London, visits are organised for boys to see and discuss art in the capital, from the big shows at the national collections to the compact and idiosyncratic, such as Sir John Soane's Museum. During their five years at Harrow, boys have the opportunity to enjoy upwards of 50 such visits. In so doing, the Old Speech Room Gallery expands its educational programme into a 'museum without walls'.

Carolyn Leder MA was a Lecturer at the Department of Extramural Studies, London University. She has been Curator of the Old Speech Room Gallery since 1989.

BELOW: *Bust of Spencer Perceval by Joseph Nollekens (1737–1823)*

The Harrow Rifle Corps

ROSS BECKETT

Form, form, Riflemen, form,
Ready, be ready to meet the storm,
Riflemen, Riflemen, Riflemen, form.
Tennyson 1859

FIFTY-FIVE HARROVIANS FOUGHT AGAINST NAPOLEON I at Waterloo so it was no surprise that Harrow responded to the call for volunteers during the French scare of 1859. France was again ruled by a Napoleon, the Emperor Napoleon III. He was regarded with considerable suspicion by many Englishmen as 'a mystery man with a deadpan face and a goatee'. The French were seen as a threat and the Queen and her Prime Minister, Lord Palmerston, were convinced that invasion loomed, particularly as the French had started to build a fleet of ironclads and were extending their fortified naval base at Cherbourg, seemingly in preparation for 'a midnight foray' across the Channel. This was 'the storm' to which Tennyson refers in the lines above.

Despite the objections of the penny-pinching Chancellor, Mr Gladstone, an Etonian, the Harrovian Prime Minister, supported by his Sovereign, demanded £11 million to strengthen coastal defences and enlarge the fleet. In addition the War Committee encouraged the formation of a Volunteer Movement to which Palmerston promised to supply the rifles. Queen Victoria and Prince Albert attended reviews in Hyde Park and at Aldershot as well as shooting matches at Wimbledon. England was to be defended.

Amidst a furore of 'patriotic slogans, rousing sentiments and xenophobic suspicions', Harrow made its contribution to the national effort. A public meeting was held in Speech Room, under the Chairmanship of Dr Vaughan, to discuss the formation of a Harrow Rifle Corps. There were speeches which expounded the duties of a rifleman, others which were calculated to arouse

martial spirit by painting a vivid picture of the horrors of French rule, and so on until some humorous banter over the matter of uniform concluded the meeting. Finally on the 30 December 1859 official sanction was granted and the Harrow Rifle Corps came into being as the 18th Middlesex Rifle Volunteers. The date is commemorated on our cap badge.

The initial response to the call for volunteers was enthusiastic and in 1860 there were some 350 who joined. However, numbers equally quickly fell away and in 1863 Vaughan's successor, Montagu Butler, presided over the reorganisation of the Rifle Corps and provided an armoury beneath the Old Schools. Butler also took a close interest in the uniform: grey-blue with dark blue facings and much braid. At one stage magnificent fur hussar hats with enormous white plumes were the order of the day.

Until the Boer War, the Rifle Corps 'remained an eccentric and minority activity'. Numbers fluctuated; for example in 1882 there were only around 30 rising to about 200 in the late 1880s before dropping back to just over 100. Frequent appeals for support were made in the *The Harrovian*. Thus *The Harrovian* writes in June 1870, 'no-one will ever be the worse in after-life for being able to "form fours" and "wheel" properly … We cannot help saying that we think the School is bound to back up the Captain of the Corps in his endeavours to improve its condition; and whilst tendering to him our deepest thanks for all his past efforts, we feel sure that as the members increase in number he will spare no pains to bring the Corps to the highest state of perfection.' The same year the Rifle Corps was presented by Lady Crabbe, in the name of her son, Eyre Crabbe, with what were grandly called 'Regimental Colours'. *The Harrovian* noted that 'notwithstanding the inclemency of the weather, a large number of spectators had assembled to witness the ceremony … the School Corps after having performed sundry military evolutions under the command of their officers, were formed into square … the colours were then duly presented to the Captain, who amidst loud applause, handed them over to the keeping of "Ensign Newall"'.

Drill was held weekly on Wednesday evenings so as not to interfere with cricket but it appears that both attendance and standard were patchy. However, shooting was much more popular, with large numbers of boys vying for a place in the School team. 'The great object of interest in the Corps is the annual match at Wimbledon … Harrow has earned the admiration and envy of all the public schools for its excellence in shooting; and the Shield (the Ashburton) has become so identified with our School, that while others might be content with a high place in the Contest, we should regard anything

short of the first place as a failure and a defeat', trumpeted *The Harrovian*. A song, 'The Harrow Blue', sadly not included in the present edition of the Song Book, commemorated the exploits of the Shooting Eight:

> So the Ashburton Shield again they bore
> To the wall where it loved to hang before,
> A prize to their shooting due,
> With a rush of triumph and wild young cheer
> Which gladden the hearts of all who hear
> And who love the Harrow Blue.

Although the Boer War was still some way distant this song was in a way prophetic, for the final verse contained the lines,

> Where bullets fly thick in no manic strife
> Where sorrow and sickness darken life
> Where men don't *say*, but *do*
> With the soldier's sword, with generous hand,
> With words of sweet comfort there'll ever stand
> Those who've worn The Harrow Blue.

The Boer War began a period of change. An attempt was made to enlist all boys over 15 and drill parades were moved to mornings. In addition grey-blue uniforms gave

RIGHT: *Harrow School Officer Training Corps marching off for Field Day, 1890s*

LEFT: *Harrow Rifle Corps training in Germany*

way to khaki, although the black buttons of the rifle regiments were retained. In 1908 the Rifle Corps was, as at other schools, re-established as an Officer Training Corps. A new range was built below Garlands and in 1910–11 a parade ground was constructed beside the Football Fields. Yet the Corps remained voluntary with just over half the School enlisting. General Sir Allan Adair, in his autobiography, recalls the Corps at that time with some fondness and humour, 'Our OTC seemed to us as professional as some Territorial battalions'. Field days were the highlight, 'our Corps, supported occasionally by a battery of Royal Field Artillery, or a troop of Hussars, or such schools as Eton or Wellington, attacked Territorial units or other schools at Richmond Park or Princes Risborough. The field days culminated in a grand supper in the evening at which a band played'. Camps too were well supported, 'discipline was good, maintained by our sentries with fixed bayonets until a squabble over jam led to a boy being bayonetted in a moment of over-enthusiasm' – no health and safety committee or detailed risk-assessments in those days.

In 1912 the OTC was inspected by General Sir Horace Smith-Dorrien, who two years later was to save the BEF in the retreat from Mons by the action his Corps fought at Le Cateau. Smith-Dorrien congratulated the 'battalion' on its progress since the beginning of the OTC and expressed a hope that to be at Harrow would soon be synonymous with being in the OTC. It was also his

hope that more Harrovians would join the Territorial Forces and Special Reserve in their country's hour of need. The same year King George V on a visit to Harrow inspected a Guard of Honour and remarked upon the good reports he had heard of the Harrow OTC.

After the outbreak of the First World War OTC parades were increased to four a week, night exercises were introduced and field days were held four times a term. *The Harrovian* provided some gloomy accounts of those field days: 'Against the Royal Military College, Sandhurst, the chief umpire was unable to give a decision beyond the fact that a large percentage of casualties would have been the toll of many of the units engaged'. And again, 'after some miles of fighting in which we crossed hill, dale, wood and moor, we ended on the golf course with a charge, shoulder to shoulder, against an impregnable position, and were annihilated to the last man'. All too close to the reality in Flanders and France.

Between the World Wars the OTC was a central feature of Harrow life, recognised as such by the Governors who decreed that it be compulsory for all boys over 15. Parades were held twice a week on Wednesday afternoons and on Friday mornings before lunch. As well as being compulsory for the boys, Masters were expected to join. Some who had been appointed before 1918 returned to teach after their war service and many of those appointed in the following years had also served. However, compulsory Corps was not popular with all boys and

Masters alike. 'Slacking at Corps' met with strong official disapproval. *The Harrovian* carried a lively correspondence in 1929–30 concerning the rights and wrongs of compulsory Corps and in particular complaints about Friday morning parades and drill on Sundays for some Houses. A petition in May 1930, *supposedly* signed by 400 boys, called the excessive number of parades 'military torture' and demanded a 'reduction to one parade a week'. The row aroused considerable press coverage, not least in Germany, questions were asked in the House and Eton offered to send a platoon to the Hill to restore order. Nevertheless Friday parades continued.

In 1940 the Officer Training Corps became the more prosaic Junior Training Corps. This in turn became the Combined Cadet Force to reflect the tri-service nature of the organisation when Royal Navy and Royal Airforce sections appeared. Many of the Beaks appointed between 1945 and the mid 1960s had either fought in the Second World War or done post-war National Service so there was plenty of military experience in the Masters' Room. The Corps also remained an important, and compulsory, element of Harrow life and, until the end of National Service in the late 1950s, many boys regarded the Corps as a necessary preliminary to their two years' conscription.

Maintaining a compulsory Corps where boys joined after three terms and remained until they left school became increasingly difficult once National Service had been phased out. Officers and NCOs had to be more imaginative, and in some cases ingenious, in an attempt to vary the routine of weekly parades and training. A large number of specialist sections sprang up, some to last longer than others. More attention was focussed on adventurous training, originally known as arduous training, which reflected official as well as local thinking. Nevertheless the bullet needed biting and in 1965 a process began which was to conclude with the introduction of a voluntary Corps in 1973.

'Echoes of Edwardian Harrow' is the verdict of a former Beak on the Corps in the 1980s and 90s. In some ways he has a point. The re-adoption of the original title, Harrow Rifle Corps, is one. The fact is that the officers are once again amateurs, Beaks whose own military experience, if any, is based on their own school CCF, university OTC or Territorial Army service. On the other hand, although voluntary, the great majority of Harrovians choose to join. Harrow's record in winning Scholarships to the armed services is second to none and the Rifle Corps provides a fruitful ground for regimental recruiters. The expertise provided by the permanent staff of ex-regulars employed to instruct (officers as well as cadets) and to administer the Rifle Corps is of paramount importance. Camps are varied and challenging. In recent years training has been carried out not only in the UK and Germany but also in Norway, France, Cyprus and Jordan with plans to visit Brunei; all a far cry from the tented camps at Tweseldown.

Change continues steadily. The armoury has moved from its original position in the Old Schools to a more secure site closer to the parade ground and fields. The 1910 parade ground has been replaced by a new one below the 25 metre range and there are now plans for a new Rifle Corps building adjacent to it to combine an armoury, orderly room, offices and stores. The School is thus determined to ensure that for the future there will be many more 'to rally round to the bugle-sound, and join the Rifle Corps'.

THE HARROVIAN

1917

HSOTC

There has been issued this term an amended order of the Army Council calling up men in groups and classes A and B. The effect of the order to that no boy may remain at School beyond 18 years of age unless he fulfils one or other of the following two conditions:

That he can produce a certificate from the OC Contingent that he is likely to become an efficient officer and will be recommended to join an Officer Cadet Unit.

That he can produce a certificate from the Head Master that he is a bona fide candidate for the Regular Army and that he has a reasonable prospect of success in the Army Entrance examination.

Even with these qualifications no boy will be allowed to remain beyond eighteen and a half years of age.

Ross Beckett OBE *was Lt-Colonel commanding the Harrow Rifle Corps from 1979–92. He was House Master of Elmfield from 1983–95 and Second Master from 2001–04.*

Harrow Football

DALE VARGAS

Again we rush across the slush –
A pack of breathless faces –
And charge and fall, and see the ball
Fly whizzing through the bases.
Stet Fortuna Domus, 1891

MOST GAMES ARISE OUT OF THE CONDITIONS of climate and terrain that prevail at the time. Harrow football is no exception. It began as an unorganised kick-about in the School Yard (fug football) and slowly developed into an organised activity. From 1803 to 1850 it was played on what is now the Sixth Form Cricket Ground and then, when the School acquired some land on the east side of the Hill, a formal game began to evolve.

Like most of north-west London the Harrow grounds are solid clay, a material which in summer months is cracked with heat but in the winter becomes a slippery miry marsh. It was in these unattractive and discouraging conditions that Harrow football was born. The rules of the games were codified in 1865 by Edward Bowen, later House Master of The Grove, author of *Forty Years On* and several other Harrow Songs. It is difficult to imagine the state of the grounds in the nineteenth century. Contemporary reports suggest six inches of mud but that it had often been up to a foot deep before the drainage had been put down in 1889. Conditions may have been dreadful but there was huge pride in the game: E. W. Howson, later House Master of Druries, added two more football songs, *Three Yards* in 1885 and *Play Up* in 1887.

Up to 1930 cricket was played into the autumn term finishing with the Goose Match at Michaelmas. The first

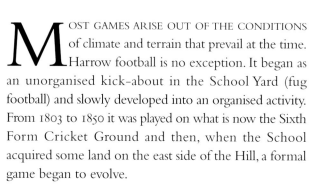

ABOVE: 'The
Football Fields' by
Thomas M. Hemy,
1887

football match was then played on Founder's Day at the beginning of October and until 1896 football continued for the rest of the winter.

Although the Harrow game was ideally suited to Harrow clay, it had two major disadvantages; first, opponents were confined to Old Harrovians and secondly, those that wanted to continue to play football at university had a problem since each school had been playing to different rules. Rugbeians, whose code allowed handling and running, could not agree with Harrovians who could catch the ball but not run with it and Etonians and Wykehamists who could do neither.

There was strong pressure, largely driven by Charterhouse and Westminster, to agree on a common

In 1999 a football was found in the rafters of Stirling Castle, supposedly above Mary Queen of Scots' chamber. It was formally identified by the National Museum in Edinburgh as being 430 years old and therefore the oldest surviving football. Interestingly, its construction is exactly the same as a Harrow football: two circular pieces of leather stitched to a central rectangular piece curved to form a cylinder. This is a neat way of forming a near spherical shape with just three components. However the Harrow ball is considerably larger than the Stirling ball, being nearly a foot across in its widest part.

RIGHT: *Football
Group from the
collection of
David Stogdon*

set of rules and several Old Harrovians were involved in the discussions which led to the formation of the Football Association in 1863. Of the fourteen rules agreed at the inaugural meeting, the first eight are clearly based on the Harrow game.

With so many Old Harrovians now playing the Association game (or soccer as it was to be universally known), the School had a brief flirtation with the idea of converting to it in 1864. Harrow football might have died then and there but the decision was made to stick to it owing to the state of the grounds. Soccer continued to be played on an occasional basis and was introduced as the official game of the spring term in 1896. Some dabbled in rugger too, with some matches played against outside opposition between 1903 and 1910.

In 1913, C.H. Byre, an OH Master, wrote 'Soccer and Rugger in the Easter term call for little comment. The ground is ill-adapted for either game and the interest is practically limited to the players themselves. The fixtures

are inclined to be dull and moderate'. It was the arrival of Dr Cyril Norwood as Head Master in 1925 that was to be the turning point. He had been a Master at Marlborough, which by then was established as a strong rugby-playing school. A year after his arrival at Harrow and following some powerful propaganda, a referendum was held; for reasons as much social as practical, rugby football was voted in and became officially established as the major game of the autumn term, football moving to the shorter spring term. Norwood wrote the *Song of the Forwards* to underline rugby's new status and dedicated it to C.D. Laborde and the XV of 1932 although their results (won 3, lost 6, drawn 1) would not appear to be cause for wild celebration. One chorus 'feet, feet, feet, feet one rush and together, let drive and let fly', smacks more of football than rugby and it seems that Harrovians were reluctant to give up their old skills; forwards were coached to dribble the ball, only heeling it when stopped. Nevertheless the standard of rugby gradually improved, although it was not until 1954 that the School could boast an unbeaten season.

Although a new Sixth Form rugby ground was laid in 1957, significant changes did not occur until the drainage and levelling of the Julian fields and the Park Ground in the 1970s. These 'New Fields', so called, were jealously guarded and football was now played solely on the Ducker and Upper Redding fields. Ducker 1 became the 1st XI ground. Several factors now began to affect the way football was played. First, the drainage of the New Fields made the other grounds much drier too. Secondly, improved technology in ball manufacture had made it increasingly difficult to get the traditional leather ball. Harrow football is essentially a dribbling game. When the ball can be kicked twenty or thirty yards the character of the game changes. The combined effect has been a faster game but one that has departed from its roots and has found difficulty adapting. The improved New Fields were beginning to make soccer a real possibility in the spring term, although the surface was rarely dry enough before the end of February. In spite of the short season the game quickly established itself and Harrow XIs have been more than a match for their opponents that now include some 'two term' soccer schools. Members of the 1st XI were awarded full Flannel status in 1998.

ABOVE: *The Queen, Dr James and C.D. Laborde with John Wells and John Dahl, 1957*

The most recent development has pushed football even further to the fringes. The levelling and drainage of the Upper Redding fields now leave only the Ducker fields and the Sheepcote fields (reclaimed from the farm) for football. It remains a popular House sport but, with good conditions for soccer, two astroturfs, and now hockey, one wonders where its future lies.

> You lie in corners dark and dull,
> An empty lump of air you!
> You sit and sulk, a frozen bulk,
> With pads and bats above you,
> Till winter comes again and then…?
> *Plump a Lump, 1890*

Note: *Forty Years On* with its football allegory has been adopted by schools – many of them girls' – all over the world. Very few could have known what they were actually singing about.

Dale Vargas (Druries 1952³) was Master in charge of Harrow Football from 1971–75. He was House Master of The Head Master's from 1983–95 and Second Master from 1995–2001.

THE HARROVIAN

1933

Old Harrovian Dinner, Cairo

TO THE EDITORS OF 'THE HARROVIAN'
Dear Sirs,
The Old Harrovian dinner was held at The Turf Club, Cairo, on 17 February when thirty Old Harrovians were present; the record number of 38 was expected, but unfortunately at the last moment, eight … were unable to be present.

A telegram was sent to the Headmaster reading: 'Thirty Old Harrovians dining Cairo send best wishes.' After dinner R. V. Jenkins got to the piano and practically every Harrow Song was sung.

Next day there was a Harrow Footer game at Gezira Sporting Club, Snowball having very kindly brought out a ball earlier in the year, for which I believe our thanks are also due to the School Stores, as no bill came with it!

Yours very truly,
E. T. CASDAGLI

Harrow School Songs

ALISTAIR BOAG

RIGHT: *John Farmer, Music Master 1862–1885, composer of* Forty Years On *and many other Harrow Songs*

I T'S THE 1920S. THE ELEGANT, MUSICAL GIRL WHO IS later to be my grandmother is filing into the hall at Roedean for the last assembly of term. Outside, the hot sun is beating down and the bustle of Johannesburg can be heard in the distance. The piano strikes up a rolled first inversion of a B flat major chord and hundreds of white South African young women burst into their school song – *Forty Years On*.

Cut back to London in 1862. A group of Harrovians are attending the International Festival and hear one John Farmer playing a piano whose virtues he is there to illustrate through daily recitals – a bit of a come down one might think for a man steeped in European music and a one-time associate of Wagner. But this is his lucky day. Harrow Boy One turns to his friend, holds up a hand and says, 'Listen (*insert established Harrow name*)! That chap … playing the piano … isn't he just the sort of chap we need to run the Music Society?' 'Good Lord! (*insert second established Harrow name*),' says Harrow Boy Two. 'You're absolutely right!' And so, later that year, Farmer is taken on as conductor for the independently funded Music Society with the more stable and formal appointment to Chapel Organist following soon.

Thus begins the story of Harrow Songs – a success story by any standards, as shown by the fact that two generations later my grandmother is singing her South African head off at the thought of 'the tramp of the twenty-two men' without, one suspects, knowing either quite what that means, nor finding the whole affair remotely peculiar. Farmer's arrival at Harrow saw the birth of what elsewhere might be called 'community singing' on a grand scale. Unison singing in Chapel and in Houses became the norm, an enterprise in which all participated. And in Edward Bowen, Farmer's chief lyricist, we find a man whose ability to put into 'poetry' his admiration for the cult of youth chimed perfectly with his Head Master Montagu Butler's desire to fix forever

Harrow's extraordinary sense of itself. Early Farmer compositions were to celebratory Latin texts – not a form destined to catch on, of course. But with *Willow the King* the thing got firmly underway and for forty years (magic number!) it never looked back – while, ironically, explicitly encouraging Harrovians to spend their post-school lives doing precisely that.

Retrospection, unsurprisingly, plays a large role in the collection of Harrow Songs. In common with all tribes – and a public school is roughly the same size as a tribe – Harrow claims its unique place by telling stories about itself, or rather singing them. And to this day the practicalities of public Songs remain indeed tribal. There is little logistical difference between 750 boys ranked in the body of Speech Room singing to a far smaller number of dais-raised dignitaries on the one hand, and the Queen, say, perched on a stage under a canopy somewhere in the Commonwealth watching danced, sung or ullulated enactments of a particular tribe's history on the other.

'Great days in the distance enchanted' (NB not '*by* the distance enchanted' which is surely more psychologically accurate) become Harrow's theme in its Songs. Bowen evokes a past that both gives meaning to and instructs the present in such songs as *Lyon, of Preston, Yeoman, John, In the Days of Old* and clearly and most whimsically in *Giants*, whose final assertion that 'All of we, Whoever we be, Come up to the giants of old' represents, in schoolboy terms, the self-defining sentiment. For Bowen, this important feature of his words – not as important as the doctrinal importance of games, but up there with it – reaches its climax in *When Raleigh Rose*, a song that is more effective musically, in a four-square Lutheran hymn sort of a way, than lyrically. Here Bowen claims for his Harrow a direct descent from the greatness of Elizabethan England, equating the *genius loci* of Harrow with the very 'winds that reared the Avon's child (Shakespeare)' in the chorus

> For we began when he began,
> Our times are one:
> His glory thus shall circle us
> Till time be done.

The details of this historical inaccuracy are recorded elsewhere, but the intention behind such dressing in borrowed robes illustrates well the workings of myth creation.

Traditions are notoriously easy to establish in schools. 'But I have always done it like that' has been, for me at least, a golden lie when I have worked in such places, allowing me to claim a permissive precedence for my

actions whose disruption would be threatening to good order and continuity. Songs at Harrow took root amazingly deeply and quickly – so much so that when Farmer left the School in 1885, his departure and contribution were celebrated in *Songs*. The practices he has established are seen as vital in every sense. 'Throats' idle pastime?' questions Bowen in his text, 'No, No, No!' After Farmer's departure, the task of adding musically to the repertoire falls to Eaton Faning and the lyrics continue to be provided by both Bowen and the more jingoistic voice of Edmund Howson, who perpetuates the notion that endeavour – above all, muscular endeavour – has a moral quality, but without the humour or fancy of the gentler Bowen. Howson's views are crystallised in the call to answer 'Duty's voice' in *Here Sir!* and the expectation implicit in the last verse of *Stet Fortuna Domus*:

> So once again your glasses drain,
> And may we long continue
> From Harrow School to rise and rule
> By heart and brain and sinew.

It was natural for such a thinker to rush into print with a recruiting song when the government told public schools in 1897 that beefing up numbers in their various Corps was of national importance. *Left! Right!*, in which young Brown's progress from undersized cadet to Major-General Brown K.C.B. is told to a piano accompaniment that imitates the bugle and the drum, is a jolly song – but it loses some of its flair when seen as the precursor to *You?* in which the awful losses of the Boer War, for which Brown was recruited, are lamented. *You?* and *The Silver*

Now and Then

The current School maintains many links with the school of the past. Boys still wear hats and sing Harrow songs. Names are carved onto boards. Harrow Football is still played in the winter. We emphasise the importance of a broad education. The House system is particularly strong. Latin and Greek are still taught. We have an annual Shakespeare play, performed in Speech Room. All our pupils are boarders. We do not, unlike virtually all our competitors, have a mass exit every weekend. We take a wider ability range of pupils than many other schools. Over 20 per cent of current pupils are the sons of Old Harrovians. We run a farm.

We are still a boys' school and that in itself is quite unusual. But demand for single-sex education is still very high – not surprisingly in our view. Why don't the co-educational schools, with double the number of potential applicants, dominate the exam league tables? Is it really sensible to put boys and girls together in the hothouse atmosphere of a boarding community during their teenage years?

Harrow is not unchanged – in many ways it is quite different. But Old Harrovians who were at the School 40 years ago would, if they returned today, recognise much of their old School's distinctive personality.

BARNABY LENON

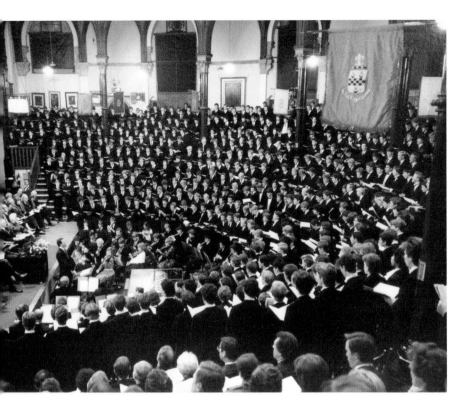

ABOVE: *Prime
Minister Margaret
Thatcher was
Guest of Honour
at Churchill Songs
in 1983*

couldn't, by definition, apply to me. The one phrase that rang totally true, however, was 'The world outside is wondrous wide, but here the world is narrow.' I believed this utterly, grateful that something penned ninety years previously could speak so directly to me. How wrong I was. Not only did I learn that Percy Buck had taught my Granny from Johannesburg the piano, but his name, along with the name of Richard Drakeford, the genius who taught me the piano at Harrow, was 'carved in gold along the boards' at the side of my College Chapel's organ when I went to university. Far from being wide, it seemed as though the post-school world was a mere extension rather than any sort of increase in scale; the world next door and not the world outside at all.

Although a few songs make an attempt to value scholarship and the life of the mind, their very nature as group activities in themselves means that they are happiest when championing the benefits and glories of other group pursuits, i.e. games. Scholars do not come out of the collection well. They are 'pale and meagre' in *October!*, voting for March with its 'theme and lesson and prize' over the athlete's favoured month of the title – a choice clearly as bad if not worse than the girls' cry of 'For May! For May!' *St Joles*, a bathroom favourite, we are told, of Winston Churchill's, is 'the friend of the lazy boy' and a thoroughly good thing as such. In *Ducker*, we are urged to 'toss (our) book and pen away'. *Euclid* sees a mathematical problem as a 'little black demon' in 'black boots tall and thin' and possession of a 'black little head' – barely concealed racist descriptions which, in fairness, must have more to do with the insecurities of Empire than with algebra. But affable Mr Bowen attempts to strike a balance in this area with *Jack and Joe*, with Jack a scholar and Joe a sporting hero, but he notably reaches no conclusion. The final verse's questions,

Can't you settle it, Joe and Jack,
Settle it, books and play?
Dunce is white and pedant is black,
Haven't you room for grey?

are answered unsatisfactorily; 'Let brains with sinews grow …'. Thus Jack becomes a Reverend Doctor and Joe becomes a General (an understandable choice in the days before professional sportsmen), and scholarship and brawn travel on their way separately. Eighteen years later, in 1894, Spencer Gore's single contribution to the

Arrow are to tunes by Percy Buck and the former, revealingly, is 'Intended to be sung as a Solo'. There is no doubting, even now, the affecting quality of this song, perhaps above all the others, as Harrovians who 'fought with Death as brave men should' converse 'from the veldt' with their successors back at school in Middlesex. Of course this is sentimental stuff but such starkness, in Harrow Song terms at least, does not ride easily with notions of mass singing and so it remains chorus-less and for solo voice. Percy Buck's other great tune – his only other contribution to the collection, alas – is *The Silver Arrow* which uses, as Elgar did and Britten would, the seventh as an interval to invoke nostalgia. The words, however, do not amount to anything as stirring as the melody and there is a trite, hollow ring to the wildly inaccurate myth-making that equates Harrovians with the archers at Agincourt.

Another theme that runs alongside retrospection is that life at Harrow is life itself writ small. This is not an idea exclusive, of course, to Harrow, but it's a happy one for the school to adopt since nowhere in the whole collection is the actual word 'Harrow' rhymed with anything other than 'narrow'. Not myself knowing how either to guard or beleaguer a base, let alone whether if asked to take 'Three Yards' I would be able to do what was required, I passed my time at Harrow feeling, regrettably, that a lot of what the songs set out to foster

LEFT: *Churchill Songs at The Royal Albert Hall, 2000*

collection tries again to reconcile mind and limb – but this time a third type is added, that of the dandy, whose 'kerchief is always a beautiful poem'. London at this time was abuzz with tales of Oscar Wilde, the personification of dandyism and a clear intellectual threat to the values of a school such as Harrow. Once again, the conclusion is lame, as the scholar, the dandy and the Athlete (significantly, the only one of the three to be graced with a capital letter) are mixed together and the result is the unimpressive sounding 'good all-round boy'.

After the two Percy Buck songs there is a gap of over twenty years before the new Head Master Cyril Norwood once again puts pen to paper, with Reginald Thatcher providing the music, and sets his own stamp on the tradition. He renders the controversial introduction of Rugby Football unopposable by writing the *Song of the Forwards*, in which he makes the comparatively casual but still essentially Victorian claim that the rough and tumble of the muddy pitch is 'not a bad outfit for life and its need'. But his main contribution is to bring the process full circle by writing words that either overtly echo or directly quote previous songs. In *East is East* we have 'scrimmages', the 'Officers' Training Corps' and 'Ducker', while in *Leavers*, Norwood quotes, unapologetically, in the second verse from *Here Sir!* What began as Songs has now become songs about Songs.

And so this unique and extraordinary process of identity-forging through the writing of songs comes to an almost total stop. A very few have been added for special occasions, such as Richard Drakeford's *The Centenarian* to words by Mark Warman and Jeremy Lemmon for the quarter centenary visit of the Queen in 1971, and the Harrow Song Book now sports an appendix of verses written to be sung to royal visitors. But the singing of Songs goes on – in individual Houses regularly and on great occasions both on and off the Hill. Harrow Beaks are frequently asked by Harrovians why such-and-such tradition is maintained. Why tails? Why hats? Why capping in the street? Why can't we x? Why shouldn't we y? What on earth's the point these days of z? They frequently have a point. This ex-Beak, however, never heard a single Harrovian claim that there was anything wrong with Songs, nor any request for their curtailment. Amazing, really. Cultish, tribal, occasionally banal, wrong-headed, frequently grammatically mangled, patriarchal, often unthinking – all those things apply. But there they are, and there they're sung and thousands of people all over the world can quote them and hum them and play them. And more importantly, given the age we all are when first we encounter them, whether we have grandmothers who've been there before us or not, they are inside us. Bowen is right – 'young voices sound still' and there's not a lot we can do about it.

I think I'm glad that's true.

Alastair Boag (Newlands 1978[2]) was an Assistant Master from 1995–98, Head of Drama at The Leys School, Cambridge, from 1999–2001 and is now a freelance writer and director.

Fifty years in the School Orchestra

John Leaf

BEFORE THE INSTITUTION OF MUSIC SCHOLARSHIPS in the early 1970s it was difficult for music at Harrow to achieve more than occasionally the heights that have regularly been reached more recently. There were indeed boys of outstanding talent, but seldom more than two or three at the same time, and never enough sound performers to fill out the School orchestra. The orchestra was nevertheless a worthwhile activity for all concerned, though depending heavily on adult support, particularly as section leaders and in concerts.

Our energies each spring term were much directed towards accompanying whatever oratorio was to be sung. In 1950 this was 'Messiah', sung by the School Choral Society and local support, for which H. J. McCurrach had taken the bold step of adding a part for the whole of the rest of the School to sing, with rehearsals on Sunday mornings. This inevitably resulted in some loss of musical balance, but there is no substitute for taking part in a great work and for many boys who would have made little claim to musical ability the experience, perhaps to their surprise, turned out to be one they would long remember. Next year it was 'The Creation' and subsequent works included, often more than once, the Requiems of Mozart, Brahms and Verdi, 'The Dream of Gerontius' and, to celebrate the School's 400th Anniversary, a Cantata specially composed by R.J. Drakeford to a libretto by J.P. Lemmon. We were indeed fortunate to have such talent in our midst and the Cantata could well stand in line with the famous works performed in the preceding twenty years. Attitudes, however, were sadly changing and two years later the inclusion of a part for the whole School was abandoned as a result of their increasing lack of co-operation in rehearsals. The loss was entirely theirs.

Other orchestral activities were playing for School Songs and with soloists in concertos. Many of the Songs are harder to play than they sound and much work would be put in before Churchill Songs and Speech Day each year. Then in 1974, to celebrate the centenary of Churchill's birth, and on the initiative of J.H. Winstanley, Songs took place in the Albert Hall. The event was an enormous success, with the Hall packed and audience and performers alike reacting to the excitement of the occasion. My daughters were even given permission off school to attend on the ground that it was the first, and in all probability the last, time that their father would be playing in the Albert Hall. In fact it was not, because there have been two more Churchill Songs there since.

Accompanying concertos has been another pleasant orchestral activity, with perhaps half-a-dozen boys most years playing the solo part in selected movements. In 1967 the whole of the Grieg Piano Concerto was performed, with Douglas Butler and Simon Lane as soloists dividing the movements between them; and the next year they did the same with Rachmaninov's Second Piano Concerto.

It was however not until 1976 that one boy played a whole concerto, Jeffrey White performing Mozart's Fourth Violin Concerto. Since then there have been many fine concerto performances, but pride of place must probably go to Graham Walker, who played major concertos on two *different* instruments – Elgar's for 'cello in October 1995 and Schumann's for piano six weeks later. His mother remarked that he was kept quite busy in the summer holidays! So were the orchestra a few weeks later, as although the notes of their parts in the Schumann are not difficult, the time in the last movement is fiendish, with the beat sounding as if it is in one place for scores of bars on end when in fact it is somewhere quite different. The usual lifelines in such a situation are to count carefully and watch the conductor, but I could not achieve anything from these and had to rely instead on listening intently to what the piano was doing and knowing how the viola part fitted. Whatever solution the other players reached certainly worked, as after much intense rehearsal the performance went with all the vigour and spirit this wonderful concerto deserves.

The orchestra of course also played many works by itself. These included the slow movements of Schubert's Ninth Symphony and Beethoven's Fifth, parts of Bizet's 'L'Arlesienne' Suite and often something fairly riotous for the concerts that used to round off the summer term. In 1969 there was the first complete symphony, Schubert's

ABOVE:
*Choral Society
performance of
Handel's Messiah,
2004*

LEFT: *The Music
Schools*

Fifth, followed in subsequent years with several by Haydn, three movements from Mozart's 'Jupiter' and in 1978 Beethoven's First. Also during this period the orchestra was led for the first time by a boy, Jeffrey White, in 1976. It would not be until ten years later that a boy, James Ross, would conduct – Saint-Saëns' 'Danse Macabre' – but during that time the orchestra, with a little non-professional help from around the Hill, had launched forth into deeper waters. In 1979 there was Dvorak's 'New World' Symphony, followed shortly by Beethoven's Fifth, Mendelssohn's 'Hebrides' Overture and both Brahms's Overtures. What a thrilling experience for young people still in their 'teens – some their early 'teens – to take part in these great works! There followed the first movement of Schubert's Ninth Symphony, which went well enough to prompt *The Harrovian* to ask when we would be playing the rest of it. As to the finale the answer is likely to be 'Never', as it is much too fast, difficult and long for amateurs! We did however play his 'Unfinished' Symphony 18 months later.

By then a flourishing string group was beginning to make its presence felt with some promising performances, as were brass and wind ensembles, and the Concert Band, just 18 players in 1957, was well on the way to packing the Speech Room stage as it has in recent times. The experience these groups acquired playing together all fed back into the orchestra, who were thus able to venture into many demanding works. Of these the hardest was probably Tchaikovsky's Fantasy Overture 'Romeo and Juliet' and the most rumbustious was the 'Festival'

Overture of Shostakovich, eminently suitable for the Albert Hall in November 2000.

As a coda perhaps I may be allowed a brief word on the title of this article. I returned to Harrow as a Master in 1951 and joined the School orchestra to play the viola, having taken the instrument up some five years earlier when I was in the Army; and since amateur orchestras are always short of viola players I was still there in 2001, long after I had retired from full-time teaching. The Directors of Music under whom I played were Hector McCurrach, John Winstanley, Richard Drakeford, Philip Cartledge and Richard Walker. I offer warm thanks to all of them.

John Leaf (Elmfield 1939[3]) was an Assistant Master from 1951–88. He was House Master of Druries from 1968–79 and Senior Master from 1983–88.

RIGHT: *Choral Society and orchestra rehearsal in Speech Room*

Enter the players

JEREMY LEMMON

ABOVE: The Taming of the Shrew *at the Bankside Globe, 1994. The groundlings are Dominic Treadwell-Collins, Tom Noad and Jeremy Lemmon*

'ALTHOUGH I AM BY NOW A COMPLETELY naturalised Yorkshireman and Politics Student,' a young Old Harrovian once wrote on a postcard to me, 'I could hardly let the month of May go by without remembering Harrow and Shakespeare.' He was probably not alone in this feeling: for many years the Shakespeare Play was one of the great full-dress festivals of the School's calendar. Of course, the excitement began long before the performances themselves. Auditions were held in November and rehearsals usually began in January when Speech Room was still chilly and deserted. In these rehearsals the focus was wholly on the words of the play; phrase by patient phrase the actors worked on the sense, shape, sound of the play's language, and movement and gesture were considered because they arose out of the words or illuminated or reinforced them. Sometimes a whole rehearsal would cover no more than a dozen lines.

In the Summer Term the pace quickened. During the preceding holiday the School Works Department had interrupted its schedule to construct the Shakespeare staging. The thrust stage was created by covering the well of Speech Room with boards on trestles; they in turn were covered with coconut matting; professional scaffolders were brought in to build the upper level; the stage posts were hoisted into place and made secure in the roof. Now it was possible to design the blocking and larger movements of the scenes, and now other elements of performance – character, motive and so on – began to emerge, spontaneously it seemed, out of the preparation that had gone before. At last, on the afternoon of the fourth Sunday of the Summer Term, came the first run-through of the whole play, in costume, nearly always a faltering and depressed affair. Clearly more ingredients were needed.

On Monday evening the little band of Watkinses, Harrises, Maurice Percival and me were joined in Speech Room by Mr Lawrence, the School Electrician, and over companionable glasses of wine we discussed how best to create the neutral light which would evoke afternoon at the Globe. Mr Lawrence clambered up ladders and experimented with direction, intensity, colour; Herbert's dog, Bracken, nosed about the stage in nostalgic search for the spot where she had given her great performance as Dog-in-the-Moon; and at last we all agreed that the lighting was just right and surprisingly like the lighting of last year, and the year before.

Wednesday was always Field Day, and while the rest of the School was busy with its activities, everyone in the play, by special dispensation, spent the whole day in Speech Room for what Ronnie Watkins called the Cues Rehearsal. The machinery of the production was thoroughly overhauled. Exits and entrances were practised again and again until the timing was precise. Music cues and sound-effects (storms, alarums, distant revelry) were slotted in. Props and furniture appeared and brought their new hazards. Costumes were worn all day (ruffs and jewellery excepted), and the Wardrobe Mistresses worked with hectic speed to finalise them, mending, altering, embellishing, nipping in waists, creating bosoms. There was a short break for the wolfing down of packed lunches, outside in the Art School garden if the sun smiled. In the afternoon there was another break – for the Derby. The cast sat on the stage in doublets and farthingales, and listened to the race on a portable wireless (as it then was). Herbert Harris produced the sealed envelope which contained the name of the winner he was predicting; it was always related in some way to the play. His greatest triumph was in 1959, when the winner was Parthia; it was the year of *Antony and Cleopatra,* the play in which Ventidius speaks of 'the ne'er yet beaten horse of Parthia.' Altogether it was an exhilarating day, and exhausting too; inevitably sometimes concentration wavered. Ronnie left a revealing note: 'The only way to get through this rehearsal … is to explode mildly at every failure to turn up on the cue, and indulge in one major volcano somewhere about three-quarters of the way through the afternoon.'

On Thursday, Speech Room was swept and the programmes were laid out. The painted marble bust of Shakespeare was carried, with much groaning and staggering from the Stage Manager and his henchmen, to the balustrade by the audience door. At six o'clock Bert appeared with his professional make-up team and the beloved jokes he always tried out on beginners ('Don't worry – the beard will come off easily with sandpaper …'). As the vanguard of the audience arrived, the familar cry of 'Under hatches!' went up, the doors of the War Memorial were closed and the actors vanished to wait in the basement for the director's pep talk. In the early years, Thursday's performance was officially the Dress Rehearsal, and Ronnie would come on to the stage at the beginning to ask the audience's indulgence in case he had to stop the play. But he never did, and soon the fiction was dropped: Thursday became in fact the First Night. It was always less formal and less crowded than the other nights, and the audience was kind-hearted. Hitches were received with murmurs of quiet sympathy, or even applause – as when Christopher Poke's Rosalind found the bracelet she was to bestow on Orlando

RIGHT: *The cast of* Coriolanus, *1968*

irremovably tangled with her sleeve; after some moments of struggle she gave up, and instead graciously assured him, 'I will give it to thee after'. Inevitably there were plenty of these hitches. The 1966 *Macbeth* lived up to its reputation for ill-fated accidents: Robert Bennett's Macduff, yelling 'O horror, horror, horror…', leapt on to a staircase which instantly collapsed in fragments beneath him; Macbeth's severed head, a horrid confection of gory canvas and straw, misbehaved spectacularly. Although these hiccups have passed into folk memory, at the time they hardly ruffled the good humour of the Thursday performances.

Friday was the School Night, and among the actors nerves were taut. The whole School attended compulsorily, the dinner-jacketed House Masters sitting with their boys. For some it must have been an ordeal: the plays were long, and Speech Room was sometimes hot and always overcrowded. The boys allotted seats in the extreme corners had only a partial view (we learned from experience, long before it became a scholarly insight, why Shakespeare and his contemporaries so often wrote of 'hearing' rather than 'seeing' a play). Yet, though this audience could be restive, and cruel if things went wrong, only once in

more than thirty years did I feel the need to come on stage at the interval and ask the audience to give the actors a fairer chance; and once – now it can be told – I had reproachful words with a House Master who was impishly egging his boys on to misbehave. By way of compensation for any difficulties, the response was wonderfully warm when things went well. In that neutral light the relationship between actors and spectators was very close: some boys sat with their feet on the stage (I remember one groundling complaining that John Thalben-Ball's boozy Porter spat on his shoe), and for most of the audience the plays were completely new. So the familiar comedy of Pyramus and Thisbe, Dogberry and the Watch, Benedick in his arbour, the gulling of Malvolio, came across as fire-new from the mint. Moreover some of the humour dismissed by critics as dry or difficult –Touchstone, Feste, Pompey Bum, Pistol, Trinculo – raised delighted laughter too. It was not only comedy that received its due reward: there was genuine excitement at Hamlet's duel, tension as Antonio faced the knife, horror at the headless Cloten, hisses for Richard Crookback, hushed silence at the death of Romeo, the rejection of Volumnia, the reconciliation of Lear and Cordelia. *The*

RIGHT: *Benedict Cumberbatch as Clarence in* Richard III, *1993*

Winter's Tale, since it contains so many surprises and was then so little known, had a particularly gratifying reception. When the statue of Hermione was revealed, in the magical glimmer of many candles, I heard a wondering whisper from the row in front of me: '*Is she real?*' Amazed applause greeted the School Gym Team as the dancing Satyrs. And since nobody expected the Bear (we had managed to keep it secret), its famous pursuit of Antigonus raised the roof. Afterwards there was much speculation about who had played the part: it was actually Adrian Ffooks, tallest and strongest actor in the cast, who took time off from

his main part of Polixenes to climb into Theatre-Zoo's best bearskin with the articulated jaws.

Saturday, the Guest Night, was the best of all. The parents were there, many friends, guests of the School, Old Harrovians, all Beaks (except a handful of rebels and agnostics) together with their families; everyone was in the full fig of evening dress. Last of all, and only when everyone else was seated, came the Head Master, Dr James. The trumpeter sounded his first flourish from the terrace outside Speech Room as the Head Master and his party left his front door; the second trumpet, also outside, sounded as the party reached Speech Room tunnel; the third and last flourish came from inside the auditorium exactly as the Head Master took his seat; and the play began. Personally, Jimmy James had no great love for Shakespeare – and indeed towards the theatre in general he admitted to feeling a little like a seventeenth-century Puritan: he was morally suspicious of it. But he was always loyal to the Play, believed it good for the School's name, and every year attended both the Friday and the Saturday performances. He insisted that the whole School's attendance should be compulsory, and he insisted too on the formality and ceremony of the Guest Night. His successor, Michael Hoban, personally loved the Play and knew his Shakespeare; he preferred voluntary attendance and informal dress, and he liked to slip quietly into his seat. He showed his pleasure by inviting the whole company to his house after the last performance; there they feasted on risotto prepared by Jasmine herself and worked off their elation under his hospitable eye.

Sometimes in the Guest Night audience there were famous folk. John Gielgud came, and Anthony Quayle, Bernard Miles, Peter Brook. A frequent visitor was John Laurie, well-regarded as a Shakespearean actor long before he found a different kind of fame as the doom-bearing Fraser in *Dad's Army*. W.A. Darlington of *The Daily Telegraph* wrote that these 'experiments in Elizabethan stagecraft have made the Harrow performances … a real contribution to Shakespeare study'. When Sam Wanamaker was struggling to create his Globe Playhouse in Southwark he often came to the Harrow play. 'Anyone interested in the Globe Theatre and original staging techniques,' he wrote, 'cannot ignore the pioneering work produced in Speech Room.' His regard was not merely theoretical. He made sure that Harrow was represented on the committee that helped to design his Bankside Globe; and in 1991 he asked that the second Annual Globe Lecture should be delivered, by Anthony Burgess, on the Harrow stage. Sam had also written, 'I look forward to the day when an eyrie of Harrow boys treads the boards of the new Globe on Bankside.' This hope led, in 1994, to one of the great moments in the story of the School Play: the first full-length Shakespeare play presented within the walls of the new Bankside Globe was performed by Harrovians.

While it is certainly pleasant to be told that Harrow has been able to add a footnote to Shakespeare studies in our time, the truest history of the Play would surely be a parochial one, a chronicle of anecdotes. Of course, the actors who grappled with the great and classically challenging parts would be celebrated: there would be high admiration for the Hamlets of Alexander Schouvaloff (who faced the Guest Night with a high temperature) and James Dreyfus, the Lears of Costa Carras and Crispin Black; Peregrine Massey as Coriolanus, Alastair Boag as the Duke of Vienna; Michael Stone's Cleopatra, Colin McLean's Leontes, Toby Dantzic's Richard III, Giles Havergal's tragic Constance. There would be celebration too for triumphs of other kinds, comic, lyrical, villainous, grotesque. And there would be special affection in recalling those actors who lavished their gifts, as 'extras', on tiny, or even mute, parts – attendants, courtiers, citizens, the twittering monks of Swinstead, the excitable Ephesian messenger, the endearing Bohemian clown who didn't recognise a filthy ditty when he heard one. In the pages of this history, well-loved images could be recreated: Hippolyta would truculently fling down her spear, and Pandulph archly wag his finger at the poor Dolphin; Aguecheek would remember that he was adored once too and Jaques would take his sulky departure to the sound of the cuckoo; Henry V's hearty nobles would fling the tennis balls at one another; the two lost princes would crawl from their low cave-mouth. The chronicle would contain a boast or two: that the School and the Old Harrovian Players have between them covered almost the whole Shakespeare canon; that for more than half a century the average Harrovian during his short school life has been able to see eight or ten different Shakespeare plays; that we did our best by the golden rules of the 'Harrow method' – nothing should be done in performance that Shakespeare's company could not have done, and the words should be the chief instrument of theatrical illusion. Above all, there would emerge out of this anecdotage a story of delighted discovery, tremendous enjoyment, occasional despair and laughter unlimited.

Jeremy Lemmon (The Knoll 1949[3]) was an Assistant Master from 1957–96 and Head of English from 1966–90. He has performed in and directed countless School and OH productions of Shakespeare plays, and has published several books about Shakespeare.

Classics at Harrow

JAMES MORWOOD

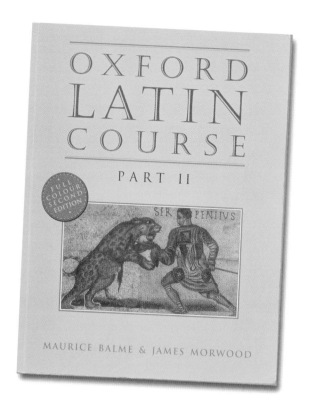

IN A FAMOUS PASSAGE FROM HIS *DON JUAN*, BYRON describes the education his hero received, surely with more than a glance at his own experience of being taught at Harrow. He directs his satirical attention to its remoteness and uselessness as well as its insistence on a lofty morality and its suppression of any sex education:

> The languages, especially the dead,
> The sciences, and most of all the abstruse,
> The arts, at least all such as could be said
> To be the most remote from common use,
> In all these he was much and deeply read:
> But not a page of anything that's loose,
> Or hints continuation of the species,
> Was ever suffer'd, lest he should grow vicious.

The most remarkable feature of Byron's description of Juan's classical studies that follows this stanza is the lively and penetrating appreciation of ancient literature that comes across. As Christopher Tyerman has pointed out, though quite a lot of Greek and Latin was read in Byron's Harrow, the pupils were subjected to the 'unrelenting monotony of construe and composition, recitation, exercises, and themes'. The School's statutes laid it down that Latin must be spoken even at play, though common sense would suggest that the rule must have been frequently broken. This is not as mad as it sounds. At the time of Harrow's foundation, Latin was the language of communication in business and government. Hence the central importance of the Head of School's annual Latin report to the governors, the Contio, a tradition launched in 1674 which has continued, with only a few gaps and one foray into English, until the present. The story I would like to tell is that of the way classics at Harrow has shaped itself to adjust to the changing and often very difficult circumstances in which it has had to operate over the past forty-five years. But before I turn to 1960, I should like to make two incidental points. First, Harrow classics teachers have at times been surprisingly progressive in their educational outlook. On a Sunday afternoon in June 1865 a society called United Ushers (UU) was born in Harrow Park. Its aim was to discuss educational issues. Indeed it was the first attempt in the English public schools to do this in a coherent way. Wider topics than the teaching of classics were of course also the subject of debate – one meeting in 1880 was devoted to the boys' sexuality and the discussion seems to have been astonishingly liberal. But there were papers on Latin pronunciation, Greek and Latin grammar, the use of cribs, and the value of repetition. Dull stuff to the outsider no doubt, but key matters when classics had so wide a grip on the curriculum. The original members of this important think-tank were from Harrow, Eton and Rugby. Soon Winchester was to join in the fun. The second point is that one Head of Classics, seemingly very much in the dry-as-dust classical mould, was in point of fact anything but. As Tyerman remarks, E.V.C. Plumptre (see page 74), who retired in 1957, 'managed the trick of inspiring enthusiasm and belief in the subject as well as expertise; postcards to pupils could as easily be in elegant Greek as in his limpid English prose'.

Now I move on belatedly to my main theme. The decision of Oxford and Cambridge in 1960 to stop demanding a qualification in Latin as a requirement for entry quickly put paid to the unquestioned place of

Plum

E.V.C. Plumptre was a scholar of Hertford College, Oxford. He taught Classics at Harrow from 1925 to 1957. He died in 1980 aged 78.

It is in his room that I best remember E.V.C. Plumptre – the Classical Upper Sixth Form Room that some six of us occupied for two years from 1954 to 1956; we were joined in our second year there by the form below us, to make a larger-than-average group of eleven. In the middle of the room was a large oblong table, and EVCP's seat was in the middle of the far side facing towards the door; on his right the bank of windows that looked out over the terrace. The table did not cramp the spacious room; there were white-painted bookcases with cupboards beneath and space to push your chair back and more.

I can visualise EVCP as he walked down the long, sloping steps that led to 'our' form room – slim, with a neat, compact step, his overcoat done up, thin greyish hair and no hat, books under his arms; glasses, a narrow wrinkled face and always a smile – a wry smile, in retrospect – as we greeted him. We all had our regular seats around the table (some faces still stand out as I re-imagine the room); our hats and books in front of us – the dark-blue (occasionally the reddish-brown) of an Oxford Classical Text especially, but often, too, an annotated edition of the Greek play or the poetry (Horace was Plum's favourite), a history or a set of speeches that helped us prepare for a period of translation with EVCP. Plum made the Classical Upper Sixth a haven for scholars like myself, whose House, The Park, was more sporting than academic. In his quiet way he supervised a very heterogeneous form, with its different nationalities, religions and social backgrounds. Slightly odd boys like myself, coping with a bad stammer and opting out of the CCF and eventually out of Chapel too, were given enormously valuable support by Plum.

Though I was marked out for History when I arrived, it was the men who taught us Classics – Ronnie Watkins, Maurice Balme, Mark Warman up to EVCP – who pulled me into Classics and made my

experience of Harrow and my academic training there so important for me. Plum was the best of that group of Masters; it was clear to us boys who were the really competent men – we often teased those who weren't. No one teased Plum or even wanted to, I think.

Murray Last

Professor Murray Last PhD (The Park 1951[3]) is Professor of Anthropology at University College London. He is engaged in research in Hausaland and northern Nigeria on both pre-colonial history and traditional medicine today.

Classical Sixth Form, 1956. Back row from left: P.L. Ghey (Class Sch to St John's Coll, Camb), R.D.E. Nichols (Class Exh to Worcester Coll, Oxon), A.P.K. Osmond (Heberden Sch to Brasenose Coll, Oxon), G.W.H. Stevenson, R.E. Melville (Class Sch to New Coll, Oxon), M.L. Gordon (Briscoe Owen Sch to Oriel Coll, Oxon), I.J. Scott (Class Sch to Balliol Coll, Oxon). Front row from left: M.S.J. Montgomery (Class Exh to Hertford Coll, Oxon), D.M. Last (Class Exh to Clare Coll Camb), F.E.R. Butler (Class Sch to University Coll, Oxon), E.V.C. Plumtre Esq., C.J. Carras (Class Sch to Trinity Coll, Oxon), D.H. Golby, N.W. Bethell (Class Exh to Pembroke Coll, Camb)

classics in the school timetable. The response from the Harrow classics department was speedy. In 1965, Maurice Balme and Mark Warman, who coxed and boxed as Heads of Classics between 1966 and 1979, produced a book called *Aestimanda*. It was a collection of Greek and Latin passages which were presented as material for literary discussion. The responses to classical literature which Byron had made automatically now began to be elicited as a conscious part of the educational process. The importance of *Aestimanda* can scarcely be over-emphasized. Suddenly, throughout the English-speaking world, students and teachers alike were not just paying lip service to the idea that the overriding aim of learning the Latin and Greek languages was the understanding and enjoyment of the works written in them; they were actually experiencing that understanding and enjoyment for themselves.

Aestimanda was the first of a stream of classical books from Harrow: Balme's *Intellegenda*, another pioneering book in which the passages chosen illustrated Roman social life, especially the experiences of marginalized groups; Balme and Mark Greenstock's *Scrutanda* (consisting of comprehension exercises), Balme's ground-breaking *Millionaire's Dinner Party*; Balme and James Morwood's *Cupid and Psyche*; and Morwood and Warman's language awareness book, *Our Greek and Latin Roots*. The most massive of these publishing enterprises were Balme's splendid Greek course *Athenaze*, a great learning experience which brings one closer than any rival to the realities of Greek agricultural and emotional life, and Balme and Morwood's best-selling *Oxford Latin Course*. Judith Affleck, the present Head of Classics, keeps the great tradition on the road as an editor of a lively series of translations of Greek drama for the Cambridge University Press, to which members of her department have also contributed. In so far as publications can come to the aid of classics in its beleaguered years, Harrow has led the way.

Another important development was the entry of Ancient History into the curriculum as an A level subject. Mark Greenstock played a key role in this both at Harrow and nationally. He edited a series of collections of historical source materials (LACTORS) which at the time seemed highly progressive, though now we take such books for granted. At a stroke, the mindless dictation of out-of-date notes was banished from the classical classroom. His initial partner in the Harrow enterprise was Sandy Smith, who produced his own book on the Athenian tyrants. Ancient History was later joined by Classical Civilization, at present the booming classical A level subject in the country as a whole.

The School's proximity to central London has led to the sharing of Harrow's superb resources with a wider world. At their zenith, a series of Sixth Form Conferences brought hundreds of students to Harrow, many of them from maintained schools, all over the south-east of England. Now Affleck is collaborating with state schools in the Harrow area to ensure that Latin and Greek A level are open to all. A significant and moving moment occurred in 2001 when a student from a local school slipped up onto the Speech Room stage on Speech Day to accept her Harrow prize from the Head Master.

So what actually happened to classics while all this labour was being expended? The story goes something like this. In a little-known essay called *The Parthenon and the Optative*, C.S. Lewis quotes, with evident approval 'a grim old classical scholar' looking up from some entrance papers and saying, 'The trouble with these boys (sic) is that the masters have being talking to them about the Parthenon when they should have been talking to them about the Optative.' (The optative, a word that nobody knows quite how to pronounce, is a part of the Greek verb even more remote than the subjunctive!) The idea is that the optative stands for hard learning, the Parthenon for wishy-washy art appreciation. A Harrow Head Master (Joseph Wood) pre-echoed this view in 1899 when he poured scorn on progressive methods of classics teaching, writing to the Hellenic Society 'If you could send me a lantern slide of the uses of the optative I could find much use for it at Harrow.' Though there are doubtless classical backwoodsmen still around who agree with this Philistine nonsense, they will not be found at Harrow. Classical civilization is far more than two languages. It is two whole worlds in microcosm. And now at last classicists, both at Harrow and in the world outside, have fully realized what that means.

James Morwood was an Assistant Master from 1966–96. He was Head of Classics from 1979–96 and is currently Dean of Wadham College, Oxford.

Tradition and experiment: Harrow Modern Languages in the twentieth century

JOHN JEREMY

WHEN I ARRIVED ON THE HILL IN 1957, FRESH from Oxford, the Treaty of Rome was barely six months old and 'Modern Languages' was still a self-sufficient little island among the other academic departments jostling for the cleverest boys – except that, like the Hapsburg Eagle, it had two Heads. One was Leonard Walton, who from his powerhouse in VI.I.ML took a distant interest in the rest of the department; the other, Eric Hudson-Davies, was in charge of the Middle and Lower School (or 'lower and slower', as a younger wit was later to describe it). Both were large, formidable men: Huddie-D was an enthusiast, who spoke in crisp, swooping phrases and nicely articulated sentences; CLW was more smoothly, even languorously loquacious, especially on the telephone, where he was a practised monologist. He was also magnificently erudite: I learnt more from him than from any of my tutors at Oxford. Each had his own hinterland: EH-D had spent much of his life in India, as an Inspector of Schools, and was now lodged in the Workshops, where he conducted the affairs of the Motor Driving Club as well as teaching French, German and Spanish, escaping occasionally to moonlight as a JP. Leonard had been old enough to catch the latter part of the War and had spent it (in his own words) 'talking to the Soviets' (in Russian, of course) in Teheran.

The teaching-aids of that era were simple and few: chalk, a blackboard and books – hundreds, perhaps thousands of books. The ML Library was housed in CLW's form room in the Estates, and the boys' borrowing-book was always full of fresh signatures for what were, by the standards of a later period, quite esoteric works of criticism. By the time I left in 1994, this same borrowing-book had become little more than a white elephant, and 'critical works' now meant little monographs (in English) on writers from the First and Second Divisions, rather than the Premiership, of European literature, those being by then the preferred areas of choice for the A-level examiners.

But even in those far-off days of the 1950s, Huddie-D already owned a tape-recorder. It was a vast wooden contraption with heavy metal knobs and levers and it weighed almost as much as he did. He seemed keen to get rid of it onto me almost as soon as I arrived and I never really knew what to do with it. A decade later every Beak was to have his own tape-recorder, but even these machines remained cumbersome and were rarely used: one Master confessed to a feeling of guilt every time he kicked the thing by accident under his desk and was thus suddenly reminded that it was there. Many years later, I discovered that there had been earlier forays into the world of sound reproduction: in investigating an old cupboard that I inherited from CLW, I found a wind-up gramophone on which still lay a dusty 78, which for some reason only very remotely connected to language teaching, was an account by Amy Johnson of her solo flight to Australia.

In those days we had no *assistant* at Harrow and so the only source of spoken French or German that the pupils heard (apart from the invaluable presence of bilingual boys in higher divisions) was Their Master's Voice. This was usually delivering a Dictation – a delightful exercise that sadly disappeared from the curriculum with the arrival of the GCSE and deprived Beaks of a pleasant and restful way of spending part of a late November afternoon. These dictations could be fearsomely difficult. I recall one about deep-sea fishing which described the poor creatures of the ocean (I write from memory) as '*arrachés pêle-mêle aux profondeurs de leurs retraites sous-marines*' – and this for boys who were barely more than a year away from their prep schools. Dictations were a delight to EH-D, whose private hobby was reading the dictionary, and also to CLW, who once revealed with incredulity (but, to his credit, relishing the experience) that one of his own sixth-formers had had to put him right about the totally unexpected direction of the accent on *empiétement* – although only in Harrap, it is true, did it seem to be that way inclined.

The photograph was taken, I suppose, in late 1957 or in 1958 and I believe the occasion was the acquisition of the vast black Daimler, presented by Sir Bernard Docker, whose stepson Lance Callingham was in the School at the time. On the right is the master in charge, Hudson-Davies, between the two instructors, whose names I have forgotten. They were sergeant instructors from the Metropolitan Police Driving School at Hendon and came over at weekends to teach us how to drive.

The Club's other teaching car was an equally vast Lanchester. We rolled majestically around South Harrow on Sunday afternoons, every other car on the road giving way obsequiously – I'm sure they were convinced it was the Queen Mother on board. It would be hard to imagine two more unsuitable vehicles for the job, particularly the Lanchester whose pre-selector gearbox enabled me to pass my test without the faintest idea of how to use a normal clutch and gearchange. None the less, this excellent little enterprise gave hundreds of Harrovians their first taste of freedom which came with the car in those days.

STEPHEN MINOPRIO

Stephen Minoprio (Moretons 1954[2]) was later a successful amateur racing driver

At last, after the age of the redundant tape-recorder, came cassettes – and a vast improvement they were: it now became possible to play, play and play again even tiny snippets of the foreign language until at last a surprised and delighted class caught what was being said – by a real French voice, for example, speaking at real French conversational speed, i.e. very fast indeed. Since the essential difficulty in coping with a foreign language is not to make oneself understood – that can always be managed somehow (using mime, if necessary) – but rather to grasp what the other fellow is going on about, the cassette-recorder represents, to my mind, the most effective breakthrough in language-learning in my time.

In the 1980s, thanks to the generosity of Anthony Edgar, we were able to buy television sets to install in the Edgar Centre in the Leaf Schools and subsequently in all the Leaf form-rooms and record foreign programmes beamed to us by satellite. I remember that to begin with there were six or seven Italian programmes and only one in French (at awkward times of the day), so what was available was of limited value to us but did no doubt stimulate the teaching of Italian which had long been a popular option. The arrival of the video meant that we now had something of even greater usefulness than the audio-cassette – we could record native programmes from the satellite system and replay them to a receptive audience – but only if the aerial was pointing in the right direction. It rarely was, because the Grove boys playing yarder next door kept knocking it sideways (by accident, no doubt) with their football.

Meanwhile, the GCSE had arrived. One of its consequences was that the Beaks themselves now usurped the role of that familiar figure at public examinations, the visiting oral examiner, and conducted the tests themselves. This proved to be quite a demanding occupation, since for a whole week one was required to abandon the familiar role of teacher and take on instead those of efficient recording-engineer, scrupulous examiner and encouraging interlocutor, while at the same time trying anxiously to get the best out of one's pupils and entering into the spirit of the thing in playing the various dramatic roles one was prescribed – laid-back shopkeeper, warden of a Mediterranean campsite, bored hotel receptionist or affable relation – usually the uncle (or aunt) of the boy's exchange partner – prepared to coax out of each pupil his stumbling account of how he had spent his day on the streets of Clermont-Ferrand or Heidelberg. For a week the Leaf Schools would be buzzing with activity, as boys and Beaks hurried up and down steps between their various assignments.

By the time I left in 1994, the eagle had only one head; but – a true Hapsburg – he now presided over a polyglot empire which taught as A-level subjects not only French and German but Spanish as well, besides offering Italian and a smattering of Russian, Arabic or Japanese. By now also two of the Beaks were in fact Beakesses, and one of these was the former pupil of a former pupil of Leonard Walton in the 1950s – in fact, he of the disputed accent on *empiétement*. We had travelled a long road since the mid-century, but in a satisfactory sort of way we had also come full circle.

John Jeremy was an Assistant Master from 1957–94. He was House Master of Bradbys from 1974–76 and Head of Modern Languages from 1982–94.

THE HARROVIAN

1 July 1926

The Prime Minister's Speech on 3 June

The School War Memorial is from this moment an integral part of the life of Harrow, from this day onwards and through the centuries so long as the School shall last; and what that Memorial may mean to the generations that come afterwards depends on what that Memorial is going to mean to the generation in possession of the School today. For that reason I propose to address my remarks more to the members of the School than to the older members of this great assembly.

Ten or twelve years in one's life when one is a boy seems an eternity, and it is difficult to realise the gulf that separates you from those who were here in 1914. No generation was ever at school, or probably ever will be at school again, under similar conditions or in similar circumstances to those then existing. With every boy, life lies before him in a vista almost of eternity in expanse and in duration, and many of his dreams are filled with what may happen to him in those vast and spacious years when he escapes from the petty thraldom of school or the wider thraldom of a university. Of all those in 1914, as every schoolmaster knows and every parent knows, every boy, though he seldom acknowledged it, knew that he had to pass literally through the valley of the shadow of death, and he knew that he might never emerge from it. That knowledge left marks on the character of thousands of Englishmen that will never be obliterated, however long they live, and I often think that if the generation of 1914 could send a message across the years to the generation of 1926 they would speak to us in the words used by Socrates when he left the Court under sentence of death, and said: "And now the time is come for us to go our ways; I to death and you to life, but which of us hath the better lot is known to none but God."

It is hard to say which is the better lot. Death is easy and life is very hard. It is not going to be an easy life for those who are now entering upon, or are on the point of entering upon, manhood in this country, in Europe, in this world today, provided, I mean and take it for granted, that you are going to play your part in this world. Many forces of good and of evil were loosed in 1914, forces which were not bound at the time of the Armistice, and there is a strange leaven at work to-day among all the nations of the world. Just as at the time of the Renascence the age devoted itself to intellectual inquiry, so to-day it is devoting itself and will devote itself to social inquiry, and all of you will have to justify yourselves to the country and to the world; to justify yourselves for the advantages you have received and to prove yourselves worthy of them in the sight of all men.

There is one question that will hammer at all our hearts for many years to come. We have heard it often, the question that the dead themselves might answer: "Have we died in vain?"' and the question you hear asked by mothers and widows and orphan children all over the world. I have got to give an answer and you have got to give an answer. The answer we can give will depend upon what superstructure we can build upon foundations that have been cemented in their blood. It will be hard work, and it will be hard work to prove to the world that those deaths have not been in vain, for there is no toil like that of trying to mend things, trying to make the world better and happier. Time after time you will find your work destroyed, you will find your best efforts misunderstood and you will be derided, and yet in spite of all that you know perfectly well there is nothing for it but to go on in faith if you mean to accomplish anything.

You cannot hope, and perhaps you ought not to hope or expect, to see in your lifetime the result of your work, but of this I am convinced, that if you can take into the world the best spirit of this place; if you will take into the world the lesson that I need not preach to you, but which your own innermost consciousness will teach you when you look at that Memorial by yourselves sometimes and let yourselves think about it; if you will take that lesson into the world and devote your lives to England as those others gave their death, then indeed the answer to the heart-searching questions may be found not to-day or to-morrow, but possibly a century or two centuries hence, when it may be that the historian, seeing the events of to-day in a truer relation and perspective, may be able to write something like this: "At that time a generation indeed was wiped out, but from their graves sprang a rebirth and a new kindling of the spirit that raised our country to heights that surpassed the dreams of those of her sons who in past ages had sacrificed most and had loved her best."

Stanley Baldwin (*Small Houses and the Head Masters 1881*)

Lions of old

ALEC RAMSAY

RUGBY WAS STARTED AT HARROW IN THE EASTER term of 1927, the term when soccer was normally played. Cyril Norwood, who had come as Head Master from Marlborough, decided that soccer on those heavy, churned up, muddy grounds was not the right game. He managed to poach I.B.M. Stuart from St Paul's as a coach. Stuart was a pretty wild Irishman but exactly the right person to get such a big change up and running. Of course the change from Harrow Football

to Rugby was not quite as great as a change from soccer, in that the ball was handled in both codes; the forwards were taught to dribble the ball forward in those days and then give it (or heel it in Rugby) to the backs 'yards' to do the scoring. Feet! Feet! Feet! was the doctrine that we forwards were urged to practise.

Ian Stuart wrote a small text book about the game and went to some trouble to explain that the dribbling technique with the oval ball was rather different from

In the Easter term referred to, after a few very scratch games trying to learn the rules etc., a Harrow fifteen did go over to Eton and played a rather muddly game that both teams thought was rugger – Eton were not much more knowledgeable about the game than we were. I forget the score.

Come September 1927, Harrow became a Rugby school and the first matches played were against scratch sides: Eton Masters; A.M. Crawley's XV; M.R Blair's XV; Harrow Masters; Harrow Club and London Scottish A.

Ian Stuart was 'in' with some of the London Scottish internationals and arranged for me to join the club and also to be selected to play for the Scottish Schoolboys against the English dittos all in the noble cause of getting Harrow on the 'Rugby Map'. Further than this, he had coached John Embleton when he was at St Paul's and when JE went to Cambridge and was Captain there a couple of years later, he must have threatened him with severe reprisals if he did not take an interest in a promising lad from Harrow called Ramsay who packed in the front or second rows. John seems to have capitulated and I pushed on JE's backside in the Cambridge XV for the 1938 season. I am not sure what part IBMS took in getting W.O'B. Lindsay playing in the Oxford XV but he certainly did a good job for Harrow Rugby in its very early years.

The furthest I got after that was playing for Scotland versus The Rest at Murrayfield in 1929 (I think) and I learned a lesson on that day. The Scottish second row comprised the Cambridge second row of that year – to wit Alec Walker and Alec Ramsay. Alec Walker was a very fine forward who had a little more worldly experience at that time than I did and he thought it a bit foolish to waste energy pushing in the scrum – in those days the scrum was a much bigger factor in getting the ball than it is now – when he could show up brilliantly in the loose instead; and this he did with the result that by half time we had hardly ever got the ball. Not unreasonably the selectors transposed the second rows and of course the Rest of Scotland then ceased to get any of the ball at all. Alec Walker played a brilliant game otherwise so obviously the fault lay with the other Alec and out I went.

However back to the Harrow days: I cannot recall why the 'colours' were called 'Lions' but I do remember that

LEFT: Harrow XV 1927. Alec Ramsay is second from the right in the back row

RIGHT: Ian Stuart coaching in a practice game in 1931

the Harrow ball and feet must be either 'pigeon toed' or 'splay footed' to control it. Not much of that now – presumably because of better grounds and lighter balls.

Ian Stuart had just the right sort of gregarious enthusiasm to get the game going at Harrow. He also knew a lot of the international players on the London scene and introduced them to the upper crust of the First XV. He may not have been loved by the more academic Beaks but I seem to remember that he could pick off a boy at the back of the room with a well-directed piece of chalk.

During that first Easter term the same organisation of the game that had been used for the soccer was used for the 'rugger', i.e. one or two top games for 30 selected School players while the remainder played in House games. In those days everyone – every day – went down to the football fields after lunch and played in an organised game. With the introduction of rugger a full game was played only once or twice a week and I seem to remember that it was something of a problem for House captains to organise what I think is now called 'training' on the days when full games were not being played, since everyone had to be out of the House before the bell went. I think that we used to call it a 'punt about'. It was pretty chaotic, that first Easter term, but it did mean that in September when the Rugby was played instead of the Harrow game things went more smoothly.

— at the time — there was a good deal of discussion about what they should be called. I believe that the Lion badges were appropriated from the School soccer 'colour', which was a Lion rampant on the pocket of their white shirts. In fact there was a great deal of fairly intense argument about the whole change of course (at a time when soccer was becoming more professional and Rugby remaining amateur) but there must be lots of documentation about the democratisation of 'the ruling class' (whisper the phrase) about that time. That

presumably was the reason for Dr Norwood introducing the changes.

I watch a fair bit of Rugby around the world but it is a far cry from the funny game that we used to play in the mud at the bottom of the Hill.

Alec Ramsay DSC (The Head Master's 1923³) played in the Rugby XVs of 1927 and 1928. He was a planter in Tanganyika and Zimbabwe and lived in Queensland, Australia. He died on 21 January 2004 aged 93.

ABOVE: Harrow v Wellington, 1955. The two Harrovians breaking from the scrum on the left are Charles Guthrie and Robin Butler. The ball carrier is Simon Clarke, later England scrum half

A future from the past

PETER SMITHERS

I ENTERED RENDALLS IN THE SUMMER TERM OF 1927. Education at my preparatory school had not been an exciting experience and at Harrow it continued to be something which had to be undergone as a matter of duty. Bored, I became interested in 'Worker' and soon became secretary of the Engineering Society. In due course I was promoted to the History Fifth, which tended to be a receptacle for those not sure of where they were going; the Master was Jackie Martin. There was a list of books to be read. I expected to continue memorizing dates and names as I had done for the past four years in Westgate-on-Sea. I little knew what was in store for me. At the end of the first week the world had changed. As I listened to Mr Martin and read what he advised, the future opened before my eyes. This was not just 'learning'. This was the story of Man and his struggles to survive and to excel and of the men and women who had directed it. This was the greatest of all games, and I would be a player in it come what might. At the end of two weeks I had finished the books for the term and came back for more.

A friend of my parents had been at Magdalen College, Oxford. I wrote to the College for information. For undergraduates there were 'Demyships', half-fellowships which in other colleges were 'Scholarships'. There were three each year in History. I went to my House Master, Billy Siddons, a rather remote figure. "Sir, I want to enter for a Demyship in History at Magdalen College." "You! A Scholar? I never heard such a thing." But Jackie Martin had lit the fire and it would not be extinguished, even today, more than 70 years later.

I talked with my parents, and, surprisingly, they agreed to my request to leave Harrow and read for a year with a distinguished Tudor historian, Arthur Innes. At the end of the year, about the time of my 17th birthday, I sat the Demyship examination. There were 300 entrants for history scholarships in Oxford colleges, the three Demyships at Magdalen amongst them. I got the second.

THE HARROVIAN

2 June 1977

Wilfred Owen's letter to his mother, 31 August 1918

My last hours in England were brightened by a bathe in the fair green Channel, in company of the best piece of Nation left in England – a Harrow boy, of superb intellect and refinement, intellect because he detests war more than Germans, and refinement because of the way he spoke of my going away; and the way he spoke of the Sun; and of the Sea, and the Air; and everything. In fact the way he spoke.

Continuing in history I missed the Gladstone Prize but got Proxime Accessit, followed by a First in History and, interrupted by the war, a D. Phil in history for my 'Life of Joseph Addison' at the University Press.

A lieutenant in the RNVR, in the bitter winter of 1939–40 I was taken ill at sea, nearly died, and on recovery was told by Haslar Hospital to go look for a bowler hat: no more going to sea for me. Not liking this I recalled that a delightful girlfriend had another boyfriend in the Naval Intelligence Division of the Admiralty. I sent her my academic record to pass on. It so happened that Admiral Godfrey, the legendary 'Uncle John', Director of Naval Intelligence, was looking for a talent to run a rapidly expanding service. Commander Ian Fleming, Personal Assistant to Uncle John, rang the hospital. 'Lieutenant Smithers is not to be discharged: he should report at once to the DNI at the Admiralty.'

My life began that day in the History Fifth. It has been fascinating throughout and attended by extraordinary good fortune and happiness. Perhaps it has even contributed a minuscule fraction to the national destiny. As my 90th birthday approaches I look back to acknowledge my debt of gratitude to Jackie Martin, an inspired teacher who fired my imagination and ambition, and indirectly to House Master Billy Siddons who provided the outrage which got me going!

Sir Peter Smithers VRD DPhil (Rendalls 1927[2]) was Parliamentary Under-Secretary of State, Foreign Office, from 1962–4, and Secretary General, Council of Europe, from 1964–9. In retirement he has won many prizes for photography and horticulture.

Sir Cecil Beaton
Photographer, writer and stage designer

Cecil Beaton (Bradbys 1918¹). Taken from his obituary in The Times *– Saturday, 19 January 1980*

Portrait of Marie Laurencin by Cecil Beaton, from the OSR Gallery collection

Sir Cecil Beaton, CBE, who died yesterday, aged 76, is likely to be seen by later generations as one of the Old Masters of photography; one in a line of inspiring pioneers during the first century of an infant art. In that succession of distinguished originals, which includes Daguerre, Lartigue and Julia Margaret Cameron, he takes a place analogous, in some ways, to that of Hogarth or Reynolds in the development of painting. In an absolute sense, his artistic achievement is not to be compared with theirs; but like both artists he wanted to elevate his art above the mechanical craft of a hireable tradesman, and equally above the fashionable diversion that others would make of it.

He went to Harrow in the summer term of 1918, just before the end of the First World War. He sketched a lot, and Edward le Bas, the future RA, was a friend. He also took muzzy but imaginative photographs of his fellows. When he was given a room of his own, he asserted his aesthetic independence by painting it blue. What finally established Beaton was his friendship with the Sitwells. Allanah Harper, who had adopted him as a protégé, brought round Edith Sitwell in 1926: Miss Sitwell's knees and joints popped and crackled as she posed on the floor. 'Chinese torture,' she said – but Beaton 'caught an approving twinkle in her eye as she left. It meant that we were going to be friends'.

By 1929, only Queen Mary and Virginia Woolf, of the subjects he aspired to, had eluded his lens. In that year, encouraged by the enthusiastic welcome Beverley Nichols had received there, he went to America. Mrs Chase, the editor of Vogue, laughed at his amateur equipment, but bought his pictures. He was commissioned to photograph beautiful women in the Condé Nast's luxurious apartment on Park Avenue. It was 'like being given a pass to photograph in the Elysian Fields.' His sitters were astonished by his shyness, shocked by his toy-like camera. Nast made him buy a large camera. 'You've got to grow up,' he said. Beaton photographed Helen Bennett, the fashion model, on a throne of ice. 'Miss Bennett suffered, though by no means in silence.' He photographed Marlene Dietrich, Gloria Swanson, Mrs Patrick Campbell.

Beaton returned to New York with many enticing offers in the following autumn. Elsie de Wolfe (Lady Mendl) lent him her interior decorating establishment on 57th Street for an exhibition. He brought back to England a contract to take photographs exclusively for Condé Nast for several thousand pounds a year for several years. *My Fair Lady* made his name for the second time, in the post-war world. For the film, first shown in 1963, he designed everything, from doorknobs in servants' bedrooms to the sandwiches eaten at Edwardian Ascot. It was a task perfectly fitted to his abilities and experience.

A deep charm is the impression his photography most often gives: but although he has sometimes caught only the superficial qualities, he has exalted them – who else could have regarded Edith Sitwell, with her 'etiolated Gothic bones' as 'the most beautiful human object I had ever seen'? He was, and remained, essentially a man of the 1920s.

The Eton–Harrow Match

ANNE de COURCY

THE ETON AND HARROW MATCH AT LORD'S, world headquarters of cricket, was an important event in the social calendar. It was attended by the wives, families and friends of Etonians and Harrovians past and present, by débutantes and their mothers, and by cricket-loving Old Boys from both schools who travelled up from the country, while the parade of fashions made it one of the recognised 'set pieces' of the Season. The match that opened on 14 July 1939 was remarkable for two things. Harrow beat Eton for the first time for 31 years; and more top hats were destroyed that afternoon than would have come to the end of their useful life in a normal decade. To appreciate the significance of this, in an age of public decorum when physical assault – let alone at one of the most elegant occasions of the year – was rare, it is necessary to understand the extraordinary

RIGHT: *The Harrow team heading for net practice on the Nursery Ground, Lord's 2004*

chauvinism of the public schools. And in particular, the traditional rivalry between Eton and Harrow (the best-known public school after Eton), carried on only half-jokingly up to and including Cabinet level.

The Match started without any particular hint of the sensation to come. Eton won the toss and elected to bat first. Although Crutchley – whose father had been largely responsible for the Harrow victory in 1908 by taking eight wickets for 46 runs – made 115 in Harrow's first innings on Friday, there was no reason to think that the long spell of defeat was about to be dramatically broken. In fact, everything seemed exactly as usual. That is, hardly a soul was actually watching the cricket. Everyone else was perambulating round the tarmac behind the stands and pavilion, so intent on meeting and greeting as many friends as possible (encountering the same ones for the third or fourth time was the signal to reverse direction) that it hardly mattered that for long spells the cricket itself was hidden from view. Yet that year, it was almost as though the dramatic finale of the match was unconsciously anticipated, for the number of coaches, wagonettes and even old-fashioned victories was greater than at any time in the past ten years.

Though a little rain had fallen in the morning, the weather had cleared by lunchtime and the afternoon was warm with brilliant sunshine. Most of the women wore floating, garden party dresses and flowery hats, many in the partisan colours of pale or dark blue – the Duchess of Gloucester, for example, who with the Duke was lunching in the Duke of Buccleuch's box, was in pale blue crêpe, and pale blue swathed her wide brown straw hat. Lady May Able Smith, on the other hand, wore a dark blue coat and blue printed dress, with a silver fox fur. Except for those who came at five o'clock or so from their City offices to watch the last of the cricket, men wore morning coats and grey top hats.

There was, of course, an enormous number of schoolboys, as attendance at the match on one of the two days was compulsory for both schools. Those from Eton wore their school clothes, but with a double-breasted waistcoat in buff or grey instead of the usual black (unless the boy in question was a member of Pop, in which waistcoats of anything from brocade to shot silk were permissible). The ensemble was completed by a black cane with a silver top and light-blue tassel, and a pale

blue carnation. The usual method of achieving this was by standing a white flower in inky water, which often presented a rather curious mottled appearance.

The Harrow boys, whose usual weekday uniform included dashing straw boaters, wore their Sunday top hats with either morning or Harrovian cutaway coats, and the lavender-grey or coffee-buff waistcoats normally worn only by 'Bloods' (those in the Eleven, the Harrow football eleven, or the rugby team). But their similar silver-topped canes were decorated with two dark blue tassels and a buttonhole that even Etonians admitted was superior: a single cornflower of a deep, pure, even blue. Traditionally noisier than Etonians ('Rugby may be more clever, Harrow may make more row,' wrote A. C. Ainger in the *Eton Boating Song*), they would give voice to a long-drawn-out, deep 'Harroo-oo-oow' from the grandstand and on the Mound when goings-on on the field seemed to demand it.

At close of play on the Friday, Harrow had been within three runs of Eton's total, with three wickets still to fall. But when the second Eton innings opened at noon on Saturday 15 July, Fiennes, the Eton Captain, in partnership with Barton, was batting so confidently and steadily that half an hour later the score stood at 66 for one wicket. So impregnable now seemed the Eton position that the few *cognoscenti* actually watching the cricket thought it likely that Eton would have to declare to have any chance of getting Harrow out and winning the match.

Then the Harrow captain, Lithgow, put on Henley at the Nursery end. In two overs this magnificent bowler took three wickets; soon after that, the Eton Captain was caught off him … and four wickets were down for 69. Moments later, another wicket was taken by Byam, the bowler at the other end.

Suddenly the whole picture had changed. With the Eton batting seemingly collapsed, the chance of a draw dwindled – and victory was in sight for Harrow. A buzz of excitement went round the ground. The *Eton Chronicle* later summed up this dramatic moment:

> Old Harrovians from all parts of England began chartering aeroplanes. Spectators who had always regarded Lord's as a clearing-house for family gossip even went so far as to face the cricket and enquire earnestly which side was batting; old gentlemen in the pavilion who generally reckoned on a peaceful

RIGHT:
J. Baskervyle-Glegg (Eton), Mark Weedon and Anthony Cable (wicket keeper) in the 1957 match

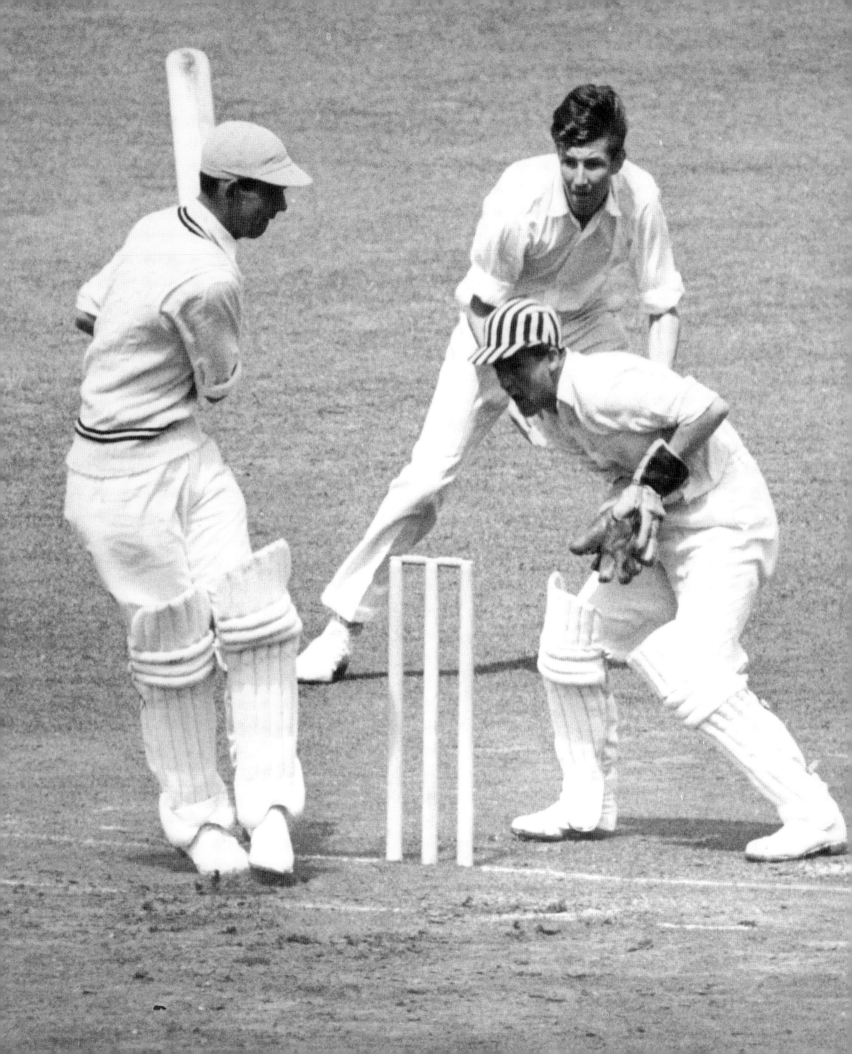

two hours' nap between the lunch and tea intervals, blew up their cushions and brought a score card.

These reactions were not without effect on the Eton batsmen, with a record of 30 years' standing to keep or lose with one careless flick outside the off stump. But they did not flick. They chose more obviously suicidal methods. For perhaps two overs, they would play safe and correct cricket and add half a dozen runs. Then a sudden rush in the Mound or the sudden clatter of yet another rudely-awakened member in the pavilion would stir them to action.

This invariably coincided with a straight, good-length ball, and each time it meant another wicket … the innings closed for 156 with a run-out which aptly reflected the state of nervous tension and left Harrow with 131 to win in more time than a Test Match would demand.

Nevertheless, this knife-edge situation did not curtail one of the main amusements of the day, the between-innings fashion parade. With the wicket roped off, spectators flooded discreetly but firmly on to the pitch where the latest creations could be displayed to full

advantage and viewed easily and unhurriedly. The unfortunate Harrow opening pair had to wait at the wicket until those more interested in glamour than cricket had finally sauntered off.

Henderson and Wallace opened the bowling for Eton. At 18, one wicket fell – but it was only a temporary setback. Steadily the runs mounted, while the excitement and tension all round the ground was almost tangible. When one of the opening pair was dismissed at 50, with the score at 96, Crutchley went in. George Lyttelton, the Eton Housemaster, reported in *The Times* that the cheers from Harrow were now 'the shout of them that triumph, the song of them that intend shortly to feast without stint or misgiving'. Finally, and fittingly, the captain of the Harrow Eleven, Anthony Lithgow, hit the winning shot, a straight drive to the Pavilion from the far end.

Instantly, the sedate grounds of Lord's erupted. As Lyttelton put it:

> The drought is over, the Arctic night is past, the chains are burst, the clouds have lifted from the Hill. No metaphors can do justice to the feeling

RIGHT: *Harrow v Eton at Lord's, 1928*

of long-depressed satisfaction with which lovers of cricket in general and this match in particular saw Harrow beat Eton by eight wickets.

Physical action was clearly the only possible culmination of 30 years of pent-up emotion. A race between the groundsmen and police, and most of Harrow, was won by the latter; half a dozen of the bigger Harrow boys – including Wyld, who sprang from the top of his carriage over the boundary rope – reached Lithgow and carried him in triumph over the heads of the crowd. Here, as women stepped hastily out of the way, top hats were bashed, and umbrellas broken. Soon ties, braces, button-holes, or anything else bearing the once tauntingly superior blue of Eton, were ripped off and torn to shreds by triumphant Harrovians past and present.

By all accounts, this rough-housing did not start with the boys, largely because there were too many Masters about; they joined in only after about 20 minutes, so that for a while it was the older men alone who indulged themselves in this form of score-settling. Next day the *Sunday Express* lamented:

When the winning run was scored, Lord's became a bear garden, and it wasn't the boys who started it, but their elders, pillars of county society, figures on the stock exchange, grey-haired businessmen. Elderly men took off their toppers, which were kicked from their hands. One distinguished-looking Old Etonian punched a clerical Old Harrovian. Two other Old Harrovians set upon their school enemy. He was thrown to the ground, his tie torn off and his coat lifted, exposing light blue braces … in a few seconds he was debagged.

The *mêlée* was thickest in front of the pavilion, where Old Harrovians and Old Etonians rolled about on the grass scuffling, and it spread into the Tavern to the annoyance of drinkers who had been to neither school. Finally, the police cleared out the combatants, but both sides continued to support their champions. 'Etonians assured their Eleven, with unconscious but appropriate irony, that it was "Jolly boating weather",' wrote George Lyttelton, 'while in the opposite camp the strains of *Forty Years On*, according to a sardonic and undaunted Old

Etonian, celebrated in anticipation of Harrow's next victory. Then the lowing herd wound slowly o'er the lea. Soon nothing remained on the scene of Harrow's splendid and deserved success save a raffle of Old School Ties and what, 48 hours earlier, had been new school hats.'

In the opinion of some, though, the outcome of the match had been dependent entirely upon Eton's decision to bat first. This, they believed, was the sole reason for her downfall: since 1901, out of the 21 matches completed only five were won by the side batting first. A letter to the *Chronicle* explained it thus:

> The Eton and Harrow Match is the big game for both sides. There is general nervous tension, even among those who have played at Lord's before … which affects a batsman far more than a bowler, as the former's first mistake is going to be fatal, while the latter can make several at little cost. The fielding side thus gains an initial advantage which it does not lose, since time heals the nerves of all and no advantage is likely to be gained in this way later in the game.

The other explanation, of course, is that Harrow, a far smaller school, was quite simply much the better side.

Extract from: *1939 The Last Season,* Anne de Courcy, Weidenfeld and Nicolson, a division of The Orion Publishing Group

LEFT: *The Harrow and Eton flags flying over the Lord's pavilion, 2002*

Harrow in wartime

JOHN LEAF

FIFTY YEARS ON FROM THE END OF THE WAR, personal memories of how the School fared in those far-off days are growing fewer and fainter and so it is appropriate to record some of them before they fade entirely. There were no Speech Days, no Lord's, no petrol for private cars, four School Houses closed and in 1941 the number of boys fell to 292. But it was a unique and stirring time, with a brave spirit abroad, and the writer, who entered the School in September 1939, would not have missed it. During the Munich crisis in 1938 thoughts turned seriously towards the danger of air raids and it was all but decided to dig trenches in the gardens of the Houses. Fortunately a persistent minority said they would rather be bombed in the Houses than die of pneumonia in the gardens and in consequence the basements of the Houses and many others were reinforced to make them proof against anything except a direct hit. A little search in the basements even now reveals the steel joists still in position. For about two years, when air raids were almost nightly occurrences, we all slept in 3-tier bunks in the shelters, and a good communal life developed there as everyone went down each evening, usually soon after House prayers. Somehow the raiders never arrived early enough to interrupt prep! Often the noise of guns could be heard and searchlights would roam the sky, but when the inky dark of a moonless black-out returned, the stars would shine forth in all their glory. Then again in the last year of the war it was back to the shelters for protection against the V1 and V2 missiles.

Harrow had been declared a neutral area by the Government, which meant that children were evacuated neither to nor from it, and this was probably a sound assessment, as for the most part we saw the blitz going on over London rather than feeling it ourselves. Nevertheless incendiary bombs fell on the Hill in 1940, setting fire to Speech Room. High explosives hit only the fields, though it was a pity that one of them landed on the newly-levelled

RIGHT: *Wartime sleeping arrangements*

Sixth Form rugger ground. Much later, in February 1940, incendiaries fell again, starting fires in the Old Harrovian Room, the Old Schools, Chapel and Druries, which were mostly put out by our own fire-fighting teams. The only injury was to one boy who tried to extinguish a bomb by putting his hat over it and then returned it rather too soon to his head! By 9am the next morning the Terrace Gardens had been tidied up, the School was given an extra hour in bed to recover from a disturbed night, and then life went on as normal.

As the U-boat attacks on our shipping, so costly in casualties on both sides, began to take their toll, everything was in short supply, with meat, butter and sugar rationed and many other foods obtainable only on a points system, though ironically it did not prove necessary to ration bread until the early days of peace. Every boy had his own small butter/margarine dish and sugar tin, and whether he could make it last the week was up to him, but for the rest it was the devoted care of House Matrons, wives and mothers that kept us fed and healthy. On a trivial level there was not one banana in the country for four years or so, though until about mid-1940 it had still been possible to go into Tom's the greengrocer at the top

of West Street, and eat 'one banana and cream' for 3d, two for 5d, or three for 6d.

Any waste was a sin – of food, materials, money, clothes, anything – 'every penny saved is a penny more to pay for the war'. To save fuel boys only had fires in their rooms on alternate evenings, taking it in turns to share their neighbour's warm room, and during the day the only heat in the House was a fire in the main communal rooms. Clothes were rationed on a coupon system and if for instance you bought a suit it would be a long time before you could get much else. Holed socks were darned, not thrown away.

Another slogan was 'Dig for victory', and much effort was put into growing food. In the summer holidays boys would go on harvest camps to help with the crops, where the usual task was putting sheaves of corn into stooks to dry. This was hard on untoughened hands and forearms, even if you were wearing fives gloves, and the favourite job was leading the horses. At Harrow, war work schemes were evolved such as timber-cutting, field-clearing and the cultivation of waste land, and in February 1943, steps were taken greatly to expand the embryo School Farm. Participation in these activities was voluntary, but once you had volunteered you had to turn up.

Warnings of air raids would last for hours, often without so much as the sound of a gun, and in order to keep the wheels of the country turning, a 'Red Alert' system was devised, which only operated if enemy aircraft really were drawing rather close. At Harrow this was not too frequent an occurrence during the day, and it was seldom that lessons were interrupted. On the football and cricket fields, brick shelters had been built where everyone could take refuge if necessary. Also on the fields long trenches had been cut to prevent the landing of gliders carrying troops; and to impede the planning of enemy air raids all reporting of weather, even long after the event, was banned. Indeed strenuous efforts were made in every way to deny information to the enemy, and you could not go far without seeing a notice 'Careless talk costs lives'. At first everyone had to carry their gas masks, but this lapsed as it became clear that neither side was going to start a form of warfare that would certainly provoke retaliation. By night there was a well-organised patrol system, with a control room in the basement of the War Memorial and first aid and fire-fighting equipment in every House.

60 Years On

Extracts from letters written to the author's mother and father from Harrow during the Second World War

Winter 1939

Wednesday, 4 October – We had an air raid practice yesterday to see how long it took people to come up from the football fields to their Houses. I did it in about 4 minutes, as I was playing on a nearish field. They are not using the far-away fields. Anyone who goes more than 7 minutes away from the House has to take a gas mask with him. Our Air Raid Shelter (the basement) has been all painted up since last term, cream & red (walls cream & girders & doors red). Makes it much nicer to remain in. We do not take gas masks up to school. No form room is more than 7 min. from the Houses; & think how they would get bashed about & lost!

Sunday, 8 October – We are still having trouble with blacking out the House, and apparently Druries is known locally as the 'Lighthouse'; people don't draw their curtains properly, or forget to do them before and not after they switch on the light, or else the material isn't thick enough.

Winter 1940

Sunday, 29 September – We get into our 'siren suits' i.e. pyjamas with greyers, sweater and bluer over the top plus socks and slippers at 6.55pm after an hour's prep, and collect our bedding consisting of flea-bag, sheet, pillow and rug (plus gas mask and anything else you want) and take them downstairs to the ground floor and dump them there. Then supper and more prep, this time on the ground floor in the Library and in the New Room until 8.50pm Prayers and then down to the shelter at 9pm plus bedding. There's a wireless in the kitchen down there so we can hear the news. Lights out at 9.45pm for most of the House, except for what the House Master calls 'Priv's Corner' which is going to have a curtain shutting it off from the rest and have an extra half hour. We get called in the morning at 7.15am, breakfast at 8am (no early school), Chapel at 9am, School at 9.20am etc.

To return to Friday: – The sirens went at 8.20pm. We descended about 8.30pm, heard the news, collected two mattresses each and proceeded to try and make ourselves comfortable, I with a sheet inside my blanket, a bit difficult to get it to stay there (however I found a better way last night, by folding it broadways instead of lengthways it was just wide enough to tuck with the blanket under the first mattress). Actually I had quite a good night and didn't hear the all clear which went about 6am.

Thursday, 3 October – Just a line to tell you that I'm absolutely OK, in case you have or will see reports in the paper about the events of last night. We had quite a few incendiary bombs on some of the school buildings about half past ten last night. The damage was absolutely nil except for the roof of a private house half way down the hill, and a bit of the roof of Speech Room and the Museum Schools. We had one on the House which was dealt with by the House fire squad and was out in about 5 minutes. Daddy rang up EDG this afternoon, having seen something in the evening papers in London.

They are the rottenest things (the incendiaries I mean) I've ever met, and familiarity certainly does breed contempt. They're not half as efficient as they are supposed to be and provided there's someone moderately near to arrive fairly soon, they are terribly easy to deal with.

Please don't fuss about me as we are better cared for here than anywhere. Last night was the most efficient thing (from our point of view) I've ever seen.

PETER HARRILD

Peter Harrild (Druries 1936[3]) was a Computer Administrator and Systems Analyst for Ferranti Computers and International Computers and Tabulators and for IPC.

THE HARROVIAN

The Prime Minister's Visit in 1940

On Wednesday afternoon, 18 December, the Prime Minister, Mr Winston Churchill, paid an informal visit with Mrs Churchill and some of his Old Harrovian colleagues in the Government to join with members of the School in singing a programme of Harrow songs in Speech Room. With the Prime Minister were Mr L.S. Amery, Secretary of State for India; Colonel J.C. Moore-Brabazon, Minister of Transport; Captain D. Margesson, chief Government Whip; and Mr Geoffrey Lloyd, Secretary of Petroleum at the Ministry of Mines. They were welcomed at Moretons by the Head Master, who escorted Mr and Mrs Churchill to Speech Room.

The Prime Minister made a short informal speech to the School in an interval between the songs, so the clapping was loud and prolonged. He said it was a great pleasure, and a refreshing treat to himself and those of his Ministerial colleagues who had come to Harrow with him that afternoon to join the School in singing Harrow songs. When he was there as a boy he was thrilled by them. He had a good memory and mastered the words of many of them and they often came back to him in after-life. He felt that they were one of the greatest treasures of the School, passing as they did from one generation to another and pointing with bright hopes towards the future. They had sung of 'the wonderful giants of old,' but could anyone doubt that this generation was as good and as noble as any the nation had ever produced, and that its men and women could stand up against all tests; and

could anyone doubt that this generation was in every way capable of carrying on the traditions of the nation and handing down its love of freedom, justice and liberty, with its message undiminished and unimpaired..

'Herr Hitler,' the Prime Minister continued, 'in one of his recent discourses, had declared that the fight was between those who had been through the Adolf Hitler schools and those who had been at Eton. Hitler had forgotten Harrow and he had also overlooked the vast majority of the youth of this country who have never had the privilege of attending such schools but who are standing staunchly together in the nation's cause and whose skill and prowess is the envy of the whole world. When this war is won by this nation, as it surely will be, it must be one of our aims to establish a state of society where the advantages and privileges which hitherto have been enjoyed only by the few shall be far more widely shared by the men and the youth of the nation as a whole.

'It is a great time in which you are called upon to begin your life. You have already had the honour of being under the fire of the enemy, and you acquitted yourselves with befitting courage and decorum. You are here at this most important period of your lives, at a moment when our country stands forth almost alone as champions of right and freedom all over the world. You, young men, will be the heirs of the victory which we shall surely achieve and you in this Speech Room will perhaps derive from these songs and Harrow associations the impulse to render that victory fruitful and lasting.'

In the summer of 1940, with most of Europe overrun, invasion was a real possibility, and though by September the daylight onslaughts of the Luftwaffe had been repelled, the winter that followed was stern indeed. December saw the first Churchill Songs, with the Prime Minister visiting Harrow accompanied by several other Old Harrovian members of the Government. We were all most excited by the prospect of his visit and pleased that when the planned programme was finished he asked for more. Most of the songs he sang from memory; the tears rolled down his cheeks and at the end he gave a stirring speech and hoped that he would be invited again.

Boys were of course not allowed out of their Houses in the black-out and so enterprising efforts were made to bring entertainment to us. Films were shown in the evening in Houses, and concert parties and groups, both boys and Masters, would go round with music and sketches catering for all tastes. During daylight hours Speech Room could be used, and concerts were given both by School performers and by the new-formed Harrow Philharmonic Society, founded by the then Director of Music, Henry Havergal, to keep music alive in the area. Dramatic activity was largely limited to the Shakespeare play, the first of the current series taking place in 1941, with the only other major events being The Park's production of *The Doctor's Dilemma* in the Music Schools and one highly popular Beaks' revue.

In November 1939 H.F. Garnons-Williams was killed on a reconnaissance flight, the first of the 344 Old Boys and four Masters who would die on active service. Their names were recorded in Rolls of Honour in *The Harrovian*, and it was not so long before the younger of us saw the names appearing there of some whom we had known as senior boys when we first entered the School. Also published were lists of the wounded, the missing, prisoners of war and those to whom decorations had been awarded. One of the first of these was E.E.A.C. Talbot, sadly to die a year later, who received the George Cross for removing an unexploded bomb. The future for all boys leaving was service in the forces in some shape or form and one certainly did not have to worry about a job. At the age of 17 everyone had to register and the call-up at 19 meant that many boys did not complete their final year at school.

In May 1942 the Hill filled up again. At a mere three weeks notice Malvern had been told that their buildings would be requisitioned to provide a safe haven for aircraft research and that they must find accommodation elsewhere. There was plenty of spare capacity at Harrow and it was quickly agreed that we should offer them a home 'for the duration'. The huge task of moving a whole school was smoothly carried out and soon after the beginning of the summer term Malvern arrived. In the interim there had been much speculation about so new a prospect – 'Shall we work together in shared forms?' 'Will there be a combined cricket XI?' But in the event both schools conducted their lives side by side but separately, with close and friendly co-operation between the staffs and the boys realising that any feuding must be out of the question. The four empty Houses – West Acre, Newlands, Bradbys and Rendalls – were all taken over by Malvern, who also occupied Deyne Court. Their Headmaster lived in Grove Hill House. Both schools retained their own uniforms and customs and the only shared occasions were Monday morning Speech Room and some Chapel services. Except for the boy, perhaps mythical, who had been destined for Harrow but went to Malvern instead because it would be safer, the whole interlude was a great success. In the event it was four years before Malvern could return home and their time at Harrow is commemorated by the clock at the top of West Street.

Long before then, the war in Europe, and indeed in the Far East, had come to an end. At 3pm on 8 May, 1945, the Prime Minister broadcast the long expected announcement that the war in Europe was finished. Celebrations at Harrow were a Service of Thanksgiving and an impromptu concert followed by a bonfire and fireworks; but perhaps the sight that really convinced everyone that peace had returned was the buildings all lit up in the night. The black-out was over.

THE HARROVIAN

13 May 1942

Malvern

In consequence of the requisitioning of Malvern College by the Government, the Governors of the School have offered accommodation at Harrow to Malvern. It is understood that Malvern College will re-assemble at Harrow as soon as the arrangements for the move have been completed.

Our first feeling, as we hear this news, must be one of keen sympathy with Malvern, who for the second time since the outbreak of war have been required at a moment's notice to strike tents and march into the unknown. The anxieties, discomforts and distresses entailed in the abrupt evacuation of schools have become in these days a too common experience; and those of us whose memory will carry us as far back as Munich, when for a nightmare spell the prospect of sudden translation hung before our eyes, will not need to overtax imagination in sympathetic understanding of the

June 1942

Correspondence

To the Editors of The Harrovian:

DEAR SIRS, – Now that we have been back for just over a week and Malvern has begun to settle down properly, might I draw your attention to what my own first reactions have been?

I came back expecting to find that some of you – probably a majority – would rather resent our arrival in your midst – in many ways a natural attitude when an army of strangers enters one's cherished home. Furthermore, I half expected you might welcome us, and then take little further interest in us and remain quite aloof. How wrong and unjustifiable my expectations were! Never could a host have been more diligent and hospitable towards his guests. Never can I forget the really magnificent welcome we have just received; not only was an immediate sympathy and understanding shown to Malvern's interests and traditions, but a spirit of co-operation was immediately shown by you, and I hope Malvern has not failed to respond.

I feel that all this reveals the great strength of the public schools in general and our two schools in particular. Our 'basher' may be a different colour from your straw hat, and it may be worn at a different angle, but it is essentially the same thing. From the top of Harrow to the very bottom, a magnificent spirit of goodwill and friendliness has been displayed towards us. From the depth of my heart, I honour and thank you for it.

Yours, etc.,

AN INSIGNIFICANT MALVERNIAN

On poetry and panache

JOHN MORTIMER

'SCHOOL SONGS' WERE A GREAT AND PROUD feature of Harrow life. We would assemble in the Speech Room and sing the compositions of long-dead House Masters and music Masters, songs redolent of vanished boys playing cricket in knicker-bockers, enjoying romantic friendships on summer evenings and going out to die in Afghanistan or on Majuba Hill: *Forty Years On*; *Jerry a Poor Little Fag*; *Byron lay, lazily lay, Hid from lesson and game away, Dreaming poetry all alone, Up on the top of Peachey stone*. That was the repertoire and then a new boy with a childish treble would pipe:

> Five hundred faces and all so strange
> Life in front of me, home behind …

And the gravely-voiced, hairy-chinned, spotty seniors would trumpet in chorus:

> But the time will come when your heart will thrill
> And you'll think with joy of your time on the
> Hill!

Winston Churchill, then First Lord of the Admiralty, came down to this strange ceremony which he apparently enjoyed. After the Songs were over Mr Churchill climbed with difficulty on to the stage. He cannot have been more than sixty-five years old, but his ancient head emerged from the carapace of his dinner-jacket like the hairless pate of a tortoise, his old hand trembled on the handle of the walking-stick which supported him and his voice, when he spoke, was heavily slurred with brandy and old age. He seemed to us to be about a hundred and three. "If they ever put him in charge of the war," I whispered to Oliver, "God help us all!". "Oh, they won't do that," he assured me. "They'll never do that. Chap in the Government told my Ma."

There were some excellent Masters at Harrow and I shall be ever grateful to a large and rather unctuous cleric who taught us English. He read poetry in a fruity voice and used to congratulate himself on his sensitivity. "You

RIGHT: *St Mary's Church and the Peachey Stone*

know, boys," he used to say after reading us Blake's poem about heaven's wrath at caged birds, "I once took out a gun. It was a fine, dewy morning and I saw a little hare sunning itself on a grassy knoll. I lifted my gun and took a careful aim and do you know what I did then?" "Yes, sir," we chorused, having heard the story from him fairly often. "You *spared its life*." "That is right," the Reverend Gentlemen would smile complacently. "It was, like me, one of God's humble creations and I *spared* it."

However, he introduced me to the Romantic poets who didn't figure in my father's anthology, and above all to Wordsworth. I think the Reverend Arthur Chalfont and I were the only people in the class who got any pleasure out of the old Sheep of the Lake District and we used to read each other long passages from *The Prelude* and *Tintern Abbey* to the fury of Tainton who said we sounded like a couple of expiring goats, and read *Titbits* under the desk with his hands in his pockets. I could see why Wordsworth was unpopular. He was clearly short on humour and capable of writing some of the silliest

LINES WRITTEN BY BYRON AT THIS PLACE.

SPOT OF MY YOUTH! WHOSE HOARY BRANCHES SICH.
SWEPT BY THE BREEZE THAT FANS THY CLOUDLESS SKY.
WHERE NOW ALONE I MUSE, WHO OFT HAVE TROD.
WITH THOSE I LOVED, THY SOFT AND VERDANT SOD:
WITH THOSE WHO, SCATTER'D FAR, PERCHANCE DEPLORE.
LIKE ME, THE HAPPY SCENES THEY KNEW BEFORE:
OH! AS I TRACE AGAIN THY WINDING HILL.
MINE EYES ADMIRE, MY HEART ADORES THEE STILL.
THOU DROOPING ELM! BENEATH WHOSE BOUGHS I LAY.
AND FREQUENT MUSED THE TWILIGHT HOURS AWAY:
WHERE, AS THEY ONCE WERE WONT, MY LIMBS RECLINE.
BUT AH! WITHOUT THE THOUGHTS WHICH THEN WERE MINE:
HOW DO THY BRANCHES, MOANING TO THE BLAST.
INVITE THE BOSOM TO RECALL THE PAST.
AND SEEM TO WHISPER, AS THEY GENTLY SWELL.
"TAKE, WHILE THOU CANST, A LINGERING LAST FAREWELL!"

THIS SLAB WAS PLACED HERE IN 1905 BY SIR J.C.T. SINCLAIR, BART.,
THE SON OF SIR GEORGE SINCLAIR, BART, OF ULBSTER, CAITHNESS,
WHO WAS BYRON'S SCHOOLFELLOW AND FRIEND.

lines in the English language. I also knew that my great friend and ally, Lord Byron, couldn't stand Wordsworth for many years and objected to his frequently ham-fisted way with a stanza and his distinct lack of breeding and panache. All the same, in those endless afternoons when the Reverend Arthur Chalfont and I read to each other I came, slowly and reluctantly, to the conclusion that as between Wordsworth and Lord B, the old fumbler from the Lake District was by far the better poet.

Brought up in a strictly agnostic household I was not only unmusical but without a religious sense. When we had been forced to kneel by our beds at my prep school I had found it embarrassing to pretend to talk to God, to whom, if he existed, I felt I should have nothing very polite to say, and so I counted up to 25 and then climbed between the sheets. On Sunday, singing the hymn:

Only believe and you shall see
That Christ is all in all to thee

ABOVE: *Byron's Lines at the Peachey Stone*

I thought I would try it. I dug my nails into the palms of my hands, stood quite alone in the playground and forced myself to believe for at least ten minutes. Even so I couldn't see it. Our house in the country was all in all to me; my strange father, my friends, my theatrical ambitions and my chances of being chosen to act Richard II. Christ, however hard I made myself believe, I could only see as a remote and historical figure, far from my immediate concerns. And yet there is, I am sure, a religion in everyone, which struggles for its own mystical satisfaction. I began to feel that my own came nearest to expression in whatever it was that Wordsworth felt he believed in:

> … I have learned
> To look on nature, not as in the hour
> Of thoughtless youth; but hearing often-times
> The still, sad music of humanity,
> Nor harsh nor grating, though of ample power
> To chasten and subdue. And I have felt
> A presence that disturbs me with the joy
> Of elevated thoughts; a sense sublime
> Of something far more deeply infused,
> Whose dwelling is the light of setting suns,
> And the round ocean and the living air,
> And the blue sky, and in the mind of man …

I read that then as I do now, feeling close to tears, and with a sense of wonder which I'm sure must be known

RIGHT: *Sketch of Alexander Fife by Oswald Birley. They were in Elmfield together in the 1890s*

The 'Saturday-nighter'

To me the Saturday-nighter was an immutable part of life before the VI form at Harrow but when I mentioned it in a letter to Ronnie Watkins about 20 years ago, he had completely forgotten about it. So when did it begin and end? In my time it was probably confined to the upper Removes and Lower Fifths. It was simply an essay, on a given topic, that had to be delivered after the weekend. It was one of those disciplines, causing groans at the time, but later seen to have been of great benefit. What it taught me principally was the value,

indeed the necessity, of false starts as a way of prodding my unconscious into life. Just as a hound has to move about, nosing the air, catching misleading scents until suddenly it hits the true and unmistakable trail, so the initial scribbles both prompt and sharpen your awareness of the right line of thought when it comes. Others may find inspiration more easily but those like me only learn this process and its value by doing it again and again. You learn to trust that some idea, some approach will emerge onto the paper so that then you can work on it, shaping and

moulding. While never a professional writer, I have written much within my profession and the lesson of the Saturday-nighter is one for which I shall always be grateful.

HUGH SAXTON

Dr H.M.Saxton MB BS FRCP (The Knoll 1942[2]) was Chief of Health Planning at the World Health Organisation, Geneva, and Professor of Social and Preventative Medicine at the University of Queensland.

It must be true: it was in all the papers

Churchill liked to choose a particular theme for his speech each year, and in 1949 for some reason he said he had always wanted to play the drums. This was my first term as timpanist of the school orchestra – I had just been promoted from the triangle – so, as a very small 15-year-old I crouched behind three large kettledrums. The snag of this post on Churchill Songs night was that at the end, when everyone else rushed out of Speech Room to cheer him on the War Memorial steps, I had to stay behind and put my drums away. The most awkward part of this involved retracting the legs, which were held by a set of screws underneath the drums. When I emerged with my spanner from floor level, I was amazed to find Churchill beaming at me, saying, "Can I try?" So I handed him my sticks, and he tried a few rolls of the drums, then invited me to demonstrate how it ought to be done. After that, he tried again, and went back in a very good mood to the platform party. I resumed my engineering, and next time I came up for air, there was another stranger waiting for me. "I'm from the *Daily Telegraph*", he said, and asked me about my encounter. "How did he do?" he asked, and I replied, "He wasn't at all bad" – the current phrase for something good. (What would it be today? Wicked? Cool?)

Finally I got my drums packed up, and went back to Druries. There was excited talk of who had got a good view of the great man, but nobody was interested in my experience – remember I was a very small timpanist. But next morning, all the major newspapers had prominent articles: 'Churchill always wanted to play the drums.' The *Daily Telegraph* had an exclusive interview with me – but never rely on the press. The headline was 'Mr Churchill at Harrow – 'not too bad' as drummer' – not at all the same thing! And the reporter had never asked my age, but said I was 14. A mortal insult at that age, but if only people did that to me now …

ALAN HAKIM

Alan Hakim (Druries 1948[2]) was a Systems Programmer with IBM.

to those who are accustomed to religious contemplation and gain pleasure from Evensong on summer evenings in country churches. I shall always be intensely grateful to Mr Chalfont for teaching me about Wordsworth and can even forgive him for sparing the hare.

There were other good things about Harrow. Martin Witteridge and I joined the Art Society and we used to go off on bicycles to make water-colour sketches of Ruislip reservoir under the guidance of Mr Nares, the wanly good-looking Art Master who used to ask us if we could 'see anything that gave us joy'. On the way home Witteridge and I would drink gin and lime in suburban pubs and he would tell me about his mother who had, he claimed, a truly wonderful sense of humour, his beautiful cousins and his uncle who had been an equerry to the King.

Witteridge asked me to stay with his family. His father was a redhaired ramrod of a man, dressed in the uniform of the Irish Guards, who went off to the War Office each morning with a briefcase which Witteridge and I inspected for secret documents. We found it contained nothing but a small bottle of milk and a tomato sandwich. Witteridge had told me that his mother loved practical jokes and she would be first deceived and then endlessly amused if I came to stay wearing a false moustache and talking in a thick Hungarian accent. Although I was nervous during my first stay I did this, fortified by a good many gin and limes, but Lady Witteridge did nothing but ask me polite questions about my family and life at Harrow, and the beautiful cousins, who were uniformly dressed in twinsets and pearls, didn't speak to me at all. After lunch I abandoned the moustache and we went out for another lengthy pub-crawl on our bicycles. We took with us Witteridge's younger brother Tom, who went to Stowe, was extremely good-looking, drew with real talent and irritated us greatly by saying that he liked to sleep next to 'young warm flesh' and '*never found it at all hard to come by*'.

Extract from *Clinging to the Wreckage*, published by Penguin Books. Copyright ©Advanpress Ltd 1982

Sir John Mortimer CBE QC (The Grove 1937[2]) is a barrister, playwright and author.

Those were the days

ANNE HALL-WILLIAMS

MY FATHER, DAVID CHRISTIE-MURRAY, CAME TO teach at Harrow in 1946, and I, his only child at that time, not unnaturally came with him. My parents were given a flat at the very top of Grove Hill House which had a steep flight of stairs. Not exactly an ideal place for a couple with a small baby and a pram. There was no garden, so most fine days I and my pram were parked in the Copse garden across the road from the flat. Being a contented baby I caused no trouble until the day that I fell out of the pram and somehow got the so-called safety harness caught around my neck. There I dangled and was rapidly turning blue, and my story might have ended had not a passing Harrovian rescued me. Who he was I have no idea, but if he ever happens to read this then I should like him to know that I am extremely grateful.

Living conditions in the School were pretty basic by today's standards. Central heating was unheard of and we were kept warm by coal fires, or gas and electric, sometimes paraffin heaters. Later when we moved to Marston Lodge on Sudbury Hill, we kept the sitting room and the kitchen reasonably warm, and often wore coats to move around the rest of the house. At Marston Lodge, Harrovians came to my father for 'specials' in English, and quite often I was the one who opened our front door and showed them into the study. Sometimes my parents had tea parties, and I used to help out with those too, but that was the extent of my contact with the boys. Just as well really. Harrow in the 1950s was completely unemancipated. Looking back it all seems so rigid and quaint. It was unheard of for girls who were the same age as the boys, but not their sisters, to have anything to do with them in public. If you happened to talk to a boy that you knew in the street, you were 'fast'; if you walked with him, he almost had to marry you; your reputation was ruined. The only way to be safe from gossiping tongues was never, ever to talk to a boy in public.

If you were a horse-loving tomboy as I was, with my cropped hair and perpetual trousers, then at least you weren't seen as a threat to the moral welfare of the boys. By the 1960s, at a black tie event in Speech Room I thought that I could get away with wearing a pair of wide evening trousers which were all the fashion then. I was already sitting in my seat when I saw one of the Masters coming towards me who was, though a very nice man, famous for having very definite ideas about what was and was not suitable wear for women. Trousers worn at any time came definitely into the 'not' category. He sat down cheerfully beside me and chatted away whilst I clenched my knees tightly together hoping that my trousers would look like a long skirt. When the interval came I remained seated, and at the end of the concert walked out very slowly with my knees still clamped together looking, I'm sure, like an egg bound goose.

If I were asked to name one thing that I miss about the old days, then it would have to be Ducker. The School has a splendid indoor swimming pool now, but the old pool was uniquely wonderful, and nobody lucky enough to swim in it will ever forget the experience. However many times you went there was always a feeling of anticipation and excitement as you approached the bridge over the Watford Road from the school fields. Then up the steps you would go to be greeted by the first sight of that huge expanse of water below you, dancing and glittering in the sunshine. The hours spent there contained all that is ever right about childhood. Carefree fun, laughter, warmth, companion-ship. We never swam at the same time as Harrovians, but we knew they felt the same. The end of the day would see us walking home across the fields in the late afternoon sun, with the school buildings and the spires of Chapel and St Mary's Church, silhouetted against the sky. Sun drenched, tired and happy, our swimming costumes rolled wetly within our towels, we would wander 'thro' the meadows, up the Hill and home again'…

Anne Hall-Williams is the daughter of David Christie-Murray, Harrow Master 1946–73, and has lived on the Hill all her life. Her brother, Martin, was in Newlands and her son, Thurstan, was in The Grove.

Naughty, really

JOHN THICKNESSE

O NE OF THE COMPENSATIONS OF GROWING OLD is that as the years slide past so memories of unhappy moments start to disappear. There may in any case have been fewer of those for my contemporaries than for most other generations because in May 1945, which was the month the war in Europe ended, everyone in England was so glad still to be alive, not least the inhabitants of Harrow Hill where at least one doodlebug had landed.

Anyway, for whatever reasons the period 1945–1950 seems to me to have been an exceptionally lucky time to have been at Harrow. In the case of cricketers that had a lot to do with the men who ran the game then: from P.A. Ledward, the Bursar, who looked after the Junior Colts, to Jack Webster (Colts) to Mark Tindall, who as Master in charge of cricket ran the Sixth Form game and 1st XI. George McConnell and Tim Warr, a 1930s Oxford rugger blue, were others closely involved. They were all good cricketers. Tindall was a three-year Cambridge blue, Captain in 1937, who also played for Middlesex. Other than Barry Richards, he was the most stylish batsman I am aware of ever having watched. His son Robert captained Harrow in 1977 and had four years on Northamptonshire's books when he left school. Webster, also a Cambridge blue (and father of Peter, a flannel from 1966 to 1968) for several post-war seasons strengthened Northamptonshire's bowling in the holidays, bounding tirelessly in off a high-stepping run, seemingly for hours at a time. McConnell, an eccentric OH who was then the Rendalls House Master, and Warr, were wicketkeepers.

None of the five could have been much nicer. In the early post-war summers, though, a cricket-mad teenager could have eyes only for our pro, the famous pre-war Middlesex and England batsman Patsy Hendren. A twinkly-eyed Irishman masquerading as a Londoner with a strong stocky body and an ever-smiling face, he was

one of the best-loved cricketers the game has known from the moment he first took guard for England, at Sydney in December 1920, until he retired in 1938, by when he had amassed 57,611 runs at 50.8, and scored 170 hundreds. Being such a natural himself, as we were shortly to discover, Patsy would never have been in danger of blinding a young batsman with science. But since all we wanted was to please him, we would all have tried to do exactly what he told us: "Watch the ball and keep your bat straight".

Just once, about the time he scored 94 for an Old England XI against Surrey at the Oval, we coaxed him into batting in a net. In he went, no pads, no box, no gloves, protesting and laughing and pretending that if Mark Tindall or Jack Webster saw him he was sure to get the sack. For boys seeing him bat for the first time it was an amazing exhibition. As word got round, so boys from every net in sight jostled for the chance to bowl at him. In ten minutes Patsy must have played a hundred balls; apart from those too wide to reach, not one of them went past the bat. Most of them were thumped resoundingly away with a noise a bat's middle makes only in the hands of a class player. It was as though he was fresh from making a century for Middlesex the day before.

Patsy was loveable and mischievous and proud: nothing gave him greater satisfaction than that, of his 170 hundreds, 75 were scored at Lord's, a record unlikely to be beaten. In 1961, the year before his death, it was at Lord's that I last saw him, on the Nursery Ground after

RIGHT: *Cricket v Wellington on the Sixth Form Ground, 2004*

a Cross Arrows game and Patsy was reliving the past: 'I remember once,' he said, 'we were playing Somerset and we needed 12 to win – so I hit Jack White once into the Long Room and once onto the balcony.' He paused a moment. 'Naughty, really,' he added. In two words that was his character. They should have been written on his gravestone.

Sixty years on from Harrow and four decades from

my final sight of Patsy, my affection for both is as strong as ever. Unhappy memories? I really think they may have gone for good.

John Thicknesse (The Head Master's 1945[2]) was in the Cricket XIs of 1948–50. He was Cricket correspondent of the Evening Standard 1967–96 and on the staff of the Daily/Sunday Telegraph 1957–66. He has been freelance for The Times since 1996.

A friend remembered

ALLAN GRAY

Ah! Happy years! Once more who would not be a boy?
Byron, *Childe Harold's Pilgrimage* C.II: st.23

LEFT: *King Faisal II of Iraq with Dr James, July 1956*

MOST OF US ENJOY UNEVENTFUL LIVES BEFORE we come to Harrow. Not so King Faisal II of Iraq, who was a direct descendant of the Prophet Muhammad and a scion of the Hashemite family, the most revered in Islam. His father, King Ghazi, died in a car accident when he was three and at six he was detained under 'house arrest' in Kurdistan. All of his early years were disturbed and uncertain.

Faisal and I were close friends for nine years though it was an unlikely relationship. In those days the School did not encourage a boy to associate with another from a different House or of a different age. However, we both came from far-away places, we both aimed to excel at long range shooting and we both laughed together at the schoolboy jokes of the day. Faisal would ask me sometimes to explain a double meaning or a play on words for he needed to know English as well as to speak it. His governess and his various tutors had not broached these topics.

Like all other junior boys, Faisal had fagged, and he took pride in this. A folded sheet of lined paper was found at Stanwell Place, his house near Staines, on which he had written:

> Day boys duties 1949
> To attend the sixth formers after eccer in the toshes.
> To let the water out of the toshes.
> To take down the sixth formers dressing gowns to toshes.
> Run to all boy calls and do them running as quickly as poss. Not stop to talk on way.
> Cutting boy calls punished severely.

Stanwell was a happy home where I first met his kinsman and closest companion, Prince Ra'ad, whose father Zeid had fought with King Faisal I and T.E. Lawrence.

There were very few reminders of any difference between Muslim and Christian. On one occasion Faisal had welcomed to Harrow the *bon vivant* Nubar Gulbenkian. His father Calouste, 'Mr Five Per Cent', negotiated many of the agreements between countries and companies with an interest in the oil of the Middle East. Nubar was quoted in 1965 for his remark: 'the best number for a dinner party is two – myself and a damn good head waiter'. Faisal showed him Speech Room and the Vaughan, and told of how the boys of Harrow stayed on the Hill during the War. I spoke of how they looked to the South East to watch London burn. Faisal remarked "That is the direction of Mecca".

I was among those school friends invited to Iraq to celebrate his 18th birthday on 2 May 1953 and his accession to the throne. In those heady days we enjoyed the hospitality of the desert revealed in Baghdad. On an afternoon, while driving back to the capital after swimming and shooting, our car came to a small village. Two elders and a young girl stood at the roadside holding a message for their King written in Arabic. As he stepped

RIGHT:
*Commemorative
Iraqi stamps*

BELOW AND
BELOW RIGHT:
*Hugh Lang,
Christopher
Cooper, David
Jones, Allan Gray
and John Hobday
with King Faisal
at his Coronation
in 1953*

from the car, the two prostrated themselves before him. The child's parents had both died and she was destitute. Faisal took her into his household where she was cared for. I felt this was an auspicious beginning to his reign.

At last the hour came for us to return to London and we gathered on the steps of the Palace to say goodbye. A large beetle crawled in front of us. Christopher Cooper, not aware, walked to crush it with his heel. My eyes met the eyes of the Emir Abdul Illah who had been Regent for 14 years and was now Crown Prince. We both knew that the King would regard this incident as a bad omen. His expression did not change. We were his honoured guests.

I am proud that Faisal felt secure on the Hill. He was moved by the Harrow Songs and looked forward to a son wearing a straw hat. He ruled the land nourished by the Tigris and the Euphrates for only five years. In July of 1958 I was in Australia when the news of his assassination was broadcast. I have never returned to Iraq.

Allan Gray (Elmfield 1949¹) now lives in Melbourne, Australia.

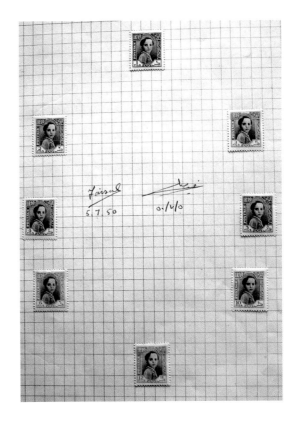

D.M. Reid
– a memoir

MICHAEL HALL-SMITH

I WAS A THIN WEEDY BOY – NO GOOD AT GAMES, AND found my schooldays undistinguished by any obvious achievement, but I did like science, particularly biology. The tang of clove oil and xylene, mixed on dogfish dissection days with formaldehyde, has always proved evocative. This was taught to us in the sixth by D.M. Reid, a bespectacled, pipe-smoking, silver-haired and moustached Scot with a bone-dry sense of humour. 'I'll have no happiness in heeere!' would precede him from his sanctum, whenever ribaldry broke out among us. The kindly lash of his tongue was relished round the room, and while he clearly cared little for the School hierarchy in its more macho and pious manifestations, he applauded good work and interest, and we were all pretty keen to strive for his notice.

I fancy he favoured the eggheads and misfits within the hurly burly and for me he was the one Beak that I could revere without reserve. He made a challenge one day to two of us to try to get to the remote island of North Rona, where he had spent some days once as a field biologist, but persuading a trawler skipper to put two schoolboys ashore and collect them again proved beyond us. Instead, Mr Reid suggested we camped for a month on an inshore island, Oldany, near to his home at Stoer in Sutherland, to which he returned every school holiday.

Dougie collected us at Lochinver, owl-eyed after 24 hours of travel, in an ancient Wolseley, and took us home to enjoy Mrs Reid's cooking before dumping us on the island next day in his boat. There we cleaned out and made rainproof a derelict bothie as our dwelling, and the Reids looked in on us now and then by boat, and took us out fishing as a welcome change from tinned food heated on our Primus. Fresh-caught scallops cooked in sea water were a revelation in those days of austerity!

Sutherland was magic. Wild, windy and with the permanent scream of seabirds around us, we explored our deserted island and made a few dilettante field notes, but it was the challenge of living without any mod cons that engaged our time. Fortune also smiled upon us when a Scottish surgeon and his family aboard a yacht anchored one evening in our bay, and discovering company, took us voyaging nearby for a few days. We both fell in love with crewmaidens and moped pitifully for at least a day when they sailed away. The month flew by and I have never forgotten Sutherland, revisiting it to camp and to climb, and keeping in touch with the Reids with a yearly Christmas bulletin to Stoer after they retired.

In 1959, with a brand-new wife that I was bursting to introduce, we were camping and moving up the west coast, when I thought I should ring ahead and warn the Reids of our approach. I was answered at the manual Achiltibuie exchange by a dignified lady, and enquiring for the Reid's number, was told 'O, Mr Douglas Reid died last week, and they have laid him to rest this very day…'. I do not weep often, but that day in a remote Wester Ross phone box, I did.

It is the privilege of the school teacher to capture minds and to inspire the most unlikely pupils. Mr Reid was the dose of fertiliser that awoke the rather barren soul in my personal soil, and I shall always be grateful to him. Ever since, I have been greatly taken by crusty old iconoclasts, and looked for pearls among their offerings.

BELOW: *A Science lesson in 2004*

Douglas Miller Reid was born in 1897, educated at Glasgow University, and became Lecturer in Zoology at Anderson College. He was appointed to the Natural Science Department at Harrow

in 1921, became a Fellow of the Linnean Society in 1922 and Curator of the Butler Museum in 1933. He retired from teaching in 1953 and died in 1959. Douglas Reid was also a Fellow of the Royal Society of Edinburgh.

Dr Michael Hall-Smith (The Knoll 1946[3]) was in General Practice from 1963–91.

Reflections of a boy of no distinction

Peter de la Billière

Winter term 1947 and the nation was in a state of poverty recovering from the recent World War. Austerity ruled; the School of 395 or so boys was beginning to return to normality after sharing the Hill with the evacuated Malvern College for the past four years. Luxuries such as straw hats could be neither found nor afforded, which pleased me. I took up residence in The Grove under the wise yet somewhat distant patronage of the Reverend Lance Gorse. It is a tribute to 'Ma Roberts', the House Matron, that she managed to produce food that was not memorably bad at a time when rationing must have made her job a near impossibility.

My father had been killed when HMS Fiji was blown out of the water at Crete in 1941 and my brave and overstretched mother found herself managing two impossibly wild and uncontrollable budding, if reluctant, Harrovians. It was in this mood that I resented having to submit to the disciplines of Harrow and for me the School became a challenging training ground for 'life' rather than a centre for academic achievement. In this respect it was an outstanding success, though the Beaks of the day may have taken a rather different view. It offered a breadth of education, which catered for the broad spectrum of boys from the academic to those who possessed other qualities – and I was of the latter breed. It was this aesthetic tolerance that made the School stand out from its peers and continues to do so even in today's contemporary and competitive world.

I remember well my mother discussing a customarily inadequate School report and pointing out that she had to pay the exorbitant fees of £95 a term and that I really ought to try to do better. But then there were opportunities for me to at least enjoy my time if not to excel. We were encouraged to participate in the usual team activities of Harrow football, cricket and rugby, but as I had a particular distaste for all of them, it is to the School's credit that they still found me an outlet for my restless energy despite 'Ducker' being closed as a war emergency measure. I was devoted to the Farm with the Friesian cattle and there was nothing like the 5.15am milking run every two or three days to divert one from the normal School routine and to justify a snooze during 'Pip' Boas's geography lesson. For the individualist such as myself, the squash court at the top of Grove Wood and the rackets court under Fred Crosby were excellent diversions. Shooting, however, appealed to me in particular and much as I disliked the boring routine of the School cadet force which, with the smoke of war just finished, we were

THE HARROVIAN

2 March 1918

Victoria Cross

Lt. (A. Capt.) Walter Napleton Stone, (HMs 1906³) late R. Fus.
For most conspicuous bravery when in command of a company in an isolated position 1,000 yards in front of the main line, and overlooking the enemy's position. He observed the enemy massing for an attack, and afforded invaluable information to Battalion Headquarters.

He was ordered to withdraw his company, leaving a rearguard to cover the withdrawal. The attack developing with unexpected speed, Captain Stone sent three platoons back and remained with the rearguard himself. He stood on the parapet with the telephone under a tremendous bombardment, observing the enemy, and continued to send back valuable information until the wire was cut by his orders. The rearguard was eventually surrounded and cut to pieces, and Captain Stone was seen fighting to the last, till he was shot through the head.

The extraordinary coolness of this heroic officer and accuracy of his information enabled dispositions to be made just in time to save the line and avert disaster.

ABOVE: *Harrow Rifle Corps training during annual camp*

I learnt my early lessons in leadership at Harrow; notably I remember CSM Moores, who was always an enthusiast, would praise boys lavishly even if they had not really distinguished themselves. Listening to him I realised that if someone in authority wants people to perform well, praise is more valuable and effective than chastisement.

I much enjoyed the opportunity to try my musical skills, which proved to be non-existent, though the music staff demonstrated endless patience and encouragement. I adored jazz, and continue to enjoy it, and longed to become a member of the School band: I tried playing the violin which was a disaster and then changed to the trumpet which led to more noise than tune. I then switched to the trombone and finally to the drums before I caved in and admitted that music and I were not really compatible. No doubt the Music Schools breathed a sigh of relief as I departed after a couple of years of teacher frustration.

Dreams of travel and adventure filled my head and when, in a career interview, I told Lance Gorse that I wished to join the contemporary guerrilla leader, Turko Westerling, in Indonesia he was not impressed but took great care to offer me additional responsibility and challenges in the School. Lance Gorse's pastoral care for the boys in his House was quite outstanding and probably had a greater influence on my life and in keeping me at the School than any other factor.

In the end I struck a deal with my mother, after failing School Certificate at the first attempt, that I would work with diligent endeavour for a term; then I would retake the exams provided that, if I passed, I could leave the School at 16. It is a measure of the excellence of the School's teaching staff that I did in fact pass with a bevy of distinctions and credits. I often wonder what might have happened had that one term's diligent work been forthcoming from when I arrived at Harrow.

I believe Harrow identified my strengths and developed them whilst not harassing me for my weaknesses. I left Harrow on a high with a sense of achievement and an intention to make a go of life by completing my National Service and embarking on an adventurous career. However my National Service extended for 41 years which were indeed adventurous,

obliged to be a part of, I found Sergeant Majors Moores and Jukes a welcome relief from the academic hierarchy. In addition to the CCF these retired NCOs ran the small and full bore shooting, and the pastime stood me in good stead for the years ahead in the Army.

Meanwhile, breaking bounds, and breaking rules of all sorts, became an ever-greater challenge. Yet my objective always was not merely to commit minor felonies, but to do so without being detected – not only to beat the system, but also to get away with it. These sorties (the Army would call them patrols) gave me a preparation for life that I shall remember with fondness and with a special respect for those who put up with my activities. They were designed to teach me field craft, planning and crisis management, to mention just a few of the skills. They demanded that nefarious activities be well planned and thought out in advance. They required in effect a military appreciation; little did I realise how much this was to assist me in my life ahead.

It would be idle to pretend that these extramural activities were an adequate substitute for the academic work on which I should have been concentrating. Yet they were useful training for my later career in the Army since they taught me a variety of skills and the ability to live and survive and plan on my own.

challenging and exciting and my respect and fondness for Harrow remains.

I hope it will continue to be a school where the development of character and personality is considered more important than squeezing out the ultimate in academic achievement.

General Sir Peter de la Billière KCB KBE DSO MC DL (The Grove 1947³) was Military Commissioner and Commander of the British Forces, Falkland Islands, from 1984–5, Commander of the British Forces, Middle East, from 1990–1 and Main Board Director of Robert Fleming 1992–1997.

ABOVE: *The assault course, 2004*

Honours List

The King has approved the award of the Victoria Cross to Captain Ian Oswald Liddell, (The Head Master's, 1932), Coldstream Guards (Chepstow).

In Germany, on 3 April 1945, Captain Liddell was commanding a company of the Coldstream Guards which was ordered to capture intact a bridge over the River Ems, near Lingen. The bridge was covered on the far bank by an enemy strong-point, which was subsequently discovered to consist of 150 entrenched infantry supported by three 88mm and two 20mm guns. The bridge was also prepared for demolition with 500lb. bombs, which could plainly be seen.

Having directed his two leading platoons on to the near bank, Captain Liddell ran forward alone to the bridge and scaled the 10ft high road block guarding it, with the intention of neutralizing the charges and taking the bridge intact. In order to achieve his object he had to cross the whole length of the bridge by himself under intense enemy fire, which increased as his object became apparent to the Germans. Having disconnected the charges on the far side, he recrossed the bridge and cut the wires on the near side. It was necessary for him to kneel, forming an easy target, while he successively cut the wires. He then discovered that there were also charges underneath the bridge, and, completely undeterred, he also disconnected these. His task completed, he then climbed up on to the road block in full view of the enemy and signalled his leading platoon to advance.

Thus, alone and unprotected, without cover and under heavy enemy fire, he achieved his object. The bridge was captured intact and the way cleared to the advance across the River Ems. His outstanding gallantry and superb example of courage will never be forgotten by those who saw it.

This very brave officer has since died of wounds subsequently received in action.

Maurice Percival

RICHARD SHIRLEY SMITH

RECENTLY, I AWOKE STARTLED AND MOVED FROM a dream where, totally out of context in a foreign market street, Maurice was before me, smiling warmly just as I and my school friends would have remembered him fifty years ago: rosy face, white hair, grey flannel suit, his empty left sleeve tucked into his jacket pocket. He lived then at Northwick Lodge, a lodging house for Harrow Masters, among whom also lived David Jones, an erudite, celebrated painter and poet. 'I never left the dinner table,' said Maurice, 'without having learned something wonderful.'

Maurice had given up the Bank of England to study at the Royal College of Art. 'They are still discovering my mistakes to this day,' he would say. He never married but he was greatly loved in many places by many people, who were dismayed each time he moved on to another civilised school where his teaching would also be understood: Eton, Downside and, years later, Marlborough, where I ran the Art School in 1969 and where he came to work with me. At the time, I was selecting a technical assistant for the Art School and the otherwise ideal candidate was upsetting everyone by anxiously talking too much. Maurice drew the man gently aside: 'My dear chap, you're simply talking yourself out of a job' – all was solved.

Maurice absolutely lived Christianity. Like David Jones, he was a Catholic convert. He regarded the pre-Reformation Church as the mainspring of European culture. He hated self-aggrandisement, novelty for its own sake or anything frantic. He loved the exquisite technique and purity of feeling of the Italian and Flemish Primitive painters. As the Renaissance progressed, man had become more glorified. 'How would you feel if you met one of Michelangelo's muscle men on the High Street? You'd run in horror.' He described van Gogh as 'Hell with the lid off'. Maurice was full of fun but he constantly surprised us with his consideration for the underdog, his

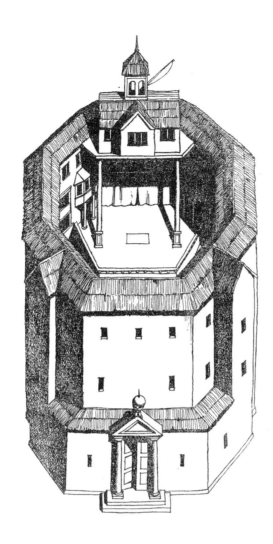

RIGHT:
Illustration for
Ronnie Watkins's
Moonlight at
the Globe

generosity and his humility. I remember complaining to him that I thought I would be passed over as a School Monitor. 'I can't think of anything that should make you happier,' he replied. The Rule of St Benedict, he said, provided that if a monk got too puffed up with his painting skills, it was time for a stint with the bees or the pigs. As a pompous schoolboy I remember saying to him that, as the word *education* came from the Latin *educare* meaning to lead out, his teaching might seem more like an intrusion. He sweetly replied, 'If you put nothing in, you get nothing out.'

The Art School under Maurice Percival was clean and inviting; materials were all prepared and the place was decorated with sculpture, books, flowers and a collection of small contemporary drawings and paintings of quality. Everything had a place and a purpose and encouraged work. Maurice described a wise abbot who, when approached by a distressed novice, would say, 'I am very busy just now, but sort out and tidy your desk and room, and then come and talk later.' They never came back.

At the Slade I learned to paint from close observation, but at Harrow Maurice had enabled us to paint what was *not* before us. He had worked out elaborate exercises to observe light from different angles falling upon cones, spheres and cubes, showing how 'the deeds of light' explain form and space. This skill has been invaluable to me in illustration and mural decoration. As pupils we never said we could not think what to paint as this would have been the perfect cue for one of the exercises. John Ryan, the inventor of Captain Pugwash, used to assist Maurice at Harrow, and regarded the exercises as rather eccentric; but changed his mind later when he found that no art school graduates had any idea of the fall of light and were therefore no use to him as assistants. He also remembered an occasion when a hideous old clock was being painted sky blue for a stage prop and he observed that two trickles of paint down the back would not be seen. 'But God will see them,' Maurice replied.

After his years of teaching at Harrow, Maurice went to study in Rome and I have on my wall a vignette which he made there and later developed with ink and crayon, as he often did. It shows something he saw in St Peter's, when a dark cowled figure produced a great key and entered a door in the front of an elaborate pedestal

These pictures were finalists in the Fox Talbot Digital Image Prize. This is the fourth year of the competition established in memory of Henry Fox Talbot who was accepted for Harrow in 1811 and who has as good a claim as any to be the inventor of photography. A junior and a senior prize are awarded each year from over 250 entries on an 'open' theme. The competition which was endowed by Dr Richard Petty is designed to promote the use of digital photography and is judged by The Earl of Lichfield (Elmfield 1952[3]).

Top: 'Harrow Nations' by Nikhil Datta
Right: 'Old Schools Tripping' by Nikhil Datta
Below: 'Old Schools' by Charlie Wemyss-Dunn

surmounted by a monumental sculpture of a Pope, such as Bernini's Urban VIII. Maurice thought this might be some rare memorial rite – but the figure soon reappeared clutching a mop and bucket. Maurice much enjoyed the waywardness of animate and inanimate things, such as a discarded bunch of fluff from his hairbrush, which wafted down the side of a long bungalow, through the kitchen window and awaited him between his bacon and eggs. While making a long row of dibber holes, each with its cabbage seedling, he noticed he was being followed by a duck, which, having removed each seedling, peered sideways down every hole in search of worms.

Maurice was a true artist. His calligraphy was superb. He designed sets and costumes for many school plays, most particularly for Ronald Watkins's Shakespeare's Globe productions; and then he illustrated them. He greatly influenced my outlook and my work. As John Ryan put it, 'He was, I am certain, one of the finest art teachers of our time. All who knew Maurice will remember him for the strength and goodness of his personality. It positively shone from his features. He was closer to saintliness than anyone I have ever known.'

Maurice Percival was Art Master, 1945–1954

Richard Shirley Smith (The Knoll 1949[2]) is a professional artist who has held numerous exhibitions of paintings, wood engravings and studies for his mural decorations.

ABOVE: *Bookplate by Richard Shirley Smith*

Of kaleidoscopes and kings

PETER GOVETT

this Sunday in **THE OBSERVER**

will Labour kill the Public Schools?

ABOVE: Observer *poster, 1964. The Harrovians are Anthony Lawrie, Andrew Nicholson, Dick Pelham and Richard Prideaux-Brune*

WHEN ASKED FOR MY MEMORIES OF HARROW, I knew they could only be scattered, fragmentary and diverse. They come to me sometimes bidden, sometimes quite unbidden in the early hours of a wakeful night. Let me shake the kaleidoscope of those years, starting in the summer term of 1949 and recall some of the pictures I see.

I see first of all the names of my father, uncle, grandfather and cousin on the Elmfield nameboards, something which must have given generations of Harrovians (a greater number, I believe, than at any other school) a wonderful sense of belonging to another family. I see my first House Songs and the initiation of having to sing a verse of 'Men of Harlech', a song which I had thankfully sung before at my prep school, but whose appropriateness to Harrow still puzzles me, although it is clearly an advantage in life to know what 'gleaming falchions' are.

Then I recall my introduction to the fagging system and my joyful realisation that most of the time I was big and strong enough not to come last. My fagging career peaked when I became the private fag of a future very eminent investment banker. After a term of faithful service, I received a beautiful presentation box with a speech of gratitude which led me to believe that a serious gift was inside. Sadly, it turned out to contain half a pound of a very down-market type of sweets.

Two other memories of those early terms come to my mind. The discovery on my first day that there were no closed doors on the lavatories came as a strange shock. Little did I know then that this would be of inestimable advantage to me later during my National Service when in the Jordan desert I sat in solitary splendour in the open latrines with the Colonel, an old desert soldier, while my brother officers lay in their tents suffering stomach cramps and agonies of embarrassment. Oh, the far-flung benefits of a Harrow education! Many years later, Patrick Lichfield, an Elmfield contemporary, related that he had mentioned the doorless loos to a photographic model. "Goodness," she said, "how on earth did you get in?"!

Sporting memories start with one of the most extraordinary games of rugger in which I played at Harrow. It was the occasion of the first new-boys' trial game. Taking part for his first game ever was Roddy Bloomfield, one of Harrow's greatest all-round games players. He was told that the object of the game was to get the ball over the opponent's line. Easily grasping this simple concept, the great man, upon receiving the ball, set off on an extraordinary run backwards, forwards, sideways, up and down the field, totally ignoring calls of "pass it" and, some six or seven minutes later, having eluded or exhausted all his pursuers, he triumphantly scored his first try at Harrow.

The kaleidoscope turns again and I see my first Eton and Harrow match at Lord's. Remarkably, these matches brought the third biggest attendance at Lord's after the Test Match and the Gentlemen v Players. Teatime, and everyone walking onto the ground in morning dress, with the women in dresses that were only surpassed by Royal Ascot. The thrill of going with one's first girl friend and desperately hoping one's friends would think her attractive … being invited to have a drink on one of the coaches drawn up by the Pavilion and looking down on everyone else.

My first winter terms brought something unknown to present-day Harrovians – the pea-souper fogs which often shrouded the Hill. After finally reaching the House in the murky evening light came the ritual of lighting the fires. I am certain that to this day Harrovians who had open coal fires in their rooms (thereby contributing

splendidly to the fog) can remember the warm happiness of sitting in front of their fires after lights out and dreaming, just dreaming. Those of us who lit the fires also became experts in later life in coaxing fire from three sticks of wood and damp coal, using that blessed piece of metal, the drawer.

When my thoughts return to winter, I remember also the extraordinary ritual of trying to get the mud of those sodden playing fields off with a severely rationed amount of hot water. The result was a communal tosh, appropriately called the Snipe Bog, in which up to ten boys sat in water of a blackness I have never again seen equalled, periodically trying to find at its bottom the solitary bar of soap with which we had to wash.

Some afternoons, of course, brought another pleasure – tea in one of the Hill's restaurants, such as the Hill itself or Ann's Pantry. In these I discovered (and have never lost) the glory of the fry-up. These teas bring back another extraordinary memory. The stepfather of one of my contemporaries (who sadly died quite young) was the Chairman of the then very prestigious Daimler Car company. He was married to one of the most extrovert women of the period, who persuaded him that he would sell more cars if she could drive around in one covered in gold stars with gilt radiator and bumpers. This car would drive slowly down the High Street to take her son to tea, while the chauffeur was then given the necessary funds to take his friends to another restaurant.

What of academic memories? Naturally human nature being what it is, one remembers one's achievements, although to a schoolboy then they could never be as satisfying as sporting success. I see myself competing with

BELOW: 'Harrow Figures' by Michael Levien

OLD ACQUAINTANCES

BLOOD

TYRANT TUTOR

RIGHT: *Sketch of
Head of House's
room in The Park
by Walter Keesey,
1914*

some confidence for the Bourchier Reading Prize, only to be rejected by an eminent and splendidly imposing Shakespearian actor, Godfrey Tearle. 'I refuse,' said Tearle, 'I absolutely refuse to give a reading prize to a boy who pronounces the word "fire"' (he spelled it out) 'as fah. It is not. It is fi-ah,' (an emphatic two syllables). 'But worse. This boy then read the word iron not as eye-ron, (which it should be) but ahn. This cannot be allowed.' I retired hurt from Speech Room and to this day am, I believe, the only man in England who pronounces eye-ron in this curious manner.

The next year I was not so confident but, inexplicably, one of my competitors pronounced Mary Magdalene as Mary Maudlin. I remember giving a quietly sympathetic laugh to draw further attention to the error – I have probably never been forgiven.

What of Harrovians of my time? I was lucky enough to have been at Harrow with both King Faisal of Iraq and King Hussein of Jordan; I suspect a rare coincidence which led a few years later to one of the more spectacular social put-downs I have ever witnessed. The scene was the British Army base in Aqaba, Jordan. King

Hussein was talking to various officers and a fellow Harrovian said to him, 'I remember you, Sir, at Harrow,' whereat King Hussein said, rather dismissively, 'I don't remember you.' My colleague, quite unruffled said, 'Oh well, it must have been another King.' No wonder General Glubb was relieved of his command a very short time after.

Ultimately one has to leave school and the kaleidoscope turns, oddly, to a rather cloudy picture. National Service loomed immediately in those days for a school leaver and I am sure, as I threw three empty bottles of Chateau Margaux into the little orchard behind Elmfield (I had read that serving this wine was a guarantee of social success and I believe it was only 10/- a bottle then), that I was more concerned with the future than looking back. It is later that the memories return, sometimes extraordinarily strongly, and I am once again reminded how privileged I am to have been at Harrow in those years and how happy I was then.

Peter Govett (Elmfield 1949[2]) worked for many years for Shearson Lehman Inc., the American investment bankers.

THE HARROVIAN

26 February 1965

Fagging

A casual visitor to the Hill may well be startled from his dreams of Winston Churchill passing through the Bill Yard by raucous shouts of "Boy!" from any of the neighbouring houses. He may be amused to hear such a relic of the past, just as he may peer into the Fourth Form Room. We no longer use the Fourth Form Room. We should no longer have fagging in this otherwise excellent education-machine.

It may be claimed that fagging, like Bill, is a custom which is so old that it would be a pity to lose it. It is instructive to note that fagging was introduced in Harrow only one and a half centuries ago. This barbarous system has too long blemished the School, and has been at the root of many bitter attacks on the public schools; attacks made by men who have noted the latent abuses of the custom of house monitors – having personal fags, or 'specials'. It may be that only in very few cases is this privilege misused; but why does the system survive at all?

Those men who believe that for a thirteen-year-old to clean shoes and run errands is good for his character must surely be decreasing in number. Those who humbly devote themselves to the service of their elders are few; most, sensibly, avoid any more work than they must do to escape punishment.

Besides, we live in an age where schools, regrettably, are judged by their examination results at 'O' and 'A' levels.

Although the method of gathering statistics for the report on the public schools last year was accidentally biased against Harrow, even if allowance was made for this, we were still not near the top. Whether it is in fashion to judge schools by the number of Prime Ministers, blues, or academics produced, it is well for a good school to maintain its 'average' in all fields. Even though it may be argued that the majority of small boys in the School, if unoccupied, might get into mischief, there must be a few who would devote time to their work. This in turn might, in time, tip the balance in one or two of their borderline subjects at 'O' level. Not only would more 'O' levels help the School; they are an essential qualification for any job, to say nothing of getting to a University. It is not even as if the fag was indispensable: all bells could be rung, and any other necessary duties performed as a punishment for small crimes.

During the last few years there have been many changes in the fagging system; each change makes a new boy's term of servitude less irksome. This is good but why whittle away at an obstacle with a chisel when dynamite would destroy it altogether. Can it be that those in a position to do so are afraid to sweep fagging from the Hill lest, being considered 'ahead of their time' they are condemned by their fellows?

We are indebted for this article to an independent contributor whose views are not necessarily those of the Editors.

FAG

Elmfield matters

RODDY BLOOMFIELD

I T NEARLY ALL ENDED FOR ME BEFORE IT BEGAN, ON my first day at Harrow, in the winter term of 1949. As I dragged my trunk up Grove Hill from the tube station I was within a whisker of being run over by a car coming out of the Elmfield entrance. I caught a glimpse of a peak-capped driver who no doubt was a chauffeur dropping off one of the boys.

My general welcome on arrival in the House was less dramatic, just a mass of noise, instructions and general confusion – then finally, a friendly meeting with Keith Fisher, with whom I was to share a room. He was as dishevelled as I was.

However, the message came through loud and clear – I must remember that Elmfield was all-important in the scheme of things, more important than the School itself! An example I liked that reflected this referred back to the 1948 Olympics, which were held in London. The House Matron was in a small group of Harrovians who were privileged to be at Wembley watching Alastair McCorquodale in the final of the 100 metres. She wasn't

RIGHT: *Harrow, Roddy Bloomfield and Christopher Strang, beat Marlborough in the final of the Public Schools Rackets Championships, 1954*

LEFT: *Bloomfield and Strang with Fred Crosby, Rackets Professional, 1954*

cheering for England, or even for McCorquodale, but in a high-pitched shriek was repeatedly heard rooting for Elmfield.

The House Monitors were rather self-important and remote to the new boys – as they are – but in between the extremes were Tom Borthwick and Bruce Ropner, two massive three-yearers with an insatiable sense of fun. It was as if they were permanently on holiday. They seemed to make up their own rules and they ran the lower half of the House like benevolent dictators. It was a refreshing aspect of growing up in Elmfield.

I was a games player and was quickly at home in the competitive atmosphere. Indeed, I couldn't believe the emphasis on sport; the House library even doubled as the billiards room. But to be fair, my House Master, Ronnie Watkins, the Shakespearean scholar, did seriously try to redress the balance between work and play, and there

were, of course, a number of academic and very distinguished Beaks. Strangely, most of them also had Oxbridge blues for soccer – a game that wasn't played at Harrow in those days.

I don't remember having much time for work because my schedule demanded rackets matches and House games during weekdays, with School cricket and rugby at the weekends. With his vast gown flapping, Ronnie Watkins would shake his finger at me and repeatedly warn that 'time hath a wallet at its back'– I knew that inevitably this must be Shakespeare, and that Ronnie was telling me not to disregard my work. In my last year when I was desperate to ensure a place at Balliol College, Oxford, I had to burn the candle at both ends to do so.

The only real rugby injury that I sustained was in a School match against Stowe when I was savagely crash tackled when least expecting it. I had been brutally brought down by John Johannessen, a short-sighted member of my own team who had forgotten to wear his contact lenses.

Rackets professional Fred Crosby and his pro's shop are high on my list of treasured memories. Dick Bridgeman, the Harrow captain, introduced me to rackets, a game that I got to love, and Dick became a life-long friend. Fred was a sweet-natured man, and he knew how much we all liked the warmth of his cosy shop and how we could relax and chat freely in his company.

Christopher Strang was my doubles partner for five years. He was a stylist, very different from me, and we got along well together. We won the Public Schools Doubles Championship at Queen's Club in 1954. The final was a tense match, and our mothers, who were watching together, had to go to the bar for a drink after each game to settle their nerves. Fortunately, the match was over in six games and didn't go the full distance.

Christopher and I met again recently after a gap of 40 years (he lives in Houston, Texas) and I'm glad to say he hadn't changed.

Fred's son Roger succeeded him as rackets professional. Roger is my age and he learnt the game playing with Christopher Strang and me. Later, as the pro, he was brilliant at communicating with the boys, a caring and understanding man who gave the same warm welcome to my son Harry that Fred gave to me.

I suppose I must have played rackets almost every other day in the winter and spring terms during my five years at Harrow. After a game, more often than not, I would have a cup of tea in Fred's room and 'rest' in a narrow and most uncomfortable little chair that squeezed in on you as you sat on it. The chair was still there when I returned to the courts in 1986 – 36 years later. I removed it when Roger was marking a match,

RIGHT: *Alastair McCorquodale – nearest to camera – (4th in 10.4 secs) running in the 100 metres at Wembley Stadium in the Olympic Games, 1948*

and substituted a more comfortable one that I brought from London.

My most loyal supporter throughout my Harrow years was my dog, Barty, a collie who trained with me on Hampstead Heath. Barty was brought to the Harrow cricket grounds in the back of a car in the summer of 1953 to watch me play cricket against IZ. He wasn't taken to see any other part of the school. Surprisingly, Barty took to the game and the following February found his way back alone to the Sixth Form Ground, *and that was seven miles on foot*. Not knowing that cricket is a seasonal game, he decided to wait around for 'further play'. Barty was fed by the owner of the sweet shop at the end of West Street for the next three months and answered to the name of George.

I met up with Barty again early in the summer term when I went down to the cricket grounds for my first nets. He was dusty and noticeably lame, but on spotting me he limped over the road to regroup, and I took him home. I had searched in vain for Barty every day for a month at the Battersea Dogs Home. He wasn't brought to Lord's for the match against Eton the following month when we beat them.

In my last year, Dr James took over as Head Master. He was immediately accessible, and I found him perhaps easier to talk to than any other Master. The occasional dinner with him was civilised and cheerful. He had a reassuring manner and was most encouraging. I am sure many other Harrovians felt the same.

Harrow suited me, and it proved to be a splendid springboard for my career as a publisher with special emphasis on sports books.

After leaving Harrow in 1954, I didn't return more than a couple of times for many years. I think we had both seen enough of each other. However, in 1973 Dick Bridgeman asked me to play in a rackets match against the School and I accepted. Before the game, we went to lunch at Elmfield with the House Master, Michael Pailthorpe. Michael asked if I had a son I wished to enter for the House and if so, how old he was. I said I did have a son I wished to enter for the House and that he was eight hours old. Harry had been born earlier that day, so I booked him in.

Roddy Bloomfield (Elmfield 1949[3]) is a Consultant Editor at Hodder & Stoughton, Publishers.

LEFT: *Roger Crosby, Rackets Professional 1962–96, at The Queen's Club in 1994*

Recollections of the School Farm 1953–1954

DAVID BOAG

JUST BEFORE I WENT TO HARROW IN MAY 1950 MY father encouraged me to take part in activities that were not available at home. I heeded his advice, and being a farmer's boy, did not take part in the life of the Farm. However, after two years I decided that I would give it a try. From that moment, it became my chief interest outside the form room.

The Beak in charge was Sidney Patterson – known to all as Sid P – in whose Maths division I was for the first few weeks of my first term. Like most boys I was very fond of him, as he was always so mischievously cheerful and friendly. There were also two full-time farm workers, both of whom were dairymen. John Backhouse, who came to Harrow as a Beak in 1952, became Sid P's assistant in September the following year.

At this time the Farm, from a boy's perspective, worked as follows; every morning (except Sunday) a group of boys would go down to the Farm in the farm van at 6am, some to milk the cows, others to muck-out the cow shed, a third group to do the milk-round to the Houses (this was before central catering). When light enough, other jobs that needed doing could also be done. We had to be back in our Houses, clean and odourless in time for breakfast. Given there were eleven Houses and only six mornings, the system was that Houses with a lot of farmers provided the whole morning workforce and those with fewer followers shared a morning between them. Each House did the same morning each week. In the afternoons, games and the CCF permitting, any boy who wished to go down to the Farm could do so, and he would be given something useful to do. In addition to the Farm there was also a Farmers' Club which had its own small room on the first floor of The Hill with comfy chairs and farming magazines to read. Meetings were also held there with talks from outside speakers and boys. I recall giving a talk on caponising chickens.

The Farm was a dairy farm with a number of pigs, which were fattened and sold for pork or bacon. The cattle were grazed on the football fields during the summer term, but some areas were left to grow and were used to make hay for winter fodder for the cattle. Boys were involved in the hay-making process which involved cutting the grass, turning it, carting it to a large stationary baler when dry enough to be baled. This baler produced large bales, which, as they were tied up with wire, were tightly compressed. This made them very heavy. The bales were then stored under cover. The most sought after role was that of driving the little grey 'Fergie' tractor.

The dairy herd numbered some 30 milking cows which were mostly Friesians and Ayrshires, plus some heifers which would join the herd when old enough. There was a modern milking parlour which had (I think) six bays. The job of those boys who did the morning milking was to get the cow into its stall, clean its udder, connect it to the milking machine, strip it (get all of its milk out of its udder), record the amount of milk given by each cow, and to release the cow so it could return to its stall in the cowshed. The stripping was a skilled job and was usually completed by the duty dairyman: though some boys became pretty adept at it.

RIGHT: *One of the Long Horn herd, 2004*

Whilst the cows were being milked their spaces in the cowshed were being mucked out and hosed down by those boys who were on cowshed duty, the muck being taken to the muck-heap. Those who did the milk round loaded up the van with churns of milk from the previous afternoon's milking session and took them to the Houses, bringing back the empty churns. I never did the milk round as I didn't consider it to be proper farming!

Sometimes, especially in the summer, boys mucked-out the pigs. It was at about this time that a new pig-house was given to the Farm in memory of Captain Grant A. Stringer, 10th Hussars, who was killed at El Alamein in 1942.

Sid P was at the Farm every morning, and at the end of my first appearance, when I mucked out the cowshed, he came up to me and said I had impressed him with my hard work and knowledge. He said that he hoped I would be a regular attendee; I assured him I would. I loved it, just as I did working on the farm at home. I was very pleased when he told me in July 1953 that he wanted me to succeed Alan Taylor-Restell as Head of the Farm. Naturally I agreed.

My taking up this position coincided with Dr James's arrival as Head Master. He took a very great interest in the Farm and in the summer of 1954 Sid P laid on a 'black tie' Farm Dinner in the club room for the head farmer from each House which was attended by Dr and Mrs James, Sid P and John Backhouse. It was a most convivial affair and it was hard to realise that the Jameses were who they were as they treated all us boys as equals.

FAR LEFT: *Wartime on the Farm: 'digging for victory'*

LEFT: *Farm Group 1954, left to right back row: J.W. Whitworth, F.G. Barker, C.G. Briscoe, D.H. Golby, D.A. Bower, J.P.C. Badcock, H.R. Bebb, A.C.L. Sturge; front row: P.D.H. Nichols, C.D. Parkinson, S.G. Patterson Esq, D.H. Boag, J.K. Backhouse Esq, J.R.W. Christie-Brown, R.A. Cumming*

ABOVE: *The School Farm, 2004*

That summer I was asked by Sid P to come to his house for tea, so that I could meet John Profumo, who was a Junior Minister in the Government. He had been appointed a Governor in 1952 and had come to see the Farm. There were just the three of us and this, too, was another interesting and enjoyable occasion.

The Farm also gave me the most frightening incident in my life. It arose one sunny summer afternoon. I had been detailed to take several boys and burn all the waste straw so that the place would be clean and tidy when a fresh lot would be delivered in the summer holidays. We had just started a couple of small fires when the wind suddenly got up and blew bits of burning straw across the yard towards the boundary hedge between the Farm and the houses in Sheepcote Road. This set alight the straw next to the hedge, which, though green, also started to burn. I sent a boy off to the Farm phone to summons the Fire Brigade, which arrived with commendable promptness.

The fire was soon put out, and no major damage was done. The scorched hedge survived and thereafter rebuked me every time I looked at it.

One sad occasion during my time at the Farm was the early death of one of the two farm workers, both of whom were well liked by the boys. Sid P took some of us to his funeral, which took place off the Hill. It was the first funeral I had ever been to.

The dairy was regularly inspected by the authorities for cleanliness, and the milk was tested for its water content (it had to be below the maximum percentage allowed), its butter fat content and for bacteria and other impurities. There was never any problem on any of these matters. We produced the best milk in Middlesex in one of these years and Sid P was always disappointed if we were not one of the first three farms.

David Boag (Newlands 1950[2]) was a Director of several subsidiary companies of the Sedgwick Group plc.

An American at Harrow

PAUL HICKS

INSIDE HARROW'S SIXTH FORM CLUB, WHICH WAS A gift to the School from Old Harrovians in America, there is a quotation from Winston Churchill inscribed in stone that reads: 'It is no exaggeration to say that the future of the whole world and the hopes of a broadening civilization ... depend on the relationship between the British Commonwealth of Nations and the U.S.A.' For many Americans, the continuing admiration for Churchill is a vital part of the special relationship that still exists between the United States and Britain.

Churchill's visit to Harrow in November of 1954 was one of the high points of the year I spent on the Hill as an English Speaking Union exchange student. After listening in Speech Room to the traditional programme of school songs, which he elsewhere described as 'a great treasure and possession of Harrow School,' Churchill spoke briefly about World War II. Inspired by the last lines of *The Silver Arrow*, he recalled the dark days of 1940, when, as he said, 'men proved that they were worthy seed of their Sires who drew the bow.' In closing he added: 'As I ventured to say at the time, this was their finest hour.'

That was an especially memorable moment for an eighteen-year-old Yank, capturing in a few sentences Churchill's sense of history and his strong ties to the school. Yet it is just one of the many vivid memories of Harrow experiences that filled my journal some 50 years ago. Among those entries is an account of a talk given to the '27 Club by Hugh Gaitskell, who shortly thereafter became head of the Labour Party. His intellect and skill as a speaker on that occasion indicated why some in Britain later claimed that he was the best Prime Minister they never had. To further my political education, I went with my very kind House Master, Kenneth Snell, to attend a session of the House of Commons. We were admitted to the Special Gallery as guests of an Old Harrovian cabinet minister, John

"Under this school exchange scheme we'll probably see some peculiar American clothes this term!"...

Profumo, who was not then as well known as he would later become.

Harrow's proximity to London proved to be one of its prime advantages for me as an exchange student. What could be more educational than attending the ceremonial Opening of Parliament by a young Queen Elizabeth, seeing a performance of *Hedda Gabler* starring Peggy Ashcroft, or joining 75,000 people at Wembley Stadium to hear Billy Graham preach? I also benefited from the cosmopolitan atmosphere at Harrow. Not only had a number of Americans been there before me, but its students came from all over the world, including such notable international figures as Pandit Nehru, King Hussein and King Faisal.

Although the Duke of Wellington may have claimed that the battle of Waterloo was won on the playing fields of Eton, the pitches at Harrow were equally good for building youthful character. This was especially true during Harrow football matches in the cold and mud, spurred on by cries of 'follow-up' and the tramp of the twenty-

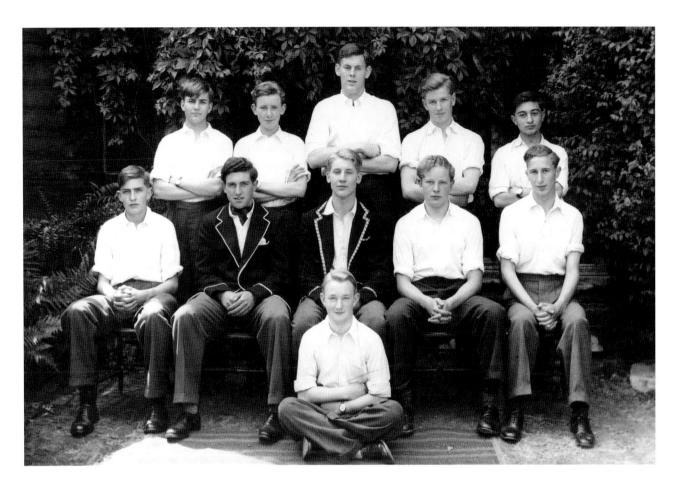

RIGHT: *Paul Hicks, centre back row, in the Druries House Cricket XI, 1955*

two men. For an American spectator, not even a World Series game at Yankee Stadium could match the excitement of the crowd at Twickenham watching Oxford's rugby team lose to a Cambridge team captained, as I later discovered, by Ian Beer, a future Harrow Head Master. At Lord's the following July, the fashion parade in beautiful weather was certainly more satisfying than the outcome of the match. Nothing, however, could top the enjoyment I had in playing tennis on grass at Wimbledon and representing Harrow in a public school tournament.

The cultural life of the school was equally rich and varied. John Betjeman, a future Poet Laureate, came to read from his latest book of poems, including one entitled *Harrow-on-the-Hill*. As an ardent fan of Victorian architecture, he also helped us look at the Vaughan Library and the School Chapel in a new light. When invited to participate in a 'balloon' debate, I narrowly managed to convince the audience that Christopher Columbus should be rewarded more for discovering the new world than William Webb Ellis should be for inventing the game of

rugby. During three nights in June, performing in *As You Like It* under the direction of the inimitable Ronnie Watkins was a singular pleasure, even though I was cast as William, the country bumpkin.

No doubt my bucolic acting role helped to get me in the mood for some early morning visits to the School Farm, where I communed with the cows, pigs and budding Harrow farmers. As a member of the school XII, I even learned to extol the virtues of early rising when we sang in the chorus of *Awake*: 'So wake, Boys, awake! The joys of the morning take! They sleep in the city, and more's the pity, but you on the hills, awake!' In contrast to such countrified life were visits to the Harrow Boys' Clubs in London where my knowledge of basketball seemed to be a useful asset.

Sunday mornings were usually more relaxed, providing opportunities to enjoy the civilized institution of 'finds' breakfasts with friends at Druries and other Houses. It was among the numerous benefits of being a senior student at a school filled with customs where rank had its privileges that were generally tempered by a spirit of *noblesse oblige*. Most of the Harrow traditions I readily assimilated, but the system of fagging and the occasional canings did run against my American grain. Sometimes it seemed as if I were living in the world of Mr Chips or even in the days of Tom Brown.

Considering all the sporting and other extra-curricular activity, it is a wonder that there was ever enough time left for academics. The Sixth Form courses, especially those taught by Messrs Ellis, Lillingston and Harris, were as stimulating and demanding as many I later had at the university level. A term report on my English History performance said I had held my own and could be forgiven for not knowing that Henry I died of a surfeit of lampreys. My French teacher wrote: 'His accent is ragged in a trans-Atlantic way, but he shows real appreciation of things French,' a judgment that still holds true, even on the second count, despite continuing friction on the Franco-American diplomatic front.

My education continued in high gear during travels over the long holidays, when, to mix Evelyn Waugh with Mark Twain, the going was good for an innocent abroad. Best of all were the weeks spent in the summer touring historic and scenic Britain from Land's End to the Scottish Highlands while enjoying the hospitality of generous Harrovians and their families along the way. Then, with my journal full of adventures, I sailed back across the pond to rediscover the new world, eager to sport my OH tie whenever the opportunity might arise.

Fifty years later, it is gratifying to see that the bonds between Harrow and those of us in America are stronger than ever. Ian Beer's first visit in 1984 drew 85 people from as far away as Toronto and Memphis, Tennessee, to a dinner in New York City. That trip was followed by Nick Bomford's equally successful visit in 1994, as the Harrow community in America continued to grow. By the time Barnaby Lenon arrived in 2001, there were nearly 250 names on the USA Register of Old Harrovians, including Sir Jeremy Greenstock, who was then Britain's Ambassador to the United Nations.

Much of the credit for Harrow's strong base in America is due to the Harrow School Foundation, which Geoffrey Simmonds and I, along with a number of others, developed as a valuable resource for the School. The Foundation not only raised more than $100,000 for the benefit of Harrow over a 25-year period but also funded an American artist-in-residence program as well as construction of the Sixth Form Club. Moreover, it helped to widen Harrow's horizons through opportunities for Masters to teach at American boarding schools and for 22 graduates of those schools to spend a year studying on the Hill.

Fortunately, there have been opportunities for reunions with Harrow friends over the years on both sides of the Atlantic. Certainly the most memorable occasion was a Harrow Association dinner at Mansion House, hosted by the then Lord Mayor, Christopher Collett. On that occasion, I gladly heeded the calls of 'once again your glasses drain', and joined in patriotic chorus with a number of contemporaries, including Robin Butler, John Harvey, Dale Vargas, and Roger Ward. Even though we were all nearing forty years on by then, I can safely say that while some may have been a bit shorter in wind, as in memory long, no one appeared to be growing older and older. But that, I realize, is what it can seem when you look back and forgetfully wonder.

Paul Hicks (Druries 1954³) was an English Speaking Union Scholar. He is a retired managing director of J.P. Morgan.

Mac

For those of us who loved her, Miss McLennan was always 'Mac'. I think of her with undimmed and devoted appreciation. 'When you look back and forgetfully wonder'. Well, my memory of Mac is as clear today as on the day I left Harrow and when I think back, my affection for all the things she meant to me remains undimmed. She was Matron of Rendalls in the early 1950s. Her sitting room, which was where we all gathered, was set apart from the rather cavernous kitchen on the basement floor. French windows led out onto the garden, which was always tidy but horticulturally undistinguished.

She had a Dachshund – a sausage dog – which she adored and which followed her everywhere. On cold winter evenings it was always possible to go down the stairs to Mac's room where her anthracite coal fire would be well ablaze. You could be sure of a warm welcome from Mac, delivered with a throaty chuckle – that husky, pleasant sound that only very serious smokers acquire. She smoked or rather chain-smoked, the fag dangling from her lips, its ash hanging precariously from the end. There was always a box of biscuits and one was allowed as many as one wished to consume; hot cocoa or tea, a chair close to the fire and always the liveliest friendliest talk, with never ever the feeling that Mac might want you to leave. Here was a place of sanctuary, where one was allowed to lick one's wounds, be they slight or deep, a lighthearted and carefree atmosphere so unlike, as I recall, the one prevailing elsewhere in the School.

She also had a very effective vocal delivery from the touch line at rugby and Harrow football matches, not many of which she missed, undaunted by the bleakest of weather. Fag still dangling, though the wind howled, she would yell encouragement and exhortations to 'tackle low' or 'tackle hard' or 'put him down' or 'push hard Rendalls' in a voice any sergeant major would have been proud to possess. It was thanks mainly to her also that I survived those seemingly endless

Above: Rendalls House Group, 1953

Left: G.R. McConnell Esq, 'Mac' and Edward Fox, in the 1951 House Group

bronchial conditions which were the bane of every single winter term. She never fussed, was always attentive and gave sensible, knowledgeable advice, stressing the importance of letting nature's powers of recovery work in their own time.

Mac was a wonderful and tremendously kind person. I owe her so much gratitude for so many glad and joyful hours during my years at Harrow. I think of her always with my most devoted love.

EDWARD FOX

Edward Fox (Rendalls 1950[3]) is an actor on stage, screen and television

Then and now: leavers

Lord Lichfield (*Elmfield 1952*[3]) started his professional career as a social photographer by producing 'leavers' for his Harrovian friends in the 1950s, in competition with Hills & Saunders. In 1993, he conceived the idea of photographing them again in similar pose and dress to the originals. Some examples of the originals juxtaposed with images 'forty years on' are reproduced here.

 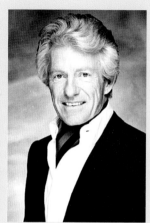

The Hon Patrick Anson   The Earl of Lichfield DL

The Hon Brian Alexander   The Hon Brian Alexander CMG   Kenneth Carlisle   Sir Kenneth Carlisle

Julian Cotterell   Mr Julian Cotterell   Rupert Deen   Mr Rupert Deen

Charles Guthrie Lord Guthrie of Craigiebank GCB LVO OBE Ian McCorquodale Mr Ian McCorquodale

Simon Orr-Ewing The Hon Sir Simon Orr-Ewing Bt FRICS Robin Pleydell-Bouverie Mr Robin Pleydell-Bouverie

Michael Sayers Mr Michael Sayers QC Richard Spence Mr Richard Spence

LEFT: Chapel chancel and nave from the vault

A city that is set upon a hill

JONATHAN STEDALL

MEMORIES ARE A PUZZLE. DOES WHAT WE HAVE forgotten perhaps affect us more deeply than what we remember? Why do the memories that I have of my childhood and youth and of my time at Harrow become more vivid as the years go by? One day, maybe at death, will I remember everything? And why does our experience of time accelerate as we get older? Those four years I spent on the Hill seem like a huge chunk of my life, yet were only a small fraction of the 65 years I have so far clocked up.

My recollections of Harrow are a jumble of incidents that rattle round in my head – moments from another life when I soaked up knowledge like a sponge, played games because we had to, was often hungry and sometimes cold. I remember on winter afternoons being covered in mud, and on summer evenings marvelling at the beauty of the place. I loved the Farm and Songs and Ducker. I acted in plays. I was appalled at the rituals of corporal punishment. But my most traumatic memories centre round those agonizing transitions from home to school at the start of each term. I suppose it taught us to be adaptable, to be flexible. The whole routine of boarding school was, I gather, intended to toughen us up. I wonder at what cost? The fact that one's teachers, however good, and one's companions were all male remains in my mind a strange and somewhat artificial state of affairs.

It is not surprising, therefore, that for those of us who did feel somewhat vulnerable a place like the Chapel was a welcome sanctuary. Despite this I remember in a Divinity lesson challenging the chaplain, Philip Bryant, about why religion was being stuffed down our throats so relentlessly. In those days we had to attend Chapel every day, and twice on Sundays. His reply was that one day we might be grateful. He was, of course, absolutely right. And even if, as in my case, I now seldom go to church he was still right. We were truly nourished and we continue, I believe, to benefit from that nourishment –

RIGHT: *Chapel choir, 2004*

even if it is only to be aware, however dimly, that in our increasingly frenetic and materialistic world there is more than meets the eye.

The one memory and its resonance over the years that I consider worth trying to share in a little more detail took place in that Chapel. A visiting churchman whose name I have long forgotten preached a sermon, the text of which I have pondered over ever since. It was, I suppose, an early awakener – a foretaste of what was going to be an important theme in my life ahead. 'A city that is set upon a hill cannot be hid' – these were the words he quoted. And he continued: 'Therefore so let your light shine before men that they may see your glorious works and praise your Father which is in Heaven'.

So what is there to share? In a sense the words speak for themselves. The preacher was, of course, talking about privilege and about talent, and the responsibility that those of us who are privileged – whether financially,

LEFT: *Jonathan Stedall with Sir John Betjeman, Trebetherick, 1982*

intellectually or artistically – have towards our Maker; or towards what that great admirer of Harrow School, John Betjeman (with whom I had the pleasure of making many films) liked to call The Management.

I was always aware as we went up the school at Harrow, qualifying for more and more privileges as we got older, that with those privileges came responsibility. It was, it seems to me, a good system. Likewise, in my adult life I have realized increasingly that the advantages with which I have been blessed are only really meaningful and of value to the extent to which I have been able to put those gifts at the service of others. Of course, our very basic and understandable instinct is to feather our

own nests. But how many feathers do we actually need to be secure and comfortable? Most of us who have paraded 'through the windy yard at Bill' are among the very privileged in this world. That in itself is not a crime. What matters, I believe, is how we handle those privileges.

We who now stand upon our respective hills are, whether we like it or not, visible – just as we were as boys when we tramped up and down Harrow Hill in those absurd hats. We are visible and we have influence and power. How we use that power is the great challenge.

Jonathan Stedall (Moretons 1951[3]) was a documentary film-maker with BBC Television for 27 years. He is now a freelance producer.

The greatest Old Harrovian

CHARLES GUTHRIE

WHEN I ARRIVED AS A NEW BOY AT HARROW in the autumn term of 1952, World War II had been over for only seven years. The War had dominated British life in a way no other event ever had, or ever seemed likely to, to all those who lived through it. There was nobody at Harrow, whether they were members of the Staff, their families or the boys, whose lives had not been touched by it. I myself was born just before the outbreak of War in 1938 and do not remember my father until he returned after Germany's surrender and there were boys in the School whose

fathers and brothers had been killed in action and never were to return.

We all knew at Harrow that one man, above all, Winston Churchill, had led the nation through what seemed the darkest, most difficult, dangerous and frightening times in our history and we were intensely proud that he was a Harrovian, a product of our School, and the greatest living Englishman.

One of the highlights of the Harrow year, if not the highlight, were Churchill Songs. In the 1950s when I was at Harrow, Winston Churchill was, once again, Prime

RIGHT: *Winston Churchill at Harrow, 1958*

OVERLEAF: *'A Distant View of Venice' by Winston Churchill, 1929, from the Old Speech Room Gallery*

Minister and he still made time to come down to hear the School sing and to sing himself. His entrance to Speech Room was greeted with a roar and the applause continued long after he had taken his place on the stage between Mrs Churchill and Dr James, The Head Master. Also seated on this stage were other distinguished Old Harrovians, including present and past Cabinet Ministers, Members of Parliament and senior officers of the Services. I particularly remember Field Marshal Lord Alexander, the victorious Commander in Chief in North Africa and Italy, who had liberated Rome.

Winston Churchill sang enthusiastically and was clearly moved by the occasion, dabbing his eyes from time to time with a large handkerchief. Towards the end of the programme and before we sang *Forty Years On* and the National Anthem, he would say a few words. I cannot remember, 45 years after the event, exactly what was said, but he never let us down and our expectations were fulfilled. But I do remember how he looked and, although he was in his eighties, and had suffered a stroke, he stood before us dressed in a black coat and striped trousers, as we had all imagined him. Indomitable and uncompromising, and we knew that any person or country who was unwise enough to try to damage our nation, would have to face the consequences if he were our leader.

What made him the man he was? He came from one of the greatest families in the land; his father was a famous politician, his mother American. He had great family advantages and great family disadvantages. But from an early time he became aware of what was possible and what was not. His education was patchy but, despite what some people said, he showed great ability when he was interested. At least two Harrow Masters inspired him. He loved History and English and when in the lowest form of the School, the Fourth Form, he won a prize which was open to the whole School by reciting faultlessly 1,200 lines of Macaulay's *Lays of Ancient Rome*, a feat well beyond any of the members of the Fourth Form when I was in it. He must have been a maddening boy to teach; exceptional when interested, infuriating when not.

He became an Army Officer and would have understood today's problems in Afghanistan and Iraq as he took part in a campaign against the very tribes who are fighting today. He charged with the Cavalry in the battle of Omdurman in The Sudan and went to the trenches in the First World War.

I like to think he learned much as a soldier: how to lead, how to motivate and, sometimes, to get people to do things they would prefer not to do when they were unsure and frightened.

He had a consuming passion for politics and great ambition. He had wide experience as a Cabinet minister wrestling with the great problems of the day. He had experience as a back-bencher and also of the wilderness when he was out of office. Even at the low points of his career his life was full — studying and working as a journalist and historian. He had a marvellous talent for narrative history and understood our heritage and where we belonged. He also knew that although history rarely repeats itself certain lessons could be learned and applied from the past.

It is as though much of his life, before he became our Prime Minister in 1940, was designed to prepare him for this high office and his time as our great War Leader. Harrow played its part in this preparation.

Like many great men, people felt very strongly about him. He was not universally admired. He was not easy, not always loyal, not always kind and, with some, unpopular. But he was also warm, interested, understanding and was often very kind and considerate. The country admired him and united behind him. He was very human with great strengths and some frailties.

What can be beyond doubt is that he was the man for the moment. He inspired the nation: he never faltered when many around him would have faltered and he gave leadership when the nation was desperate for leadership. He gave us hope.

As an Harrovian I believe we should view him as our greatest Old Harrovian and be proud that he was educated on the Hill. I will never forget and know how proud I am that he came to Harrow when I was a boy and that I spoke to him.

General Lord Guthrie of Craigiebank GCB LVO OBE *(Newlands 1952³) was Chief of General Staff from 1994–97, Chief of Defence Staff from 1997–2001*

A sporting education

JULIAN WILSON

IN THE SUMMER OF 1957 IT WAS TIME TO SIT MY A levels. I had specialized in French and German – sound advice from my father – and with the benefit of my trip to Nancy sailed through my French. I failed my German exam, which was a mixed blessing: with a further year to spend in the School, but with no wish to go to university, I did not have to move on to scholarship level in the coming year. Instead I could gently go over the A-level syllabus again. A year of free-wheeling – what bliss! I had already decided my destiny in my early years at Harrow. I harboured the idea of becoming a schoolmaster, for which the motivation was simple: I adored school life – never wanted to leave – and envisaged becoming a sports master so as to be able to continue to play games every day. I had not got as far as working out academic responsibilities; this was simply a free passage to a Peter Pan lifestyle. What could be better?

Mercifully, by the age of 16 I had grown out of this fantasy and was determined that my career would be in the world of horse-racing. My father and grandfather had been journalists, so what could be more obvious? I would be a racing journalist. I think that it was widely accepted that my future lay in this direction. In my last year, studying some mandatory 'optional extra', I was rewarded with an end-of-term report from the benign master in charge, Roger Ellis, which read as follows: 'Wilson has sat quietly at the back of the form throughout the term, evidently pursuing his own agenda. I can only hope that his deliberations have been of profit!'

With a true spirit of adventure my mother allowed me to use her credit betting account with a firm called 'Derridge' and sent on any winnings through the post. Conveniently there was an old-fashioned, red telephone box outside West Acre, and one Master described me to another as 'that boy who is always hanging about outside the telephone box'.

There were several contemporaries with racing connections. As well as Peter Ohlson, there was Peter Robertson, whose father had horses trained by the late Ryan Jarvis, and Sandy Taylor, whose father was Chairman of Newcastle Racecourse. Sandy and his friend Patrick Hume suffered a desperate blow when their betting account was intercepted by their House Master and they were 'gated' for the Lord's Exeat – the weekend of the Eton and Harrow Match. At the time it was difficult to think of a more severe punishment. Of course we had setbacks. Peter Ohlson took a long time to forgive me for persuading him to back a horse called Brother Birdbrook, which (as he correctly anticipated) was 'having a run'. We were greatly assisted by information from Jeremy Rugge-Price, whose stepfather, Tom Blackwell, was a leading owner and member of the Jockey Club. We therefore had a useful network.

An individual on the fringe of our group was a large, untidy boy called McCririck. This individual was not pleasing to the eye, being scruffily dressed, looking thoroughly unwashed, and invariably sporting a damaged straw boater. He had, though, one notable talent: he was an able table tennis player, with the help of the latest of Chinese foam-covered bats. He was a good opponent and enjoyed a bet on the outcome. Eventually he became the School's 'third bookmaker'. In our last year he invited me to watch Royal Ascot on television in The Head Master's House senior boys' room.

And so my last year at school drifted pleasantly by. I was a House Monitor and life, as they say, was easy. In the spring term, James Lotery, who had left the School but kept in touch, took me surreptitiously to watch Swindon at Brentford one Saturday. Swindon won 2–1. Not surprisingly, I was undetected.

West Acre won the Harrow Football House Matches and looked certain to win the Rugby Cock House Match.

RIGHT: *Polo v Eton at The Guards Polo Club*

However, for me the week leading up to this climax of the term was traumatic. I was again inflicted with the poisoned leg that had ruined the holiday with my father in St Mawes. I spent several days in the sanatorium in a race against time to be fit to play. Released on the eve of the match, I trained hard in the afternoon and slept fitfully, dreaming of a glorious win against our arch-rivals Rendalls, Michael Connell's House. But there was to be no match: the playing fields froze solid overnight, so the match was abandoned and the trophy shared. The summer was an idle paradise of playing cricket for the Outcasts XI and lazing in my room listening to the music of Eartha Kitt. The Outcasts was a team of older boys, of Second or Third Eleven standard, who were leaving that summer and resigned to not playing at Lord's. We had entertaining fixtures, mostly away from Harrow, at grounds like the Rothschild Estate near Tring and the Hendon Police College. Alcohol was allowed on the journey home.

It was a bitter disappointment to me, and no doubt to my father, that I failed to play in the Eton and Harrow Match at Lord's. It was probably the biggest disappointment of my life. But thanks to my friend, Anthony Cable, and the reputation of my card school, I was selected just once as twelfth man for the Harrow XI. At least I had sniffed lightly at the scent of success.

There was one great day at Harrow yet to be lived. Every morning I would read the astrology column in the now-defunct *News Chronicle*. On one Saturday the star sign of Gemini was promised:

This is a day on which everything that you attempt will succeed!

My bet was doubled – to £10 – on a horse called Radiancy, running at Wolverhampton that afternoon. The horse duly obliged at 100/30. I bowled with unusual accuracy for the Outcasts – five wickets and my Outcasts cap was my reward. It was such a perfect day.

Now the day that we pretended to welcome, but some of us secretly dreaded, was drawing closer. It was the custom, on leaving the school, to present the House Master with a small token of appreciation. I had a friend, in Bradbys called Julian Barrow, whom I had seen painting in oils and watercolours from time to time and whose work, to the untrained eye, looked exceptional. I commissioned him to paint West Acre as my leaving present to Philip Boas. I think I paid Julian, who is now a world-renowned landscape and portrait painter, 30 shillings for that effort. The West Acre painting has subsequently been reproduced in prints and enamels and is familiar to almost all West Acre Old Boys.

Mine may not have been an outstanding scholastic career, but at least it ended on a worthy note!

Extract from *Some You Win – A Life in Racing*, Collins Willow, 1998

Julian Wilson (West Acre 1953[3]) was BBC Television Racing Correspondent from 1966–97. He is now a freelance journalist and broadcaster.

Pat McSwiney

From the Obituary in the Daily Telegraph

Portrait by Edward Halliday

Major J.M. 'Pat' McSwiney, who has died aged 83, was awarded an immediate MC in the Western Desert in 1941, and an immediate DSO in the Aegean two years later; he went on to become a House Master at Harrow.

On 21 November 1941, McSwiney, then a lieutenant in the Royal Artillery, was commanding three Bofors light anti-aircraft guns, as part of the force defending the ridge at Sidi Rezegh. In the confused fighting of the fourth day of the British 'Crusader' offensive, this ridge was attacked from the east by elements of Rommel's 15th and 21st Panzer Divisions.

McSwiney's position came under attack on three separate occasions by more than 60 German tanks. Showing great coolness under fire, McSwiney trained his anti-aircraft guns on the advancing tanks, engaging them at a range of 800 yards. Moving from gun to gun, he encouraged his men to keep up their fire, which played a major part in driving off three determined attacks.

McSwiney's MC citation attested that his 'complete disregard for his own safety, his quick action and handling of his anti-aircraft guns was a fine example'.

In 1943 having become, at 21, the youngest major in the Army, McSwiney was sent to join the garrison of the Aegean island of Leros. For a while during the illness of the brigadier, McSwiney found himself doing his job with the rank of acting brigadier until reinforcements arrived. When, in November, the Germans attacked the island, McSwiney was in command of the anti-aircraft defences. These defences were soon swamped by the weight of the air attack and the gun detachments were also under constant mortar and small arms fire. Again, McSwiney found himself employing anti-aircraft guns in a ground-defence as well as an air-defence role; and once more he set a fine example to his men

under fire, maintaining their morale and determination until the defences were finally overwhelmed.

The island fell with the loss of 3,000 prisoners, but McSwiney was not among them. With a few companions, he crossed a minefield, commandeered a small, leaky boat and rowed 20 miles to the Turkish coast. It was for his conduct on Leros that he won his DSO – an award held by his father and his grandfather before him.

John Murray McSwiney was born on 19 September 1920 at Weybridge, Surrey, and educated at Sedbergh, where he was Captain of Rugby. On leaving school, he attended the Royal Military Academy, Woolwich, and, commissioned into the Royal Artillery, was sent to France in 1939 with the British Expeditionary Force. As the Germans advanced across Belgium and France, he took part in the retreat to Dunkirk, and after four days on the beach, swam out to a destroyer and was evacuated. In March 1941 he went with his regiment to the Western Desert, where he won his MC, after which came Leros.

In 1946, he went up to Brasenose College, Oxford, to read Geography. There he was given his Blue for the Javelin and the

Low Hurdles and played for the Oxford University XV. After a term as schoolmaster at Redruth Grammar School and a year at Merchiston Castle, Edinburgh, McSwiney moved, after a six-month attachment to the London School of Economics, to Harrow.

In 1958 he was appointed House Master of Elmfield. As in the war, McSwiney had found himself assuming responsibility at an unusually early age, but he brought to the task the qualities that had stood him in good stead as a gunner: adaptability, administrative flair and an insistence on the highest standards.

Under the care of McSwiney and his wife, Judy, the House flourished, producing a succession of sporting triumphs and an impressive quota of scholars. Colleagues and former pupils remember the couple as a never-failing source of humour, kindness and hospitality during their 13 years at Elmfield.

On his retirement in 1971, McSwiney moved to Child Okeford in Dorset, where he was able to indulge his passion for golf.

He died on 21 December and is survived by his wife Judy (née Lee-Booker), a Wren he met 10 days after Dunkirk and whom he married in 1944, and by their son and two daughters.

On seeing things ... and Jimmy Porter

JONATHAN DUDLEY

I THINK I SPENT MY FIRST TWO YEARS AT HARROW IN a state of quiet awe. Not something that trips easily off the tongue, but awe is probably the word. Like some kind of New World tourist, I was very much taken by the School's old traditions and historic customs and somehow believed that they were enduring and unchanging. Unlike the tourist, I derived a very particular satisfaction from the thought that I was there being part of it all. Frankly, it feels odd to be admitting that, as a schoolboy, one of the aspects of Harrow life which appealed to me most was the School's esoteric regulations and controls. I came to relish the complex system of rules, myths and conventions which taught us how we should behave. And the private world of 'eccer', 'toshes' and so on did much to confirm a cosy sense of belonging to a privileged community. The dressing up and dressing down kept me alert, and I learned to appreciate the peculiar status bestowed by a button, or a tie, a hat or a waistcoat with the critical enthusiasm of a bird-fancier. Of course, symbols like these helped to promote the integrity of our world at school. More importantly, perhaps, they kept it insulated from outside distractions. News of fresh defeats from Haydock, Headingley or Highbury would get through, but (as I remember) very little else.

In my first few years at Harrow, it was these conventions and codes of conduct which seemed to have the most powerful effect on the way I saw things. Maybe doing Classics didn't exactly help me sort out contemporary ideas about class, race or gender in any coherent way. But even if there had been opportunities to wander off the Hill during term-time to gather ideas about the Real World from other sources, I probably wouldn't have taken them. Why bother to get caught up in all the complex ambiguities of the Real World when the Hill provided an altogether reliable framework of certainty and progression?

"'I'll build,' quoth he, as he looked down, 'a road to far off London Town.'" Looking east from the Hill across the all weather pitches laid in 2003

In the 1950s it was never a simple matter for boys to walk off the Hill. I did slope off with my good friend Myles Ponsonby to the pictures in South Harrow a couple of times, but that was because they were showing films featuring the delicious Françoise Arnoul. It would have been a serious matter if anyone had seen us. Normally, to get 'off the Hill' permissions had to be sought and good reasons given. Of course there were formal, organised coach-party visits to other schools for sporting fixtures and so on. I remember Maurice Balme taking the Classical Lower Sixth to Mill Hill School to recite passages of choral verse in Greek. It was some kind of inter-school competition. Our small but perfectly groomed chorus hadn't chosen to do very much rehearsal for this, as it seemed to us a bizarre if not altogether pointless venture and potentially quite embarrassing. When the great day came and we were comprehensively beaten, what surprised me most about the event was the complete absence of irony in Godolphin and Latymer's performance. They were brilliant, superbly drilled in a long passage involving complex vocal harmonies. Worse still, these young women seemed to be taking the thing seriously. It was never pleasant to lose at anything, but to lose to a team from a girls' school who knew what they were doing and were good at it … It seemed, well – shocking, in a funny kind of way.

At that time, going off the Hill was mainly confined to outings which were more-or-less routine and predictable. Even when they were not connected to sport or the CCF, they tended to have little to do with the world of ideas. True, we could go on periodic visits to the Harrow School Clubs, but I took this as a chance to see whether I was really as good at table tennis as I believed I was. I don't recall having any sort of grasp of the foundation of the Clubs or what they were intended to achieve. I had no political awareness at all. Why, I wonder? Probably because I was far too busy getting on – keeping myself visible and productive, getting myself into teams and winning things. Did I understand that I was seeing the world in a very partial way? I don't think so. And at 15, I probably wouldn't have wanted to do anything about it in any case....

A huge change in my attitude to things came about in 1957 when four young men were appointed Harrow Masters. John Jeremy, Jeremy Lemmon, David Gaunt and Tony Davis were fresh from Oxford. Not only were they young, they seemed strangely under-awed by the weight of all the precedent and tradition. While each contributed to the School in a variety of different ways, these young men were full of ideas drawn from what was going on in the wider world. These bubbled over in all the chats and discussions they had with us. Their talk, their way of seeing and thinking about things, had the effect of making me feel uncomfortably parochial. And hopelessly inward-looking, it seemed to me. Self-satisfied, too. Smug, even.

I came to know John Jeremy through the play-reading society. John was passionate about theatre – he had directed a stunning (we had it on good authority) production in the gardens of The Queens College, Oxford the summer before joining the School. One day he talked about a new play called *Look Back in Anger* which was presently being performed at the Royal Court, and about

why there was such a fuss being made about it. He told us about the dismissive approach taken by the majority of newspapers and about Harold Hobson's outspoken support for the play in the *Sunday Times*. Some time later John announced to the play-reading society that he was taking us all to see the play at the Court. I have no idea how he managed to swing this with the boundary-keepers at Harrow, but it must have felt to them as if John's approach was different from anything that had happened before.

It's clearly silly to make too much of this, but it still seems to me as if that trip to the Royal Court was something of a turning point. Certainly John Osborne's play had a profound and lasting impact on British theatre. I hope it's not too fanciful to suggest that John Jeremy's action in taking boys to the Royal Court signalled a watershed of equal significance at Harrow. There were to be other visits too – Ingmar Bergman films at the Academy Cinema and a further schedule of London theatre visits which John arranged for his Modern Languages group.

My sense that Harrow rules were bending under John's influence was further sharpened when, in the summer term of 1959, he directed a production of Jean Anouilh's romantic fantasia *Ring Around the Moon*. This was a House play, to be performed in the Head Master's garden, but with a difference. John wanted to offer the women's parts to – difficult to believe, this – women. The case made and the necessary permissions given, the women's parts were taken by Masters' wives. The production was well received, and the boys who came to see one of their peers smoke cigars and kiss women *in a public place at School during term-time* certainly got their money's worth. But the New World tourist of my younger days would not have been so much impressed. Nothing quaint or exclusive here at all. No old traditions or historic customs. Just a silly old play.

But for those who were involved in it, that silly old play seemed quietly radical, if not subversive. Maybe the culture pendulum at Harrow had been swinging a bit too far in a conservative direction, and maybe this production, and the values that went with it, did something to correct the tilt. Here was evidence of the dynamic tensions between reaction and innovation which characterise all new developments at Harrow. John's creativity and initiative were important and precious to Harrow at that time: as important and precious – but not more so – as those famous old traditions and historic customs.

Jonathan Dudley (The Head Master's 1954³) worked in the theatre and in higher education, where he specialised in the continuing professional development of university teachers. He is now retired and spends a large part of each year in Hungary.

BELOW: *The Head Master's House and garden from a Sketch Book of Harrow by Walter Keesey, 1914*

The power of music

JOHN STENHOUSE

BREAKING A RECORDER OVER MY KNEE SO AS NOT to miss the fun on sports day at prep school was my first instrumental act of rebellion. My father – a discriminating music lover of eclectic taste – had dabbled in playing the trumpet. I remember feeling emotional when discussing with him which orchestral instrument to learn at Harrow. I was sent to the bandmaster, Campbell, to have my teeth and embouchure inspected. I had a lesson on the French horn but he needed a clarinettist in the orchestra. After about a year of very fast progress, Campbell – an experienced oboist – suggested that I took lessons with a specialist.

Clarinet lessons 'off the Hill' in London provided an opportunity to explore the outside world. Leaving a partial viewing of a Brigitte Bardot film to meet my curfew, I was interviewed for a radio programme. A boy who had been 'roomed', burst into the dining room where the Monitors were still sitting. To my embarrassment, he excitedly declared that he had heard my voice on the radio commenting on Brigitte Bardot.

As a new boy, I was warned to sing badly at audition to avoid the time-consuming Chapel Choir – which I now regret considerably. Professional colleagues who have attended Cathedral Choir Schools and other specialist institutions such as the Purcell School, display a particular development of 'ear' and musicianship. At House Songs, new boys individually had to stand on the table in Hall and sing the first four lines of *Men of Harlech*: a pure treble

RIGHT: *The Head Master's House Glee 1960. John Stenhouse is second from the left in the back row*

ABOVE: *The School Band, 1959. Mr Campbell, the bandmaster, is in the centre*

rendering was unwise. I was warned and duly delivered a somewhat rough and ready performance to considerable acclaim.

My first public orchestral experience, playing the side-drum, was in front of the Queen. Another time my contribution was on the triangle, after which I received the shocking comment from a boy in the audience that I had ruined the concert – to this day I am not sure if it was genuine or a joke.

James Crossman and I formed a dance band. He was an extraordinary character who helped produce a magazine called *Goulash*. We rehearsed wonderful Broadway songs by Rogers and Hart and Sandy Wilson of *Valmouth* and *The Boy Friend* fame. We were restricted

to rehearsing in the basement of Music Schools on Saturday afternoons when everyone else was playing cricket, swimming or eating egg and chips in the tuck shop. For the band to perform in front of the whole School before Film Society, the Head Master demanded an audition by the Head of School – regardless of his musical discernment.

Corps (or CCF) was compulsory. I decided to start a military band partly to avoid the weather, spit and polishing boots and crawling on our bellies. We recruited elementary players, rehearsed indoors and were not much good. We were so bad that for the big day (General Inspection) with a very senior guest of honour arriving by military helicopter on the parade ground, a professional military band had to be engaged at short notice. Playing while stationary was bad enough, but marching at the same time was beyond us and rendered the musical content unrecognizable; so it was the National Anthem only – from the far corner of the parade ground.

I became one of the music critics on *The Harrovian*, reviewing the Chamber Concert Club evenings of visiting artists playing mostly masterpieces by Beethoven, Mozart, Brahms etc. I 'lifted' chunks from my books on chamber music. I wonder if anyone noticed. These great works were revelatory and I remember that the first time I was reduced to tears by the power of music was hearing a performance of the Elgar violin concerto in Speech Room.

A love for jazz has played a large part in my life. I thanked my father for introducing me to his small collection of great 78s including Duke Ellington, Coleman Hawkins and Earl Hines. One long summer

holiday was spent immersed in about 50 LPs I had been lent. That truly changed me for ever.

My father donated the Stenhouse Prize for Woodwind while I was still at Harrow. As I was still winning it, the title had to remain anonymous. So all this and more seems to have paved the way for my joining the music profession. For the last 39 years I have experienced the vagaries of this hard but sometimes glorious way of life. After a variety of jobs in light music, opera, teaching, examining and freelance playing, I now enjoy the relative security of a position in the clarinet section of the great London Symphony Orchestra.

John Stenhouse ARCM (The Head Master's 1956[1]), formerly Professor of Music at Trinity College of Music. He is currently teaching at Guildhall School of Music and Drama and is a member of the London Symphony Orchestra. He is a Governor of the Purcell School of Music.

RIGHT: *Ben Eadon and Graham Walker in an orchestra rehearsal*

Domesday and all that

RICHARD FLETCHER

PREP SCHOOLS ALWAYS HAVE BEEN, AND STILL ARE, eccentric places. The prep school I attended from 1952 to 1957 was Aysgarth in the North Riding of Yorkshire, and its then Headmaster was R.W. Thompson who was also a Governor of Harrow. One of Mr Thompson's eccentricities took the form of a strict rule that whenever the names Nelson or Churchill were mentioned every boy within earshot must spring to his feet and stand rigidly to attention until told to resume his seat. Enquiries among friends who attended other schools revealed that no such performance was required of them. It was just a peculiarity of Aysgarth, perhaps best kept quiet about beyond its walls. When in March 1957 my friend Peter Phillips and I were despatched to sit for entrance scholarships at Harrow, Mr Thompson's final words of advice reminded us in the firmest terms of how we should conduct ourselves if, in the course of our interview with Dr James, the Head Master should mention the name of a certain very famous Old Harrovian who only two years before had resigned the office of Prime Minister. Inwardly dubious, we muttered assent. In due course I was summoned for an interview with Dr James, to be conducted in the hallowed – and for a classroom, luxuriously appointed – quarters of the Classical Sixth beneath the Vaughan Library. As I made my way down the steps towards the dreaded rendezvous I prayed with all the fervour that I could muster that the Head Master would not mention either Churchill or Nelson, because I was obscurely convinced that the acrobatics which I had promised to perform might prove an occasion for surprise or even, and much worse, mockery. To my huge relief neither name was mentioned. That is all that I can recollect of the interview. It was my first experience of the Vaughan Library; well, strictly speaking, of what lay beneath it.

I suppose that I must have visited the Vaughan Library at least from time to time in the course of my first three terms at Harrow, though I have no recollection of it except as somewhat intimidating, awesomely quiet, almost invariably empty of humans, a daunting space pervaded by the smell of old books. I had loved books since my earliest childhood and had already discovered that few pleasures in life could match browsing and reading among them; but the Vaughan somehow did not encourage exploration or familiarity. All this was to change in the course of the summer term of 1958, my fourth term at Harrow. Under the encouragement of my parents I had from a young age taken an eager interest in history, the earlier the better, and read all that I could lay my hands on among the plentiful books at home. During the early months of 1958 my interest focused – for reasons which I cannot now recall, presumably arising from some chance bookish encounter – upon the history of the pre-Conquest or Anglo-Saxon period of English history. (Little could I have guessed that the interest would still be with me, as strong as ever, nearly 50 years later.) Among the sustenance which I found at home to feed this appetite was a book about Yorkshire place-names. It excited me to discover that the history of a national community could be read through its place-names; that Celts, Romans, Anglo-Saxons, Danes and Normans had all contributed something to the complex patchwork of names which clothes the English landscape.

During that summer term I shared a room in my House, Moretons, with a contemporary called Huw Vaughan. The room we inhabited was next door to one occupied by a senior boy in his last term at the School, one of the House Monitors, by name Nigel Firth. Among Firth's shared duties was the job of going round the House at the end of an evening to check on lights-out. Naturally, as next-door neighbours, Vaughan and I were his last port of call. In the time-honoured manner of boarders the world over, we would attempt to delay the moment when the light would be switched off by

A HARROVIAN'S
ENGLISH

Now that you have come to Harrow, one of your first responsibilities is to make sure that you can talk and write the King's English. On this card, which you must keep close at hand until you no longer need it, you will find stated the minimum that is asked of you.

Before you leave the SHELLS, you will be expected to be able to account for the *Clause-Construction* of any sentence which you write or speak. You must be able to identify

I the *Main Clause*, and say whether it is statement, question, exclamation, command or petition; and

II the *Subordinate Clauses*, and say whether they are
(a) Noun Clauses—the indirect forms of statement, question, exclamation, command or petition—used as subject, object or complement,
(b) Adjective Clauses—relative clauses—used to define or to comment, with corresponding difference in punctuation,
or (c) Adverb Clauses—final, consecutive, causal, temporal, conditional, concessive or comparative.

Before you leave the REMOVES, you will have had the opportunity of studying the following points, and will be expected to apply your experience in your written work:

III The points of *Emphasis* in a sentence, whether spoken or written. You will have practice—both by reading aloud and by written exercises—in throwing the emphasis on different parts of speech.

IV The *Connection in Thought* between a series of sentences. The use of the semi-colon and colon and full-stop, and also of parenthesis.

V The *Paragraph*, with its double purpose—unity in itself, connection with its context.

VI The *Structure* of a continuous composition—sequence of thought, climax, summary, beginning and ending, &c.

In the LOWER FIFTHS, you will study to add the following arts to your equipment:

VII *Metaphor.* You will become aware of its constant use and its purpose: you will learn to avoid the dead metaphor; and to create your own metaphor, and extend and prolong its use over a paragraph.

VIII The extension and enrichment and selection of your *Vocabulary*; colour of words, their association, their individual history, &c.

IX The control of the *Rhythm* of your sentence; order of words, the suspension of interest, the sound of words in combination, &c.

X Various "*Graces*": irony, epigram, paradox, allusion, &c.

LEFT AND RIGHT:
'A Harrovian's English' was issued to all boys in the 1940s

engaging Firth in conversation. Nigel Firth, most unusually for a Harrovian, was an Orcadian: his home was on the island of Rousay. For Vaughan, from Wales, and me, from Yorkshire, the Orkneys had all the attractions of a distant, exotic region of which we knew little. Firth was fond of his native islands and it was not difficult to get him to talk about them: their treeless landscape, their remarkable prehistoric monuments, their most un-Scottish dialect – and then, one evening, their place-names. I pricked up my ears at once, and

PUNCTUATION

Think of punctuation as being the means of showing your reader how your sentence is grouped : help him to understand your meaning at first glance ; don't leave him in doubt.

You have four routine signs, which mark pauses of different length in your sentence: shortest is the comma; next the semi-colon; next the colon; and longest is the full-stop.

Begin by making sure of the *full-stop*. Except when you are asking a question or exclaiming, there is no other means of bringing your sentence to rest than the full-stop. If you forget it, you leave your reader in the air. Even if you are in a hurry to finish, never forget to put the finishing touch—the full-stop.

N.B.—It should also be put after initials and abbreviations.

Then master the use of the *comma*.

(a) First form the habit of marking your clauses with commas: but you will find that this is not always necessary. Consider that most Noun-Clauses, being either subject or object of the main verb, and those Adjective-Clauses that define—see II (b) overleaf—are an integral part of the Main Clause and so need no commas. The commenting Adjective-Clause, which interrupts the flow of the sentence, must have commas. With Adverb-Clauses the commonest exception occurs when the main emphasis of the sentence lies in the clause itself. Here, for instance, you will see that there is no comma before "when."

(b) Mark any interruption in the course of the Main Clause with commas at the beginning and the end: such interruptions, gentlemen, are the vocative address and, in many cases, an adverbial phrase.

(c) A list too should be separated with commas—whether nouns, verbs, adjectives, cats, dogs, shoes, ships or sealing-wax. Notice that after "ships" no comma is needed.

(d) Commas are also often used to prevent doubts as to the grouping of words or, in a long sentence, to give the reader a chance to draw breath. You now understand full-stops and commas, and semi-colons and colons should cause you no difficulty.

The *semi-colon* marks a pause a little longer than a comma; the *colon* a little longer still: neither is so long as a full-stop. If you read this sentence again with an attentive ear, you will find that you want the first two clauses to hang together more closely than the last two. The expression of a train of thought often needs such grouping: ask your Form Master for further examples; and then frame your practice accordingly.

As final as the full-stop are the *question-mark*, which marks a direct question,—do you sometimes forget it?—and the *exclamation-mark*, which marks a direct exclamation. But if you exclaim more than once or twice in a page, what a bore it is !

Don't forget to *indent* your paragraphs clearly and at a regular distance from the left-hand margin. Copy this page.

Parenthesis is used—it is a weakness to use it too often—when the writer or speaker wants to interrupt his Main Clause with a sentence or phrase which is not grammatically connected with the construction of the rest. *Dashes* are better than brackets—leave brackets to the mathematician—for this purpose. But don't let these dashes look like careless hyphens.

Quotation, whether of single words or whole speeches, is marked by *inverted commas*. "What happens," you will say, "when someone tells you what someone else has said?" "You ask me 'what happens?'" is my reply. Note especially the use and position of the ordinary *comma* in these two examples:

"I wonder if he is a Harrovian," I said.
"You can always tell a Harrovian," he answered, "by the way he writes and speaks his own language."

listened eagerly to talk of names ending in *–ister* and *–setter* and *–stather*, wholly unlike anything that was familiar to me at home. But it was the parting shot which (if I may mix the metaphor) sowed the seed. As he began to finger the light-switch preparatory to plunging Vaughan and me into darkness, Firth said, 'The trouble is, in Orkney we haven't got much in the way of early sources recording place-names. You're lucky in England, you've got *Domesday Book*.' '*Domesday Book*?' I said, wonderingly. I knew of the existence of *Domesday*

Book as the record of the great survey of his new kingdom commissioned by William the Conqueror and conducted in 1086; but I knew barely anything about what was in it. 'Yes,' said Firth, 'thousands and thousands of eleventh-century place-names. Go and have a look for yourself. It's in the Vaughan. Goodnight.' And off went the light.

A day or two later I made my way to the Vaughan and looked it up in the catalogue. Yes, there it was: *Domesday Book seu Liber Censualis Wilhelmi Primi Regis Angliae*, edited by Abraham Farley, 2 volumes, folio (Record Commission: London, 1783). I copied down the shelfmark and after a few false starts managed to track the volumes to a lower shelf towards the far right-hand corner of the library (looking from the door). I carried the unwieldy folios over to a table and decided to make a start by looking up the village where I lived, by name Wighill. After much searching I did eventually run Wighill to earth on folio 326. Trying to understand the entry was quite a different matter. I knew that the language of the text would be Latin, but I had not been prepared for the abbreviation of words, nor for the unfamilar typeface which, as I learned years later, was a special font known as Record Type designed to reproduce as closely as possible the form of the original text. It took several visits to the Vaughan, much puzzlement, and some moments of near despair, before I was tolerably certain in a rough and ready way of what the Domesday text said in Latin, and even more approximately what it meant in English. But I did it: my first sustained encounter with medieval records, my first steps on a ladder whose rungs I am still climbing.

The ice had been broken. Thereafter I plunged into the waters of the Vaughan with zest, extending my early medieval enquiries in all sorts of directions. There I first sampled the *Anglo-Saxon Chronicle* in the 'Rolls Series' edition; there I pored over R.H. Hodgkin's *History of the Anglo-Saxons* and F.M. Stenton's *Anglo-Saxon England*; there I puzzled over F.W. Maitland's *Domesday Book and Beyond* (a great work but not one for beginners).

Encouraged by my teachers, there I tried my hand at Gibbon's *Decline and Fall of the Roman Empire*. On my election to the august society of the Essay Club – founded by Vaughan in the 1850s and meeting in the Library named after him – it was there that I researched an essay to be read to the Club in 1961 on the Venerable Bede, England's earliest and most influential historian, encountering in the process the incomparable edition of and commentary upon Bede's *Ecclesiastical History* by Charles Plummer. There I dipped into E.A. Freeman's *History of the Norman Conquest*, and read J.H. Round's devastating attack upon it entitled 'Mr. Freeman and the Battle of Hastings'. There I first sampled the work of foreign scholars: Henri Pirenne's controversial views on the economic history of the early middle ages, Marc Bloch's brilliant evocation of feudal society in the work of that title.

I was extraordinarily fortunate in my teachers at Harrow. Roger Ellis and Geoffrey Treasure were outstandingly gifted teachers of history, to whom I can never be grateful enough for stimulating an interest and inculcating a discipline which would lead in time to a career which continues to give me fulfilment. But excellent teaching was not alone among the impulses which led me to become a medieval historian. Having the run of a first-rate library was also critically important. Laboriously discovering how to make it work for you, how to get the information you want, how to evaluate it, what questions to ask of it, are important skills, and they are most enduringly acquired by means of a do-it-yourself process of trial and error, of learning on the job. That's what I started to do as a fourteen-year-old when I first looked into *Domesday Book* in the summer term of 1958. This was the opportunity for which I look back with appreciative gratitude upon the Vaughan Library.

And I'm still, nearly half a century later, trying to make sense of *Domesday Book*.

Richard Fletcher (Moretons 1957²) was Professor of Medieval History at York University and is the author of many books, articles and reviews.

German, not Greek

ANTHONY GRENVILLE

I MUST HAVE MADE AN UNUSUAL NEW ARRIVAL AT Harrow when I entered the Head Master's House in autumn 1957. My parents had come to England in 1938, as Jewish refugees from Vienna escaping Hitler. We lived in modest prosperity in a pleasant semi in Golders Green – at that time hardly the background for recruits to the top echelon of British public schools. Though I had been at a private prep school, it had been a very small, rather disorderly institution that bore more resemblance to Nigel Molesworth's St. Custard's than to the more orthodox feeder schools to Harrow. If I had not won a scholarship, no one would ever have dreamt of putting me down for Harrow.

My first encounter with a major public school was a shock for me, especially as I arrived late, because of illness, and missed the induction period during which the other new boys learnt the ropes. I felt intimidated by the School, by its size, its arcane rules and rituals, and by the social class and evident self-confidence of those around me, and I don't think that I ever really got over that feeling. As a scholarship boy, I felt even more of an outsider, as my academic achievements were regarded, it seemed to me, more as a curiosity than as cause for admiration. Even when I won the top scholarship in Modern Languages to Christ Church, Oxford, in 1962, this seemed to come a poor second to representing the School at rugby football.

To say that I was fortunate in the education in Modern Languages that I received at Harrow would be an understatement. Thanks to Leonard Walton and John Jeremy, I had read more French and German literature by the time I left Harrow than had most of the final-year students whom I taught at the University of Bristol in the 1970s and 1980s. I happily answered a question on Goethe's *Urfaust* in Finals at Oxford simply by drawing on John Jeremy's notes, while Leonard Walton thought nothing of introducing his sixth-formers to the most demanding of recent literary criticism: Lucien

Goldmann's structuralist analysis of the influence of Jansenism on Racine's tragedies, for example, or Martin Turnell's Freudian reading of the same dramatist's *Phèdre*. How Leonard ever found time to keep up with contemporary lit. crit. when he spent untold hours teaching, marking essays or correcting our French and German proses, I shall never know.

By way of a distraction from languages, we did some history with Roger Ellis, whose teaching of C.V. Wedgwood's classic history of the Thirty Years' War instilled in me an enthusiasm for European history that has remained with me for life. I also had the advantage of being among a group of highly gifted, and not uncompetitive, Modern Linguists. Whereas my natural skills were those of a smoothly efficient machine for passing examinations, I learnt to admire the creativity and flair of contemporaries like Francis Kyle, Peter Phillips and Carey Harrison. When I arrived at Harrow, the unquestioning assumption had been that scholars became Classicists, and the top three scholars of my year all did. I can still remember the role call of their names: Annesley, Gilbart-Smith, Osmond … But I was determined to take German, not Greek, and in this instance the spirit of the

LEFT: *The Terrace in the spring sunshine, March 2003*

second half of the twentieth century triumphed over Victorian values, though not without some traditionalist harrumphing along the way.

I cannot say that I was happy at Harrow, but looking back, I have to admit that most of the unhappiness was probably due to the isolation that I created around myself, rather than to anything that was done to me. I never encountered any sign of anti-Semitism, for example. I escaped fagging after a year, was not bullied or picked on, and though I did once get beaten, it was for the grievous crime of telling a rather preposterous 'four-yearer' to go to hell; even in 1960 this was so mild a use of bad language that the ensuing disciplinary farrago, instituted by an earnest House Monitor who fancied himself as an interrogator and completed with due relish by the Head of House, merely appealed to my sense of the ridiculously disproportionate.

In fact, I made a number of good friends. I remember how pleased I was at the end of my first year when Barney Powell, one of the House's most popular characters, asked me to share a room with him. The first person to invite me to stay with him at home was another room mate, Alastair Malcolm, whose family mansion in the Thames Valley greatly impressed me, but with whom I remained on the sort of casual schoolboy good terms in which lasting friendships are rooted. I also greatly valued my friendship with James Benn, who

invited me to travel across Canada with him shortly after we left Harrow, and I can't see how one can easily beat that.

The Harrow that I remember was an austere and rather forbidding institution that made little allowance for the emotional frailties of young boys. It was profoundly conscious of the tradition of public school service to King and Empire in which it stood, and of the values of discipline and of institutional and group loyalty that were its code of honour. The strongly hierarchical structure of School and House cast those values, one has to say, in a form perhaps more suited to the running of the Indian Empire than to a post-1945 Britain shorn of its imperial grandeur and economic pre-eminence. Inevitably, by the 1960s the rhetoric of imperial grandeur cut little ice with Harrovians, who mostly went their own ways; some were still very 'old school' in their view of life; others were keener to strike out in the new society of the dawning 1960s. I, too, felt that my choice of career set me apart from the conventional mould – Old Harrovians are rare in academic life – but then again it was Harrow that gave me my start on that path through life.

Anthony Grenville BA, DPhil (The Head Master's 1957[3]) formerly Lecturer and Senior Lecturer in German at the Universities of Bristol and Westminster, is now Senior Research Fellow, University of Bristol. He is Historical Consultant to the Association of Jewish Refugees.

ABOVE: *Landscape*
by Spencer Gore,
c. *1908*

That gentle, civilised art

HUON MALLALIEU

PEOPLE OFTEN SAY THAT IN A GENERAL SENSE THEIR schooldays dictated the course of their later lives, for good or ill. I can claim that two specific days during my time at Harrow provided the triggers for what became my career and lifelong interest.

A little while ago I had lunch with Ian Willis, a Harrow contemporary whom I had not seen for several years. Naturally we fell to reminiscence, and among his memories was a day on which we both had no doubt uncomfortable after-lunch appointments with our House Master. While we waited shiftily in the library which led into his study, apparently I attempted to distract myself by reading *Country Life*. In those days the correspondence pages were much more extensive than they are nowadays, and they were full of eccentricity and out-of-the-way information. However, on that occasion I immersed myself in Frank Davis's weekly 'Talking about Sale Rooms' column, and according to Ian, I said, 'That's the job I want.'

At that time, in the early 1960s, Frank was only a few years into what he had taken as a retirement job in 1957. In 1990, a week after his death, the last of his inimitable articles appeared. At 97 he must have been the oldest working journalist. I had the privilege of writing his obituary, followed by the greater privilege of taking over the column.

BELOW: *'Distant View of Lincoln Cathedral' by Peter de Wint (1784–1849)*

More significant still for me, and as little noticed at the time, was a cold Sunday in 1960 or early 1961 when I had been in the School for about a year. I had vaguely noticed the collection of watercolours then hanging in the protective gloom of the War Memorial stairwell, but I had never taken any note of them. Although I thoroughly enjoyed drawing, especially cartoons and caricatures, and spent much time in the Art Schools, I knew and cared little about art history. Indeed I have an embarrassing memory of sitting sulkily in the car parked in Orange Street during a family visit to the National Gallery.

However, my father was a very accomplished amateur watercolour painter, a taste that he had got from his mother. He had heard of the watercolours that had been left to the School by an Old Harrovian, C.J. Hegan, in 1935, and on this Sunday he turned up to take me out to lunch over an hour early, demanding to be shown the collection. I was deeply engaged in something else and grumbled a bit, but lunch was lunch in those lean times, and off we went to the War Memorial building. An hour later I had fallen in love.

The principal object of my passion was a green vision of the Grand Canal after Turner by another Old Harrovian, the splendidly named Hercules Brabazon Brabazon (1821–1906) – or Sharpe as he would have been during his schooldays. As a younger son he had determined to become an artist and had studied with good Masters, but his brother died, and he inherited large estates in Ireland – thus the name change – Durham and Sussex. He was an absentee landlord in Ireland, and a vicarious one in England, but as a very rich man he did not need to earn a living by the brush. Thus, as an enthusiastic amateur, he was freed from any need to follow fashion, and he developed his own brand of Turner-inspired impressionism. Late in his long life Whistler persuaded him to show his work in public, becoming, in the critic Sir Frederick Wedmore's phrase, 'a country gentleman who at 70 years made his debut as a professional artist and straightway became famous.'

Once, years after that first encounter with him, I was shown a collection of watercolours by Brabazon and others in a Yorkshire house. Often there were two or three which at first sight appeared identical. A lifelong bachelor, it was his habit to travel to Venice, the Near East or India with what he called his 'harem', the educationalist Mme Bodichon, her Leigh-Smith sisters and other ladies and they would all paint the same subjects, often in his manner.

During the remainder of my time at Harrow I got a great deal of enjoyment from the Hegan collection. My eye developed, expanded and refined. On a recent visit to the collection, now handsomely re-housed in the Old Speech Room Gallery, I looked at that Brabazon again. My puppy love for it has long faded, although naturally a gentle affection still lingers. It is now too bright for my middle-aged taste. By the time I left my favourites were probably a 'Distant View of Lincoln' by Peter de Wint, and John Sell Cotman's blue and gold 'Mont St Michel' of 1818, which is like a trumpet fanfare.

The latter packs great power into its 9¼ by 16¾ inches, and one has only to observe the casual touch of a few ribs from a long-disintegrated boat half-buried in the sand to understand why Turner so approved of Cotman. Not only does it anchor, so to speak, the composition, but it is a tiny reminder that all works of man, even this strong citadel erected to the glory of God, must eventually crumble.

A few years later I went for a job interview at Christie's. It was short.

'I see you were at Oxford.'

'Yes.'

'Did you actually get a degree?'

'Yes!'

'Well, you'll have to forget all that arty-farty nonsense when you start here. Is there any area that you know anything about?'

'I like English watercolours.'

'Well, you'll have to go wherever there's a gap. Start on 5 May.'

Luckily, after a few months there was a gap in the Drawings department, and I found myself learning the subject in earnest, under the rigorous tutelage of yet another Old Harrovian, Noël Annesley.

When I left Christie's, it was to write a reference book, *The Biographical Dictionary of British Watercolour Artists*, and even though I have diversified over subsequent years of writing on art and antiques, that gentle, civilised art perfected in England remains close to my heart. For which I thank my father, Harrow and Mr Hegan – only regretting that almost nothing beyond his name appears to have been recorded about that generous benefactor.

Huon Mallalieu (The Grove 1960[1]) is the author and editor of numerous books on antiques, painting and the property market. He is also the saleroom writer for Country Life.

ABOVE: *'Riva degli Schiavoni, Venice', attributed to Hercules Brabazon Brabazon (1821–1906)*

Sentimental education

CAREY HARRISON

NO CENTRAL HEATING, NO GIRLS. NO FRILLS OR furbelows or pampering of any kind. It's 1957, and we imagine ourselves to be the last generation to attend the old Imperial Harrow, a place where young men are made ready for the rigours and responsibilities of a vanished art: colonial administration. Delinquent junior boys are to be roused after lights out by a single ominous 'day boy' call, the drawn-out cry that summons them to be caned by a senior boy; fagging-chores turn adolescents into valets, adjutants, body slaves; School customs and School argot will bind former schoolmates forever in the jungle or the desert or the boardroom. There are a hundred arcane rules to be learned and obeyed, many of them patently absurd – only the fittest, already hardiest boys, the sporting heroes, are allowed to wear scarves in the depths of winter – though many rules make a Darwinian point: the small and sickly are foredoomed, and serve them right. This is the whole antique public school package, blown to smithereens in Lindsay Anderson's film *If*. We are of that screenwriter's generation; we too yearn for change. We want to belong to a vanguard and not to the fag end, so to speak, of an outworn authoritarian tradition. In reality the full extent of our rebellion will be to vote, as House Monitors, not to administer the cane.

The very word 'Monitor', brings back much of what it meant to be a boy at Harrow 50 years ago, dodging teenage tyrants barely a year or two older than yourself. School Monitors, in distinctive headgear; Phil, societies of the laureated. For some it would be the high point of their lives. I had a promisingly undistinguished Harrow career, as did my closest schoolfriend. We were both unkempt malingerers, 'shag', as the phrase was. In truth I wasn't 'shag' at all (in the sense of listlessly cool), just scared and out of place, a Jew unresistingly attending Anglican services and wishing in vain to be, and to feel that I was, a part of it all. I had come to England from the French Lycée in New York. My German mother often got the name of the School wrong and said, 'My son attends Harrods,' eliciting puzzled looks. I myself had no idea where I was. I arrived drowning in nostalgia for a preparatory school I had briefly attended between the Lycée and Harrow, and was thrust into Room 40, West Acre's only 4-bed room, an eyrie at the very top of the House.

My first morning in Chapel: I've been told I'm to sit in the choir loft but I can't find the way up to it and stand in the nave mortified and confused, close to tears, as the service begins. Out of nowhere a tall thin boy, a figure topped by a small neat head that makes him look taller still, descends on me to ask if I'm lost and to guide me to the choir. This saviour, as I later discovered, was Johnny Dudley, the elder brother of my good friend the editor of this volume. At college Johnny and I became friends for life, but at Harrow he remained godlike and distantly adored, whether on the cricket field, scoring 150 in a House match, or on stage in Anouilh's *Ring Around the Moon*, a majestic, tender, infinitely gifted spirit whose kindness that morning remains vivid to this day. I felt very isolated then, but there was nourishment to come. I soon found that the arts flourished at Harrow. There were memorable outings to London theatre; I saw my first Brecht at the Mermaid; walked, with the School Architecture Society, around Sir Christopher Wren's city churches, a trip culminating in my first visit to St Paul's. At school there was the great A.R.D. Watkins, supreme Shakespearean, to whom I have attempted to pay tribute elsewhere; there was also Ronnie Watkins's bearded, pipe-smoking sidekick, 'Bush' Harris, who memorably set fire to himself during rehearsals for *A Midsummer Night's Dream*, while showing me how to exhibit passion. I was Demetrius; Bush, forgetting the pipe he'd stowed in his pocket, was standing in as my Athenian maid, until he caught fire.

In class, under C.L. Walton's gaze, I discovered Racine; on my own I came to the other author who determined my life's course: Chekhov. And then I found John Gielgud's recordings of Shakespeare. I had known Gielgud – a friend of my actor parents – since childhood, but it was neither he who introduced me to his own recordings nor my parents nor even Ronnie Watkins, but Patrick Hutchinson, a fellow Harrovian so 'shag' that in winter he usually kept his pyjamas on under his trousers. At Patrick's urging, we made our own tape recordings of King Lear. Many years later I was to write a play for Sir John, called *A Last View of St Paul's*, about Christopher Wren at the age of 90; Gielgud performed it, aged 90 himself, the BBC broadcast it and, strange to say, it's only now, writing this, that I've connected up the dots and seen how the pieces of a life hang together; how much I owe to my old School – and to Patrick in trousers and pyjamas, unshaven, intoning, 'You do me wrong to take me out of the grave'.

All around me at Harrow, I can now see, artists were being born. In my House there was a strange boy called Birkin, who drew swastikas on himself and inked in his knees where the holes in his trousers might otherwise have revealed skin; Andrew Birkin, for whose sins I was caned on one occasion, when I was caught helping him perform a chore (cleaning rugby boots) that he'd left too late. I was caned by the owner of the boots, the captain of School rugby – a towering redhead. By contrast: spindly Andrew Birkin, about whom a friend and I penned a mocking end-of-term play for the House's amusement; inky, spidery, gawky Andrew, who amazingly … but the punch line to this tale must wait.

Racine and Gide inspired me; otherwise I was so afflicted by classroom tedium that for three years I replaced listening to the teacher with counting the number of times – I ran a book on it – each particular Beak, would utter an 'um' or an 'err' of hesitation in the course of a single class. Centuries; sometimes double centuries. I certainly achieved a measure of cool, or shag, through my habitual inattention. And I survived on my lazy wits. In my first term at Cambridge I was astonished to run into Garth Wood, a Harrow contemporary, whom I knew only for his sporting skills and had taken to be a handsome, stylish dimwit; he was just as surprised – 'I thought you were stupid,' he exclaimed, and I glowed with secret, Puckish pride: I had succeeded in making myself invisible.

Beneath the invisibility there were growing pains. We were adolescent boys, after all, and afire. Photographs of Brigitte Bardot and Diana Dors adorned our rooms. My school holidays were spent with celebrated adults in exotic places where my parents were filming or were currently domiciled for tax purposes, but I would have traded this upbringing any day for teenage parties in a place and language I knew. A single-gender boarding school was a torment at a time when the erotic imagination was running riot. Mine predictably ran riot into words on paper; paper lost or discarded and somehow finding its way, to his intense embarrassment no less than mine, into the hands of my kindly bachelor House Master. He felt obliged to explain to me what he termed the 'anatomical discrepancies' in my erotica. It was a memorable interview. Unabashed, I turned our interview into a one-act play called *26 Efforts at*

LEFT: *Andrew Birkin in 1963*

Pornography which reached many small acting spaces during the 1970s and, finally, BBC Television's 'Thirty-Minute Theatre' to embarrass my poor House Master once more – this time before a national audience.

One day, in an event almost too strange to relate, I contemplated going into a shop – it stood opposite The Park – which sold wool. I had an idea I wanted to knit a scarf (a peculiar ambition – many years later I knitted several scarves and even made a shirt and tie, out of pure curiosity), and stepped up onto the doorstep of the shop, thereby saving my life. As I rose up onto the step I heard the sound of brakes and a car speeding out of control. I turned to see a Morris Minor, with a panic-stricken female face above the wheel, veer wildly and jump onto the pavement to head directly for me at full speed. I was certainly going to die within the instant. The car's nearside front tyre hit the doorstep where I stood, hypnotized, as it bounced off back onto the street to career down the Hill and up past Druries and away. It was a bleak Sunday afternoon in winter; there was no-one in sight. I never went into the shop, but walked off on rubbery legs, feeling sick and obscurely fingered by destiny.

I was only just beginning to learn about destiny, however. Shortly after leaving Harrow, a contemporary brought me a piece of gossip too bizarre to be anything but true. Andrew Birkin, our inky spider, had entered the film world (to which, in fact, both his genius and his family heritage amply entitled him, though we knew nothing of such things at school), and was currently Brigitte Bardot's toy-boy lover. A world in which it was possible for an Andrew Birkin to wind up as the lover of our goddess, Bardot, was not a world in which any verities could ever be found, much less predicted. It wasn't even a parallel universe. It was an insulting and impossible world.

In unremarkable reality, of course, it was the case (even the predictable case) that Andrew would swiftly grow from a gawky stick insect into a remarkably handsome young man, not to mention that he already possessed an artist's soul and a single-mindedness which would draw the admiration of more demanding spirits than Brigitte Bardot's. It was not really remarkable that Garth Wood, the silky cricketer, would turn into a noted psychologist, or I from one who dreamed of anatomical discrepancies, into a plausible author. At Harrow we were each of us, like schoolboys everywhere, a creature in a chrysalis, trying to deduce the shape of the world to come from within its foggy membrane. Transformations and reversals, the stuff of Aristotelian drama (stuff which the young imagine to be merely far-fetched) were to come.

As I write this I am preparing to teach my New York City college graduates a 15-week class on the bible of reversals, Proust's *A la Recherche du Temps Perdu*. (Transformation: I am back at my French and New York roots.) Another Harrow friend and contemporary, Richard Fletcher, introduced me to Joyce and Eliot as we trod and bicycled the roads of Tuscany and the Dordogne, aged 18, inspecting churches and castles and reciting Eliot's *Four Quartets*, antiphonally; and it was Richard, the future historian, who introduced me then to an ancient motto – thoroughly Proustian in its world view – which has served me well over the years; a motto which would have soothed my schoolboy anxieties, if only I had trusted it: *cavete, felices; sperate, miseri*. Beware, ye happy! Be hopeful, ye unfortunates!

Carey Harrison (West Acre 1957²) is Associate Professor of English at the City University of New York. He is a novelist and playwright.

Unfaded copy – editing *The Harrovian*

SIMON WELFARE

THE TELEVISION TYCOON WAS IN A MOOD. THE pressures of ensuring that his new ITV station would be on the air in only a few months' time were clearly affecting him. I sat nervously on the edge of my chair waiting for the dark cloud to blow over, so that the job interview could begin. I was still at university, but had wangled a meeting with the great man through a girl I had met at a party. Suddenly, a career in television didn't seem such a good idea. At length, he looked up from his script-covered desk, and, waving my *curriculum vitae* impatiently, threw me a question:

'It says here that you worked on your school magazine, a *weekly* magazine. What was that like?'

I took a deep breath, relieved that I had been given an easy start by a man famously unwilling to suffer fools gladly. But I never got the chance to answer. Instead, I had to duck as a huge ring-binder, bursting with paper, whizzed past my ear.

'Sorry, boy,' said the Director of Programmes, as it exploded on to the floor. 'They *will* keep sending me the corporate plan, and I can't abide it. Don't think it's got much to do with programme making. Anyway, I suppose you can have the job. Get a good degree and I'll see you after your finals.' So I left without ever answering the question. Here is what I would have told him.

By the time that I became one of its editors in the early 1960s, *The Harrovian* had been a key feature in the life of the School for almost three-quarters of a century. With its distinctive thick cream paper and a layout that had remained unchanged for decades, it was an institution, but it would not, each of us vowed as we were recruited, be a moribund one.

Then, as now, there were about half a dozen editors, drawn from different Houses and in different years. When we joined the team, we were told that *The Harrovian* was primarily a journal of record: news of School events and the achievements of Old Harrovians would take pride of place. Rather more alluring was the revelation that the School authorities also saw each weekly issue as a chance for members of the School to let off steam anonymously, safe in the knowledge that the editors were sworn never to reveal the identity of even the most controversial or cantankerous contributor. As I grew into the job, I realized, too, that *The Harrovian* helped to unite a School which, in those days, might otherwise have formed a rather fragmentary community, with boys eating meals and finding their friends, for the most part, within their fiercely independent Houses.

Though we sometimes envied the writers from other schools who could fill their publications with photographs and satire – Shrewsbury's *The Salopian*, edited by many of the founding contributors to *Private Eye* was the epitome of subversive cool – and though we often longed to be allowed to outdo the *Eton College Chronicle* in outrageously provocative editorials that were written up in the 'real' newspapers, we rejoiced in the opportunities that *The Harrovian* gave us.

We were at the very centre of School life: the first to hear the gossip and to learn of changes. We – and only we – knew the identity of the letter-writer who had stirred up the latest controversy, and, because we had to proof-read every word of every line of every article, we had a detailed weekly snapshot of the rich and varied activities on the Hill.

Our routine seldom varied. On Sunday night, the copy for the next edition was gathered together and sent off to the printers in Uxbridge. Although we handed out a rather nannyish *Advice to Contributors*, the articles came in many different forms. Some – usually the reports of obscure societies – arrived immaculately typed, but others were handwritten and often only vaguely legible. Only the Editor for Old Harrovian News could be relied upon: week in, week out, his brief notes on the successes of our predecessors appeared on time and in the clearest of scripts.

THE HARROVIAN

22 October 1983

An Interview with the Prime Minister

We would like to thank the Rt. Hon. Margaret Thatcher, MP, for agreeing to be interviewed by The Harrovian.
On 4 October, Simon Sebag-Montefiore and Scott Martin met the Prime Minister at Number 10.
These are extracts from their interview.

In view of the doctrine of monetarism, will you pursue a policy of reflation eventually if unemployment continues as it is?

No, certainly not, because if you start to print money you very soon run into a situation where you have even higher unemployment than you have now. You call it monetarism. It's a new name; it doesn't mean very much. I will tell you what it is. It is honest money. It is a system that means that the supply of money is equal to the production of goods and services in the economy. Now that is honest money. Anything else is dishonest money and it is totally wrong for a government to have dishonest money.

Is it right to use the antics of Scargill and Livingstone to discredit the Left?

I don't use the antics of Scargill and Livingstone. I don't use the antics of Scargill and Livingstone ever. I point out as I have done just now, reasonably and honestly, why I think their policies won't work.

How important was Saatchi and Saatchi to your image in the election campaign?

Not important at all. They had nothing to do with my image.

Really?

Nothing whatsoever to do with my image. They are trying to put across a message, not an image at all. We are the image; no-one can alter that.

How important do you see the role of public schools as being in this country today?

Very important indeed. Far more important than the 5 per cent who benefit from independent schools. If ever you have a total monopoly of education by the state, you have nothing to compare their performance with. So every single person in this country profits from there being independent schools. Also, it is a part of a free society – the right to spend my money as I wish.

What sort of attributes do you think someone leaving public school should have?

The greater the privilege you have experienced, the greater the responsibility you must shoulder: responsibility to your country, to your community, to your family for upholding the standards of this country, for being leaders. I used not to understand when people said to me that what we want in this country is leadership. I now do understand it and I think you understand it in a way at school when no-one knows what to do and someone gets up and says, 'I think we should do this, for this reason'. That is leadership. We all of us sometimes fail, but we must try again. You must be seen to work hard, seen to be willing to go and help with anything in the community – it may be to help with disabled, or it may be going to teach youngsters cricket. You must be seen to be bold and brave if you go into the armed forces. The greater the privilege – and it is a privilege to go to Harrow – the greater the duty and the responsibility to your family and your school, to your community and to your country.

Are you personally governed by any particular philosophy of life, or do you take decisions day by day, expediently?

No, I don't take decisions by expediency. I never have done. That is why I do believe we have to try to get personal responsibility in our society. The moment people start to look to the state for everything you find that if the state does everything for you it has to take everything from you. That would be the end of personal liberty. I remember when I was just about your age being taught by my parents that we were people who didn't have to be told what to do. If we were in a tight corner we could take the initiative, because we were the sort of people who were used to using our own loaf if you like, using our own nous, because this was the way we had lived. You can't get that if you run the state in such a way that the moment a person has a problem they come to the state to solve it. You have got to have personal responsibility and personal initiative. There are certain things that only government can do – the defence of the realm, law and order and defence of the currency. Then you have a safety net; that's where your welfare state comes in.

Many of the other reports, particularly the letters to the editors, had been picked up during the week by the Senior Editor from a pigeon-hole in the Bookshop. This, I found, when I occupied that exalted position, was my greatest treat: the contents of the box were invariably surprising.

By Tuesday evening, the compositors had deciphered everything and long sheets of proofs had arrived for checking. Geoffrey Treasure was the Master-in-Charge, and we descended to a poky room in the basement of his house in the High Street for our meeting. One of my colleagues (I know who he is, but, of course, the oath of silence still holds) described the scene accurately, if rather archly, in an article we published in May 1964. Amazingly, the writer went on to have a notable career in the media:

'It is the Harrovian holy of holies, a sacred, chaste temple, impenetrable save to the editorial hierarchy. Bound volumes of fifty years ago lie haphazardly on the dusty shelves, musty proof-sheets are scattered amok on the uncarpeted floor, past copies litter the battered table. There are no curtains: there is one decrepit armchair, with horse-hair spilling out in unsightly tufts....'

With a glass of cider in one hand and a ruler in the other, we set to, measuring the columns, cutting and occasionally rewriting to make everything fit. Above all, however, we gossiped. Our excuse was that we needed to gather stories for the 'Inside Out' column, which was the nearest *The Harrovian* dared to get to Nigel Dempster or William Hickey. Little of it, of course, was publishable, and, in a thin week, 'Inside Out' usually grew out of paragraphs cut from over-length reports of the School's societies or stories culled from the education pages of the national newspapers and given an Harrovian spin. We had our modest scoops, of course. Most of them very modest: an owl that had become a pet in Newlands and the failure of the School bell to toll on Whit Monday 1964.

Late in the evening, we wandered back to our Houses, to await the arrival of the finished copies a couple of days later. Most weeks, our efforts were greeted with an indifferent silence, but, once or twice a term, we managed to stir up controversy or to include an article that got everyone talking.

Today, leafing through some of the editions of the magazine that I helped to produce, I am struck by the effort that must have gone into producing so many words each week. Though the house style is rather stilted and distant, almost every copy contains something that catches the interest: a necessarily long article about the extraordinarily large number of Old Harrovians elected to Parliament in 1964; the inside track on Harrow's first professional pop group, the Band of Angels; and obituaries of Beaks and Old Boys full of colourful detail and anecdotage that would have escaped the august writers of the broadsheets.

We did our best to vary the diet — for ourselves, it must be said, as much as for our readers — by producing thick Christmas and summer numbers, and, in the year of Shakespeare's quatercentenary, we persuaded a host of distinguished actors and writers to help us compile a tribute to Ronnie Watkins's 'Harrow Globe'.

Astonishingly, some 40 years on, the copies that I have kept have not faded, despite having lain in a rather damp box for all this time. The print is still crisp, the heavy, woven paper looks brand-new, the calendar on the front page appears oddly timeless.

Only the stories seem dated, which is as it should be. For *The Harrovian*, in its modest way, is, as I later learned, what grown-up journalists always dream of: the first, fresh draft of history.

Simon Welfare (The Grove 1960²) is an author and an independent television producer.

No easy way down – The Harrow Marmot Club, founded 1929

MARK GREENSTOCK

IF IT IS TRUE THAT ANY GOOD SCHOOL NEEDS TO provide space for alternative expression and for divergence from the mainstream of school life, then perhaps 'The Marmots' may offer a modest example of what boys can safely be allowed to get up to in a liberal society.

The Club celebrated its 75th anniversary in 2004. Started by 'Holdy' Holdsworth, a Beak who was also a member of the first team to scale a Himalayan 8000 metre peak (Kamet), the Marmots started life as a walking and downhill skiing society in days when only a few parents, and even fewer Masters, took the boys on skiing trips. It changed character after the Second World War under the leadership of Tim Warr, who encouraged parties to visit his remote and comfortably basic cottage in the western Lake District, for fell-walking and elementary rock-climbing.

In more recent years the rock-climbing element has predominated, enhanced by the building of a double climbing wall on the outside of the Sports Centre and the addition of a smaller indoor wall. It would be impossible to do justice in a short article to over a hundred Marmot expeditions between 1967 and 2001: weekend trips to the sandstone rocks of Kent, the limestone cliffs of Dorset and the Gower, and (most popular of all) regular visits to the Peak District with its superb gritstone faces; longer holiday expeditions to the granite cliffs of West Cornwall above the wild foam of winter seas, or to the hills of Snowdonia and the Lake District, the Scottish mountains and the gabbro of Skye; abroad to Norway, Corsica, and the French, Austrian and Swiss Alps; and, in an expedition lasting nearly the whole of the Christmas holidays of 1989–90, to Mt Kenya and Kilimanjaro and outlying areas of Africa and Tanzania. Potent sources of annual inspiration were visiting lecturers to Speech Room such as Don Whillans, Doug Scott, Chris Bonington, Peter Boardman and Joe Simpson, who

showed slides of their usually hair-raising exploits and met members afterwards over a glass of beer.

Two members of the Club who subsequently won fame were Tom Prentice, who became a front-rank climber and has written climbing guides as well as editing *Climber* magazine; and Tom Avery, who went on to lead expeditions to the Andes, Pamirs and Africa and in December 2002 became the youngest person ever to reach the South Pole on foot. While not originally a Marmot, Rupert 'Pen' Hadow, upon becoming the first explorer in history to walk from Canada to the North Pole alone and unsupported in May 2003, received the supreme accolade – that of being made an honorary member of the Club!

No Marmots expedition was ever typical, except perhaps in the tendency of its members to exaggerate both their own exploits on the rocks and those of the Beaks at the wheel of various long-suffering minibuses. Since this is a book of portraits, a few snapshots will have to suffice.

When doubt was expressed as to the precise location of the summit of the Fluchtkogel (3500 metres) in thick mist, 'Pigeon' Edward suggested that his compatriot 'Bernie' Rowles, whose bulk required size 13 boots, should crawl to the edge of the snow to get a better view,

while being belayed by everybody else at a safe distance. The next day was fine, enabling the horrified party to see from a neighbouring peak the huge cornice on the top of the Fluchtkogel, on the overhanging lip of which Bernie's tracks and body-impression were clearly visible.

In fact there were few really heart-stopping moments, but one of them was in Africa just after completing the ascent of the remote and difficult main peak of Batian on Mount Kenya (5199 metres); an entire rope peeled off one by one from some ice above the Gate of the Mists and were saved from a speedy descent to the plains below by our very experienced guide Andrew Wielochowski: Andy (who was a chemistry teacher at Lancing College at the time) modestly attributes this feat not to his own superhuman strength but to their collective lack of weight, none of them having eaten anything for several days thanks to the effects of altitude on the appetite.

One of the policies of the Marmots was to encourage boys of sufficient seniority and skill to rope-

lead climbs that were well within their capability: the dangers inherent in this policy do not need spelling out, but it paid off in greatly enhanced confidence and personal judgment, and many fine routes on British and French rock at 'Hard', 'Very Severe' and even 'Extreme' grades were led by boys suitably kitted out in helmet, fleece, climbing harness, rock boots and an impressive array of nuts, karabiners and slings. An exception to the equipment rule was John Meredith-Hardy who climbed in a dark-blue school overcoat held together by a single button, together with an umbrella which he managed to fix somewhere on his person: John is alive and well and recently launched his *Directory of Sporting Activities* at the Alpine Club.

Speaking of idle dogs, the member who holds the record for tardiness must be 'Oz' Stuart Lee, who would always be in his tent putting his boots on when the rest of the party had already set off, and who was memorably a whole day late starting for one holiday expedition

(Austria 1978). The current *Harrow School Register* records that Stuart Lee became a PhD student at the Scott Polar Institute, Cambridge University, so his ability to pass time doing nothing may have been put to good use in the winter darkness of Antarctica.

Over the years there have been some memorable individuals: Roddy Newman, who wrote a *Guide to Climbs on Harrow Buildings* while still at the School (the Old Knoll provides a particularly fine array of chimneys and corners); Tom Kenyon of Druries, who made himself useful by rescuing the House cat from a tree in the Elmfield garden, thus demonstrating that Marmots didn't spend their whole time nipping up and down the Old Schools or putting Monitors' bow ties and other articles on the top of the Chapel spire (a formidably vertiginous lead for whoever was bold enough to do it, quite apart from the dangers of getting caught, which they never were).

Taking into account the regular annual achievement of exceeding the height of Mount Everest from sea-level in rock-feet-per-man climbed on expeditions, it is a matter for great thankfulness that no boy was ever seriously injured on a Marmot meet, with the single exception of Charlie Blount who, having wandered off with his geology hammer while everyone else was concentrating on climbing the sea-cliffs at Portland in Dorset, managed to fall 20 feet off the Easy Way Down

and had to be scooped off a boulder-strewn beach by the local rescue team. On the Cuillin Ridge on Skye, Paul Dearden was hit by a huge rock which bounded upon him out of the mist, but he emerged grinning and unhurt from his ordeal, which was just as well as he became an outstanding cragsman: his book *Extreme Climber* is in the Vaughan Library, together with many other volumes that have been presented over the years to the Marmots.

The Marmots do not appear in Tyerman's official *A History of Harrow School*, probably justly, though they do manage to squeeze a photograph (clad in ropes and civvies) into *An Illustrated History (1986)*. If the Club didn't exist, it would need to be invented – and indeed, perhaps, it needs to be reinvented every few decades. Not only has it produced expedition leaders, climbers, pioneers, explorers and authors, but it has enabled boys to discover unexpected characteristics of Beaks they had hitherto thought were all too sane, and Beaks to experience the unique terror of being held on a rope by a boy to whom they had given a hundred double in a fit of irrational temper the week before.

'None so narrow the range of Harrow.'

Mark Greenstock was an Assistant Master from 1966–2001 and House Master of Newlands from 1985–97.

BELOW RIGHT:

Marmots in Norway, 1971: Christopher Hughes, Philip Vaughan, Tony Crofts, Nick Stuart-Lee, Norman O'Driscoll, Roddy Newman

Belonging

JOHN RAE

FROM THE POINT OF VIEW OF A YOUNG BEAK WHO left to become eventually the Head Master of a no less traditional school, what was distinctive about Harrow in the years we were there, 1955–66, was the way in which the School so quickly made us feel that we belonged. All schools have their strengths and weaknesses, their good periods and their bad, so I do not know whether this gift for inspiring loyalty and affection and a sense of belonging was always typical of Harrow, or was a reflection of the personality and style of the Head Master, Dr R.L. James, who was then at the height of powers.

I am fascinated by the way Dr James operated as Head Master of Harrow. He was the antithesis of the hands-on headmaster but while he appeared to do little except stand in front of the fire in his study, drinking tea or reading *The Times*, the School enjoyed something of a golden age when its reputation as one of the great schools was secure.

Where other headmasters want to be seen to be active, appointing committees and working groups, talking about strategy and five-year plans, writing discussion papers and haranguing the troops, Dr James was happy to be the still centre of a busy and successful school. He hated committees, especially if they wanted to discuss education, and he kept his public occasions to a minimum. If he talked to the School in Speech Room, he did so quietly and with no theatrical flourishes. To say that he was a low-profile headmaster would be an understatement.

He told me that the secret of headmastering was to appoint the best Masters and let them get on with it, but in saying that he did not do himself justice. His genius was to make a common room of different talents and temperaments work together because we were all keen to win his praise. If you had difficulties, he was always ready to see you. No one would enter his study saying, 'I know you are very busy, Head Master', because he so obviously was not, but he made himself available to his staff to an extent that was probably unique among headmasters.

He was also a master of psychology. If you went to see him with a complaint, you came out half a hour later convinced that Harrow was the best school in the world and that your complaint was unimportant. He flattered junior Masters by appearing to take them into his confidence and senior Masters by giving them the impression that he was acting on their advice. I recall being told on more than one occasion by Charles Lillingston, then House Master of Druries, that he had persuaded the Head Master to change his mind and that Dr James had confessed to him, 'You were right after all, Charles.' As a skilful manipulator of men, Dr James would have had a long and successful career at the Tudor court.

Devoting his time to making his staff feel valued instead of chasing them with new directives and initiatives, he brought the best out in them and with the help of his wife, Bobbie, he made their families, too, feel that they belonged. I sometimes had the feeling that the dinner party was the only formal gathering in which he was entirely at ease, for he knew how to use these social occasions to encourage Masters and their wives to see themselves not so much as part of a hierarchy as of a joint enterprise in which their contribution was just as important as anyone else's. Of course, none of this would have worked if he had been purely manipulative. He and Bobbie were warm and welcoming people with no hint of self-importance.

Dr James was conservative by nature as well as by political calculation. When I applied for the Head Mastership of Westminster, he wrote to say, 'If you go there, you will be very much in the grip of tradition. Personally, that sort of thing appeals to me. I hope it does to you.'

His reluctance to countenance change – one of the incidental amusements of Harrow life was to watch him

RIGHT: *The Royal Visit, 1957*

kicking proposals for reform into the long grass – no doubt made life more difficult for his successor but it preserved some of the best Harrow customs when other schools in the 1960s were throwing tradition overboard. I am thinking particularly of those customs that contributed to our sense of belonging.

Was Harrow the only public school where senior boys invited Masters and their wives to a full English breakfast before Chapel on Sunday morning? Outsiders may mock the idea of fags cooking breakfast for their Masters (in both senses of the word) but 'Finds Breakfast' had the admirable result of establishing a relaxed relationship between the senior boys in a House and Masters. In a similar way, we were made to feel that we belonged to the community by being regularly invited to House songs which was preceded by a formal dinner.

Even the simplest and, no doubt now unfashionable, customs helped to encourage the new Beak to identify with the School. There were no House Tutors in those days but John Morgan asked me to be an unofficial Tutor in Moretons. I went to lunch, coached the House rugby team and sometimes took evening prayers, after which, as was the custom, I shook every boy's hand and wished him goodnight.

One of the boys I wished goodnight was Michael, the only boy who was causing me trouble in the classroom. I had been appointed to teach mathematics to the junior forms though my degree was in history, an academic mismatch that had not worried Dr James at all when he appointed me. Under the fatherly eye of those two fine mathematicians and schoolmasters, Kenneth Snell and John Morgan, and with the help of my wife who knew her maths and taught me the next day's lesson each evening, I survived. When I went to see Dr James about the troublesome Michael, he talked about his own difficulties with some boys when he started teaching and suggested that if I had more trouble, I should send the boy to him. But I never did; just to talk it over with Dr James was enough. It was somehow typical of Harrow that the troublesome Michael should become a friend whom we saw from time to time when we had left Harrow far behind.

For a young man straight from Cambridge, Harrow under Dr James was the ideal place to learn the art and craft of schoolmastering. Harrovians of that period were

not angels or free from vice but so may boys became good friends and it is so easy to take up with them again despite the years between that I cannot help wondering why this should be. The answer, I believe, is that Dr James's Harrow gave us all such a strong sense of belonging.

John Rae PhD was an Assistant Master from 1955–66. He was Headmaster of Taunton School from 1966–70 and Head Master of Westminster School from 1970–86.

THE HARROVIAN

March 6, 1971

Bill

A sudden silence fell on the Yard as we removed our hats; the cameramen appeared retreating up the steps; and finally Her Majesty arrived. Mr Morgan, W. G. S. Massey, The Knoll, the Head of School, and Mr T. M. Wilkinson, Custos, were presented to her. Then, standing on the Old School steps with the Head Master, she witnessed Bill.

To some the capping, passing and hurrying on of this event may at times appear anachronistic. Not so on this occasion. For the tradition of Bill regained its full significance and was vested with a new life when conducted in the presence of our monarch. As Her Majesty studied the list of names and the corresponding procession of boys, we felt that she was doing more than grace the occasion with the calm and enormously impressive dignity of her person; she was, in addition, transmuting the old Harrow custom into an altogether meaningful expression of discipline and respect. Ceremony and decorum were gloriously enhanced on this proud afternoon.

We are confident that Mr Morgan felt that taking Bill that Friday was a magnificent conclusion to his career at Harrow.

Ducker

TIM BENTINCK

I FIRST HEARD THE WORDS 'BENTINCK AT HIS BEST OFF the spring board was worth going miles to see' when my father was showing me around his old school when I was deciding which one to go to in 1966. We started the tour at Ducker, and Ducker was the reason I went to Harrow. The alternative that I'd been given was Bryanston, and they only had a river. Upon such 12-year-old's decisions (I was a very fast swimmer) whole lives turn.

The quotation was from *The Harrovian* in 1899 – clearly not about my father (though he too was a fine swimmer and won the Senior Ebrington Cup three times in a row) but about my great uncle Major Henry Bentinck, who was killed at the battle of the Somme. On his last leave before he died, he spent most of it resting and swimming at Ducker. The tranquillity and peace of his time in that leafy sanctuary contrasts poignantly with the horror of his slow death in the trenches.

As you can probably guess from the name, it used to be a duck pond. Boys started swimming in it and eventually it was concreted in and changing huts for each House were built around the sides. It was 150 yards long and L-shaped, about 25 yards wide at the corner and completely surrounded by the tallest trees. Until the 1960s it was unheated, and then only a fifty-yard stretch at one end, between a footbridge and a telegraph pole. Wooden slats divided the heated from the cold water. The difference in temperature was seldom very great and early-term training was just bollock-freezingly cold – if it got above 60 degrees we were ecstatic.

When I look down now from the balcony, where my and my relations' swimming feats are recorded on panels of English oak, at the white-skinned, warm-watered, chlorine-smelling Harrovians in the oppressive heat and chemical smell of today's 'Ducker', I bemoan their loss. We were sun-kissed, water-hardened and before they built the hospital from which could be seen our cold-shrivelled willies, naked. My father told a story of how they once had a swimming gala with a school from Germany in the 1930s who were all Hitler Youth. Starkers Nazis. Quite a thought. Harrow won. Pa said that gave him hope sometimes in the war.

My best friend Noël Diacono was king of the log mill. The idea was that any number of people from two Houses fought to get a great four-foot sodden log to their side of the pool. You weren't allowed to actually hit people, although Noël did, but it was like rugby in water up to your armpits. Semi-drownings, wood splinters, concrete grazes and black eyes were common. Health and Safety hadn't been invented. I've just Googled 'drowned in a log mill' and 'drowned at Ducker' on the

internet and nothing comes up, so maybe they weren't needed then.

There was a shop, and a caretaker and a caretaker's wife. Mr and Mrs Campkin had been there when my father was a boy, which seemed to me at the time an unimaginably long time ago. They sold Ducker Biscuits and Coke which we ate walking back across the footer fields that in the summer were grazed upon by cattle, so you had to beware being shoved into the cow-pats by your friends along the way.

Campkin was also the official timekeeper for all school records and I had two years of trying to break the 50 yards freestyle. I'll never forget looking up each time I tried it to see him shake his head as if to say, 'you'll never get it boy', with a certain mean satisfaction. He wasn't actually at all malicious so I suppose it was his way of trying to spur me on, which it did — I got it eventually, 50 yards in 25 seconds dead. As far as I know that was never beaten before the place was abandoned, and I know I still held the 200 yards individual medley relay when records closed. One of the reasons I loved swimming fast

RIGHT: *'Ducks and Ducklings': relay races on Speech Day, 1971*

was because it was so bloody cold – the sooner you got to the other end, the sooner you could get out.

The Senior Ebrington was cancelled the first year I could do it, due to ice. The next year it had gained a bit of a reputation; also the morning was foggy and cold so that only two of us turned up. My opponent was Gibson of Rendalls, vice-captain of the school team. I was captain and we were the formidable freestyle duo who with Tillotson at butterfly, Baird at breaststroke and Neal at backstroke, gave Harrow an unbeaten swimming record that year. Away matches were sometimes tight, but we creamed the home fixtures. Firstly of course because of the cold – a lot of the other schools had heated pools so we, like Mill Hill who had no heating either, made sure the opposition were freezing first. Then there was the telegraph pole. As I mentioned, you dived in off a level footbridge. Fifty yards further on a wooden pole was lashed with ropes across the pool. You turned on this and swam back. Our advantage was that the pole was covered with slime, and it was almost impossible to kick off. We practised our tumble turns so that one foot landed on top of the pole, and the other found the sweet spot from which you could just maintain a grip. This gave us about a second's advantage in the race, usually quite enough.

Gibson and I agreed that we'd race the last 100, so we duly plodded up and down the pool until we turned for the last two lengths and upped the speed. At 50 we were still dead level and we went flat out for the final spurt. We touched as one and the cup was shared.

Eating biscuits, drinking Coke and avoiding cow-pats on the way back up, we agreed it would have been a hell of a lot easier to have divvied up before the race and saved the effort.

I swam the last ever length at Ducker. I felt it was only right.

Twenty years on, Noël and I returned for old times' sake and got drunk in the King's Head. We went down to Ducker, and although derelict it was not yet half filled in as it is now, but fantastically romantic and a quarter full with leafy rainwater. With my great uncle Henry in mind, I stripped off and swam the full 150 yards, while Noël messed around with a log that was still floating in the semi-stagnant water. We got out and dried ourselves with our clothes. My mother died when I was young and I've never felt her presence since, but I swear that Uncle Henry spoke to me that day, and he was happy. Either that or we'd had one beer too many.

Ducker is the place for me.

Tim Bentinck, Earl of Portland (Moretons 1966[3]) is an actor, well known for his role as David Archer in The Archers.

Long Ducker 25 years on

PEN HADOW

THIS YEAR I DID LONG DUCKER. THE LAST TIME was 4 December 1977 – the Queen's Silver Jubilee. No-one alive has done it so long ago – because 25 years ago I was the first person to have done it for 50 years! It started simply enough for me. I heard two senior boys in my House (The Park) on different occasions letting it be known to their peers and juniors that they would be doing Long Ducker before they left. They never did – and I felt strongly that to claim to be capable of doing such a thing and then not following through the claim for such a prestigious challenge was a classic case of 'talk is cheap'. I decided I would show the senior boys a thing or two on the basis that action speaks louder than words.

Most Sundays I'd set off alone, while others watched the telly, building up the number of Short Duckers I could string together. Actually I worked it up to two or three 18-milers (i.e. six consecutive Short Duckers), but ran out of time, and enthusiasm, to run further – it's a hilly route compared to Long Ducker and very dull on your own on a Sunday afternoon!

I decided to make the most of the charitable fund-raising opportunity the challenge presented – and 1977 was the year of The Queen's Silver Jubilee Appeal. I was exceptionally rigorous in my collection of pledges from fellow boys, especially if they had titles or were known by me to be well resourced. I'd position myself in strategic places like street junctions, The Hill tuck shop, outside Speech Room before functions etc and solicit whatever funds I could – generally something like 1p–5p per mile. Half a penny a mile was not uncommon and 10p a mile signings were red-letter moments. A letter, after the run, from HRH The Prince of Wales, couriered by special royal messenger in the following Christmas holidays (dated 10 January 1978), thanked me for raising the princely sum of £101.36 for Her Majesty The Queen's Silver Jubilee Appeal.

I really enjoyed the run to the Arch. I had kept a gentle, steady pace. The priority was to finish – not set a fast time. It was unknown territory. At the Arch I was joined by my friends and fellow Parkites, Alex Budworth and Simon Marsh. Half-way home I felt the strength slowly ebbing away, legs losing their spring, starting to feel wooden, disconnected from the rest of my body. My glycogen reserves in muscles and liver were depleting and inevitably the dreaded 'wall' was approaching. At the bottom of the Hill, I was having to work hard to keep a jogging pace up the steepening pavement. Alex and Simon ran on to The Park to tell all the boys, who by now were having lunch, that I had nearly made it. They leapt from lunch tables, reached for their Sunday headgear and ran down the Hill. I had reached the top of the Hill when they came hurtling round the corner towards me. It was one of those special moments. I knew I had it in the bag now. I could relax and savour the moment. I felt no pain. I was floating.

The run had taken 3 hours 47 minutes. In retrospect I like to think I could have done sub 3 hours, with more

ABOVE: *Pen Hadow ascending Sudbury Hill on the last lap of Long Ducker, 1977*

LONG DUCKER

This traditional run from Harrow-on-the-Hill to Marble Arch and back, a distance of 26 miles, was completed by R.A.P. Hadow on 4th December, 1977 in a time of 3 hrs. In honour of the attempt, the central gates of Marble Arch were opened specially for him to pass through. Long Ducker had not been run for exactly 50 years, the last time being in 1927.

training and more of a race situation, but completion was everything back then. The next day, at the regular morning assembly for the School in Speech Room, The Head Master, B.M.S. Hoban, formally announced I had completed the challenge and confirmed that The Long Ducker had not been done since 1927 – exactly 50 years before. Twenty-five years on I now run the world's only guide service to the North and South Poles – The Polar Travel Company.

Long Ducker taught me several useful lessons that I have tried to apply since. The most important of which is this. 'A ship is safe in harbour, but that's not what ships were built for.' Seek out your 'Long Ducker' and try going that extra mile to achieve it. I wish you success.

Rupert (aka 'Pen') Hadow (The Park 1975[3]) was Captain of Harrow football and rugby and Deputy Head of School in 1980. He is founding Director of The Polar Travel Company and a noted polar explorer.

Mark Tindall

Mark Tindall (Moretons 1928[1]) was Head Master of Bradbys 1960–74

In the late 1970s there had been an outbreak of graffiti (in large whitewash letters) on numerous buildings and Beaks' houses during the night. First lesson of the day was English with Mark Tindall who started with "I suppose you've all seen this stuff written all over the walls?" He then surveyed the grinning class and said in that famous gravelly voice, "Strubber," (he always had a nickname for everyone in the class) "go along to my house and see if anyone has written anything about me, and if they haven't, ruddy well write something. I don't want to be the only one left out."

As I said he had a nickname for everyone, mine being Elm. On one occasion when he noticed my absence he enquired "Where's Elm?" … "Ill, sir," came the reply … "Ruddy Dutch Elm disease I suppose."

LINDSAY ASH

Lindsay Ash (The Knoll 1973[3]) is Business Support Manager for Barclays Private Bank & Trust Limited.

A mass of contradictions

JAMES DREYFUS

LEFT:

James Dreyfus

M Y RECOLLECTIONS OF MY TIME AT HARROW, (four years in total, as I left a year early), are an intriguing mass of contradictions. On the one hand, there were a few wonderful 'Beaks' and House Masters, who had the good sense to realise that I was interested in only one thing, acting, and did their utmost to support and encourage me; for that, and to them, I shall be ceaselessly appreciative. I was not obligated to remain in Harrow's CCF, nor was I press-ganged into participating in any sport I had no interest in. Golf was the singular exception. On the other hand, although the School itself is a truly stunning place, like being forced to read Shakespeare, I did not appreciate it while I felt imprisoned there. I spent much of my time, in 'civvies' off the Hill, pursuing other interests; I kept a gerbil named Juliet in a tuck box under my bed, along with a mini black-and-white TV, which I watched well into the early hours, undisturbed. Martin Tyrrell, an English teacher and

Head of Drama, was an enormous influence on me, and encouraged my acting, but he also had a healthy anarchic streak, which appealed to me.

Because of the acting – and I appeared in approximately 20 different productions – most boys in the

LEFT: *James Poole, James Webb, Harry Robertson-MacLeod and James Cooper in* A Servant to Two Masters, *Bradbys House Play, 2004*

School knew who I was. Thankfully, I was never bullied, although the size of my nose was the source of much merriment. In Speech Room, our seven-hour-long production of *Nicholas Nickleby* was an astonishing experience, with a frantic Martin Tyrrell shrieking orders at all and sundry, and inhaling Rothmans with a ferocity that only an asthmatic finding a lost inhaler could reproduce.

Equally exciting were Jeremy Lemmon's annual Shakespeare productions; Speech Room was transformed into a replica of the now-rebuilt Globe. These epics were conducted by Mr Lemmon from his lectern, instilling in us all the beauty and thrilling nature of 'The Bard', sometimes calmly, sometimes quivering with anger. The entire room hushed as he slowly pronounced, 'Someone has taken the black cloak, who?' Silence. 'I repeat, someone has taken the black cloak, WHOOOOO?' The hassled costume lady timidly put her hand up and said, 'It needed darning, Jeremy.' He slowly turned back to his lectern, smoothed his parting to one side, and began giving me a lecture on how Hamlet 'WASN'T some yob', and would I 'pull my breeches up and do the speech PROPERLY!'

The Music Schools doubled as a more intimate space and the Drama Studio, which was built at the end of my second year, allowed for more experimental works and rather risqué poetry evenings.

A brief word about the, ahem, straw hats and the tails on Sunday: personally, I couldn't abide them. But, if a school, an advantaged school, chooses to retain the archaic dress code of years gone by, a dress code that signals superiority and wealth, no less, and that school happens to be in the middle of a public thoroughfare, surrounded by other less well disposed and less well-off educational institutions, it can and did lead to problems. With privilege comes responsibility, and one must take that responsibility seriously; hopefully the School has now learnt that particular, rather obvious, lesson. (The glazed exterior of the hats, by the by, make extremely effective Frisbees, if thrown with accuracy; so it is useful to keep one handy in a plastic bag or something.)

I spent many hours in the magnificent Library, usually reading, and rereading the naughty bits from Gore Vidal's *Myra Breckinridge*. For a while I was a bass in the choir, and loved hearing various music scholars bashing out Widor's *Toccata* or the Nyman-esque riffs from Purcell on the mighty Chapel organ. The antique muskiness of the Old Schools, the Butler Museum, the War Memorial Building and finally, the triumphant and unforgettable Speech Room; all are entrenched in my memory for one reason or another.

BELOW: *Tom Micklem and Louise Goldstein in* Me and My Girl, *1999*

BELOW RIGHT: *Martin Tyrrell, Head of Drama from 1983*

LEFT: *Rob Micklem, Nick Horton and James Lea in* Arsenic and Old Lace

My House, The Head Master's, was like a Harry Potter maze: concrete steps, winding wooden corridors, endless doorways and nooks. I rather liked it. It was infinitely preferable to the Barratt Home look of new buildings: characterless rooms, flickering tube lighting that give you constant headaches, and breeze block upon breeze block, painted institutional lime green, which last about a year before they crack. Oh, the eternal monotony of those bleak cloned edifices! So, the squeaking warren I lived in gave my soul colour and spirit. Whereas most boys chose to adorn their walls with posters of tennis girls scratching their bottoms to reveal no underwear – ahh, the genius of Athena posters! – Santana album covers, tie-dye cloths pinned above beds, traffic cones and flashing road lamps hanging everywhere, I chose to hang my own appalling artwork merely to irritate and offend visitors, as the 'paintings' were incomprehensible, pretentious and gratingly amateur. They were eventually stolen. Coveted or burnt? I shall never know. I suspect the latter.

And there you have it; my memories of that eccentric establishment on top of a hill: perhaps one of the most famous schools in the world, which I experienced, and where I lived and learned for four years. I chose to take my A levels at a dodgy college in Holborn, and THAT was when real life began.

On a final note, I never believed that 'my eyes would fill at the thought of the Hill', but it happened, once, about fifteen years later. I took a friend to pay a visit one gloomy winter's afternoon. After a few hours of rambling, my friend noticed me rubbing my eyes:

'Are you ok?'

'Yes,' I replied, wiping my cheeks. 'It's this bloody freezing wind … it's making my eyes water.'

We wandered on, and as we passed familiar sights and smells from many years ago, I secretly acknowledged to myself that I had just told a lie.

James Dreyfus (The Head Master's 1982³) is an actor. He has won an Olivier Award for Lady in the Dark *at the RNT and an Ian Charleson Award for classical acting as Cassius in* Julius Caesar *as well as the Top Comedy Award for BBC TV's* The Thin Blue Line.

Harrow Rugby

DAMIAN HOPLEY

MY FIRST INTRODUCTION TO RUGBY AS A Harrovian came in the late summer of 1986, when my older brother Rupert and I, having come to Harrow in our mid-teens, joined our new school-mates on a pre-season training camp to Roger Uttley's home patch of Kielder Water in the beautiful surroundings of Northumbria.

The School had an excellent rugby reputation, and had gone undefeated in 1985 – a feat not to be repeated until the 2002/03 season. Some of that success in part had been down to a tremendous pack of forwards, and a certain Canadian by the name of Gareth Rees, who

went on to become one of the most recognisable figures in world rugby. One of the great Corinthians in the sport, Gareth was a prodigious kicker of the ball, but also has a tremendous rugby brain and went on to make a considerable impact with all the teams he played for, both on and off the pitch. Having arrived on the Hill with a reasonable rugby reputation of our own, there was a lot of pressure on the two new boys to fill the considerable boots (and shorts) of 'Reesy'.

Inevitably, we were tentative about making our first foray into the closed ranks of such a tight-knit School community. But as is so often the case in sport, our worst

fears were allayed when we met up with some extremely colourful characters who couldn't have been more welcoming. Our introduction to life at Harrow was helped enormously by the fellowship of the rugby team, which made our integration into the School far easier. The pre-season training was going well – there were some outstanding athletes and natural rugby players in the group, and the competition was fierce as everyone set out to impress. Add to this the excellent tutelage and experience of 'Big Rog', and it was clear to see this was a team that had tremendous potential.

What I hadn't been prepared for was the mischievous element in Harrovians. Being stranded in the middle of a training camp, hundreds of miles away from the glamour of the Kings Road, it was inevitable that all would not run according to plan. Roger treated the squad like the mature young men he hoped we were and permitted a modicum of drink to help break up the boredom and fatigue after a full day's training.

The ice was well broken as a few of the boys decided to explore the camp, and see what trouble they could find. Being a team man, I felt obliged to join them, and enter into the spirit. Two broken windows later the guard dogs were barking ferociously as the searchlights came on. Instantly, we knew that if we were caught out of our rooms, all hell would break loose, so being the new boy

I did the right thing and disappeared as quickly as I could through an open window into the room I was sharing with the Ist XV Captain, Gavin Hughes. Quick as a flash I dived into bed, ruffled up my hair, threw the duvet over me, and played dead. Within seconds RMU had appeared in the room to catch Gavin clambering through the window, and proceeded to read our skipper the riot act about setting standards for the team.

I was extremely honoured to be appointed captain of the School XV in my final year, and we had a team that promised great things. We were fortunate to have some outstanding players in the team. Our South African duo of Chris Keey and Peter Gordon, had joined the School in the previous Lent Term and both had a tremendous impact on the style of rugby we played. Peter was a complete footballer with an electrifying turn of speed, while Chris reinvented himself as an open side flanker, blending his outstanding creative skills with his fearless approach to defence. In so doing he became the terror of schoolboy fly-halves throughout the land (and dare I say a few other folk since then.) Add to that our 6 foot 7 inch goal-kicking lock, Alex Snow – who later went on to play professional rugby for Harlequins – and it was inevitable we would be one of the teams to beat on the schools circuit that year.

LEFT: *The all-victorious Rugby XV of 2002*

LEFT: *First XV v Radley, 1998*

After a successful season, where Wellington were the only team to spoil our otherwise unbeaten record, I was fortunate enough to be selected for the England Schools team of 1988, which went on a very successful tour of Australia, beating both New Zealand and the host team. Of that team, five of us went on to be capped by England at full test level, including the 2003 Rugby World Cup-winning Captain, Martin Johnson.

I was always convinced I had the talent to play for England, and in hindsight I know that my time at Harrow gave me the confidence in my own ability. I am extremely privileged to have played with some outstanding individuals and household names during my time at Wasps and with England and realise just how blessed I have been. However, I still cherish my rugby experiences at Harrow as some of the great days, playing alongside so many good friends. Unfortunately my professional career was ended in 1997, aged 27, when, after six knee operations, the surgeons couldn't put me back together again.

My father maintains that schoolboy rugby is the purest form of the sport, and it is very important that the School continues to produce first-class players, and uphold its strong rugby traditions. Only last year I returned with my parents to watch the unbeaten School XV defeat Merchant Taylors'. I was pleased to see that time had not caught up with the Hill – the same Masters were still pacing up and down the touchline blissfully unaware that nowadays it is no longer three points for a try, whilst proud parents watched their sons put on an outstanding display and there was the ever present RMU offering his inimitable advice.

My rugby career has taken me all over the world playing in front of capacity crowds from Twickenham to Sydney, but without the support of my family, and the encouragement of my team mates and coaches at Harrow, starting out on that road would not have been possible. For that reason alone the Sixth Form Ground will always hold some of the best rugby memories for me.

Damian Hopley (The Head Master's 1986) was a member of the England rugby squad from 1991 to 1996, and a member of the Rugby World Cup winning 7's team in 1993. He was forced to retire from professional rugby after a series of knee injuries in 1997 and went on to found the Professional Rugby Players Association, where he is still Chief Executive.

Diary of a director

TOM NOAD

Wednesday, 9 September 1998
Dress Rehearsal (supposedly) for *The Winslow Boy*. Six weeks of preparations and four weeks of rehearsal (in its 'loosest' sense) have come to some sort of conclusion. I can't help feeling nervous. The play opens tomorrow night, to a house which, not surprisingly, looks set to be full. The set is fine but for the fact that the set decorator has decided for his own bizarre reasons to paint the doors of an otherwise superbly replicated Edwardian drawing room a gaudy, almost fluorescent, green. One or two nicknacks still to find. However, Peter [O'Toole] announced yesterday that he can't make it to the Dress

RIGHT: *Ed Lyon, Peter O'Toole, Kate Chalkley, John D. Collins in* The Winslow Boy, *1998*

Rehearsal!!!! What would David Lean have done? Peter has regaled us nightly after rehearsals in the pub with some very amusing anecdotes – eat your heart out, Parkinson – but I don't recall any which included '… and then I told the director that I wouldn't be at the "dress"! Ha! Ha!' or what the outcome of such a bombshell might have been. I suggested moving the 'dress' to tomorrow afternoon, before the first performance, which would be convenient for technical reasons anyway, but he feels he is too old to cope with two shows in a day.

So! The upshot is that we will do the 'dress' tomorrow. Sent everyone else home for an early night – without Sir Robert Morton. Could make for quite an interesting play in its own right … Ronnie Winslow exonerated with the help of an unannounced, unseen, mysterious *deus ex machina*. Perhaps we could include some green thunderflashes … hmm … John [*D. Collins, playing Arthur*] says that's the biz and just get on with it. We'll see … Otherwise this has been a totally delightful experience. The cast has worked very hard, no doubt buoyed by having a genuine intergalactic supernova star in its ranks – one who has not only shown what it is to be an utterly magnetic and brilliant actor, but who is the ideal of a dedicated, generous professional, without a scintilla of the disheartening attitude one reads and hears about other 'stars'. The School, and especially those at the Ryan Theatre, have been especially generous in their support of, let's face it, the whim of a gap year student to put on a play, even going so far as to write me a virtually blank cheque to fund it. It does drive home to me quite what an asset the Ryan has proved to be and makes me wonder what I would have done in the last three years of my time at Harrow without it! I certainly would not have had the guts to attempt something (as foolish?) as putting on this play unless I had the experience of acting in the theatre and familiarising myself with the arts of acting, directing etc.

Sunday, 13 September 1998
The Winslow Boy was a tremendous success. Peter O'Toole may have missed the 'dress', but he was as sharp as a needle on each of the three nights.

Post script: I returned two years later to direct *The Importance of Being Earnest* and in September 2003 to act in Ayckbourn's *Taking Steps*, which leads me again to ponder the legacy of Harrow in my life and the continuing generosity it shows me as an OH. But I really should not ponder; it speaks for itself.

Tom Noad (Druries 1992[3]) has directed a number of Rattigan Society and OH Players productions. He read Classics at Corpus Christi College, Cambridge and has been at RADA since 2003.

Sir Terence Rattigan CBE

Terence Rattigan (The Park 1925[2]). Extracted from the Obituary in The Times, *Thursday, 1 December 1977*

Sir Terence Rattigan, CBE, the dramatist, died yesterday in Bermuda after a long illness. He was 66.

He must rank with Sir Noel Coward as one of the leaders of the twentieth-century stage in what has come to be known as the Theatre of Entertainment. It can be a misleading label; frequently Rattigan worked in depth. But it is true that, without venturing into what he regarded as unprofitable minority experiment, he wrote some of the most enduring narrative plays of his period, designed for a 'commercial' theatre and using traditional techniques Pinero and Henry Arthur Jones would have recognized.

From *French Without Tears* (1936) to his last work for the stage, Rattigan was unashamedly a West End writer, an absorbed craftsman with a wit that reflected his own friendly, generous nature. It was a pity, no doubt, that he invented, as a symbolic playgoer, the well-to-do, middle-class 'Aunt Edna' whose tastes, he said, deserved as much attention as those of the avant-garde. Her name slipped into a catchphrase. Rattigan's opponents, at an hour of theatrical rebellion, took every chance to belittle a probing storyteller.

Born on 10 June, 1911, son of William Frank Rattigan, a diplomatist, who served as Acting High Commissioner in Turkey and British Minister in Romania, Terence Mervyn Rattigan won a scholarship to Harrow and went on, as a history scholar, to Trinity College, Oxford. His earliest play, *First Episode*, with Philip Helmann, was transient, but two years later he appeared as the author of *French Without Tears* which had over a thousand London performances.

The second play, also set in wartime, was a brisk farce. Rattigan proceeded (1944) to a competent comedy, *Love in Idleness* (in New York, *O Mistress Mine*) which he wrote for Alfred Lunt and Lynn Fontanne. *The Winslow Boy* (1946) was much more than simply competent, either as play or film. Inspired by the Archer Shee case of 1908 in which, after much legal and parliamentary conflict, a young naval cadet was vindicated of a charge of petty theft (a five-shilling postal order), Rattigan produced a strong, dramatic plea, a petition of right, for the liberty of the individual.

Resolved not to repeat himself, he turned in 1948 to a double programme: *The Browning Version*, a study, grimly compressed, of a failure in work and life (a schoolmaster, grey, weary, unlovable, and soured by a bitter marriage), and a flippant, superficial romp, *Harlequinade*, about a Shakespeare rehearsal in a Midland theatre.

Besides writing fluently at times for television, Rattigan was the author of nearly thirty film scripts – nine from his own work, as well as such celebrated films of their periods as *The Way to the Stars* and *The Yellow Rolls-Royce*. Always he was a superb technician. It is irrelevant now to insist on the acrimonious and arid debate over 'Aunt Edna' from Kensington. As a critic said, rebels were themselves ruled by an equally demanding symbolic figure, Aunt Edna from Hoxton. It is better to let both abstractions fade into the haze.

Harrow: my first impressions

BEN KERRY

RIGHT: *Barnaby Lenon, Head Master, addressing New Boys in the Fourth Form Room*

2 September 2003. Day 1:
My first day at Harrow! Last night, I started the biggest adventure of my life so far. Three years of prep school had built up to this day! I had mixed feelings about starting at Harrow. I was excited – I had heard from people what Harrow was like, I had visited the School before, and I couldn't wait to start – but I was also nervous – what if it wasn't all I had thought it would be? What if I found it hard to settle in? The thoughts swirled around my mind throughout the entire journey to Harrow.

When we arrived, I was met outside my House by my shepherd, and after unpacking all my belongings, saying goodbye to my parents and eating supper, the tour of Harrow began. Walking amongst the old buildings, I tried my best to take in all the names of the classrooms, games pitches and buildings, but it was so vast and overpowering. As I looked up at the Chapel, Speech Room, the Old Schools and finally back to my House, I found it very hard to believe, although I welcomed the thought, that this was to be my home for the next five years.

6 September 2003. Day 5:
Almost a week into my Harrow career and I faced a weekend full of activity. I rushed to my lessons with little time to think in between. I have now learnt my way around the School, and it is surprising how much more friendly everything seems when you know how to find everything, and almost every face in the High Street is a friend or Beak. Almost the entire school turned out to surround the beautifully groomed pitch to support the School's first team in their first game of the season. After a little while, I realised just how brilliant this event was. The atmosphere was incredible. Harrow chants and songs filled the air. The crowd gradually grew as players and spectators from other games moved over towards the Sixth Form Ground. In the last five minutes, the

atmosphere and support was like nothing I had ever experienced. I could not wait to pull on the Harrow shirt and represent the School in some way or another. I could not wait.

14 September 2003. Day 13:
The days and weeks have flown by like a breeze. The long days filled with lessons, Chapel, meals, play rehearsals, rugby sessions and music lessons etc, passed so quickly. It is unbelievable that I have been here for two weeks already. And yet on the other hand, it seems as though I have known the School for years. I know the lay-out of the School like the back of my hand. There is still a lot to learn though. My new-boy's test looms in a week's time.

Rushing to and from lessons, my head is filled with so much information. There is no time to think. In the evenings, I find five minutes when I do nothing. I just think. Two weeks ago, this seemed like the biggest, scariest thing of my life. The alien buildings loomed down on me from all around me. But now, after just thirteen days, this feels like home. I feel comfortable here. I spent years looking at the School in awe, as someone else's adventure; a distant, unreachable life. But now, the experience is mine. I can live these dreams. I am a Harrovian.

Ben Kerry (Rendalls 2003³) is an Entrance Scholar from Lockers Park, Hemel Hempstead.

THE HARROVIAN

7 June 2003

Iraq War
Letter from the Front Line

Not all Harrovians in Iraq were regular officers. The following letter has come into our hands and
is reproduced with permission.

The war is now thankfully over and we have begun 'phase 4' or force protection as it is known. Currently I am in a small village in Iraq where the Tigris and Euphrates meet (the Garden of Eden in the Bible) carrying out patrols in vehicles and on foot, as well as guarding key installations in the town (hospital, fire station etc.) The looting has now finished, although to be honest, there is not much left to loot. The poverty here is shocking; there is no clean water, no sanitation and the place stinks of faeces. It is so horrendous that I can't bring myself to take photos. I meet people daily who have been tortured by Sadaam and his regime: people with cut off fingers and scars across their throats. As we talk to people we are made to feel extremely welcome. They are so glad we're here and the children pester us all day. It is still very active on the arms front and we confiscate weapons daily. At night we can hear gun shots on the other side of the street but unless they attack us we leave them alone. The country now has a much better future with our help. We've made it clear to them our intention is to assist them back onto their feet but not to run the country. With 10% of the world's oil reserves, this could be the Switzerland of the Middle East.

So what's it like out here? To be honest, pretty unbearable. The first six weeks were spent in open desert living out of our vehicles. We've not seen fresh food for over a month so our rations get boring pretty quickly. Water is such a precious commodity that we wash in mess tins and then launder our clothes in the remains. It was well over two weeks before our first shower and even that was recycled. The thought of putting on clean clothes … Naturally we are seriously short of kit – no desert combats, boots and body armour plates (bloody essential when being shot at!). There was not even any oil until three weeks in theatre. Try maintaining a fleet of 48 vehicles without oil.

We spent the first month training in the UK, which was followed by two weeks' intensive brush-up here. As we are prepared for nuclear, biological and chemical contamination we dress up in lots of rubber – frequently. When the war started this came in very handy as we received several sudden gas warnings per day. We were often masked up and under cover for hours. On day two we moved into Iraq and headed for one of the main gas/oil separation plants where we sat and waited. We were mightily relieved never having to carry out our training as serious casualties would have been sustained. We have, however, found the chemical munitions, which were stored in their masses.

Being attached to 16 Assault Brigade, we were a divisional asset and therefore looked after considerably better than many units. My crew and I get on extremely well and we've kept each other going through the harder times. Mail is more important to a soldier than food and ammunition and luckily everyone back home has been wonderfully supportive. At times we received nothing for weeks and this undoubtedly took its toll on morale. Even now the system is not working properly.

I was amazed at the graphic detail the public has been exposed to. In many ways it has helped but I'm not sure all the bloodshed was for civilian eyes. The Iraqis shocked America with their level of resistance as plans had always revolved around an instant defeat. The weather is now baking – in the mid-40s during the day. We probably drink six bottles of water per day just to keep hydrated. When we first arrived the nights were bitterly cold and even with our clothes on we froze. Now we sweat even at night. Next holiday – Iceland or anywhere cold!

Now I can't wait to get back to work as I've missed it enormously. You don't get quite the same mental stimulation here. I've not run in over two months and I can't wait to get around Hyde Park again. Out here when we're not working we rest and sleep. Some days we can work for 18 hours and there is little time even to write letters.

I will tell you all the war stories when I get back and may even offer to present something to The Harrow Rifle Corps. After all, it was my days there which made me join the TA later on. What you go through there is excellent training for the real thing.

From 25138133 Tpr Edward Bowen, Newlands, 1991[3], MPDS Troop, G Squadron, Joint NBC Regiment, Iraq.

The ancient river flowing

JEREMY GREENSTOCK

FOR A BOY AT HARROW, IT IS SCARCELY CONCEIVABLE to acknowledge that there can be life after Forty Years On. But time, the ancient river flowing, forces me to confess that it is now 41 years almost to the day since I played host, as Head of School, to Sir Winston Churchill. He paid his last visit to Harrow Songs in November 1961, aged just short of 87. He was frail, stooped and slow-moving. But his pleasure at being back in Speech Room for Songs radiated through the assembled company. And our reciprocal delight and awe that he was ours for a day seemed to communicate back to him on the stage.

He sang intermittently, perhaps because of failing memory or sight, but perhaps also because he enjoyed the chance to gaze reflectively into the massed faces in front of him, casting himself back seventy years or more to a Harrow experience of which he was always wise enough to remember only the good parts.

He did not make a speech, but very evidently enjoyed the journey back to one of his principal boyhood inspirations. Afterwards at a reception in the Head Master's drawing-room, Churchill parked himself in an arm-chair in front of the hearth and gathered the boys around him. Masters and other adults were kept at bay. Even the Head Master was left to his idiosyncratic habit of placing new coals on the fire and licking the coal-dust off his fingers. Since Sir Winston's voice was low and his hearing almost gone, I knelt beside the chair and acted as interpreter, ear to mouth and mouth to ear, of a conversation which traced questions and answers in both directions and touched, with some humour, on the rigours of academic work, on his painting, on the future of Harrow and other things long since forgotten. Then he quickly tired, maybe even fell asleep for a while, enclosed and comfortable in a place of pleasant memory and peace.

The inspiration lingers on of such a personal contact with the figure not so long ago chosen by popular vote as the greatest in English history. That he should belong to Harrow, as Harrow belonged to him, touches us all.

Sir Winston would have been at ease with globalisation. Our abiding image of him remains one of the British bulldog standing alone in defence of his country, against the odds. Yet his fundamental legacy is one of collectivism: nation states united for freedom, democracy and the rights of the law-abiding individual. He would have approved of the global web, so long as the gap between the 'haves' and the 'have-nots' was not too wide. The modern world is in danger of ignoring that message. Almost half the people on the planet are trying to live on an income of two dollars a day or less, three billion people living on the same as 50 million Americans. The Island of Manhattan consumes more energy from non-renewable resources than the whole of India; and possesses more telephones than the whole of Africa. Disease is taking a monstrous toll of the poorest societies: life expectancy in several Southern African countries, which might have exceeded 70 years without HIV/AIDS, will within the next decade amount to less than 40 years.

The growing tragedy of this inequality, with all its loaded implications of resentment, polarisation, economic migration and political conflict, has to be addressed collectively.

I worked as Britain's representative at the United Nations. You may not know that Sir Winston played a part in naming the UN. Staying at the White House over Christmas 1941, just after America had entered the War, he and Roosevelt one day discussed the founding of a new institution for global peace; the Associated Powers, they called it. Over a late glass of scotch however they together decided that the new organisation should be called the United Nations.

The UN, in a globalising world, is the only global institution, the place *par excellence* for strife without anger and art without malice: a unique, compelling and in many ways flawed institution. Without it, we would not have the rules and standards that underline everything international: every flight we take, letter we post, ship we sail in, message we send, relies on UN-based systems.

The United Nations is not a separate and higher authority than national governments. It is a forum of 191 member states, which only reach important decisions between them by attempting to create consensus. The highest level of political decision-making in the world remains the national level. You cannot, in your own country, be subjected to any law or regulation from outside, including from the United Nations, if your own Parliament has not itself accepted it.

So far, fine. A world of distinct political and cultural identities seems a sensible arrangement. But there is a snag. At the United Nations, when these 191 governments meet, there is no leader, no hierarchy, no party organisation or discipline; only pure sovereign equality. It is as if the Head Master, Assistant Masters and Sixth Form at Harrow were all, as individuals, equal in authority: one vote and one voice each, regardless of age, experience or wisdom. Interesting, but chaotic: even, given Harrow's reputation for individual expression, anarchical. Now, you can see that the youngest and weakest individual in such a group has a much stronger interest in it than the most powerful. The newest member of the Sixth Form would be delighted to have an equal say with the Head Master, whose interest would be correspondingly slim. But at the United Nations, the United States and Tonga have equal status in the General Assembly, taking no account of the fact that the gross

national product of the United States exceeds that of Tonga by a factor of 10,000.

To a certain extent this may not matter very much. The world's business plays itself out on many other stages than the UN. But for a collective programme to address what is going wrong in the world, there has to be leadership of it.

Traditional leaders, not least the United States, the great power of this age, appear not yet to have taken on board that the world is changing fast. There is a third dimension, beyond economic and military strength, in an increasingly open and democratic international structure: that of the power of free choice. A thousand myriads of individual decisions can, if they flow in a similar direction, create an irresistible torrent; or if they interact haphazardly, represent a maelstrom of disorder.

The resolution of the problems of globalisation comes back to effective leadership. Imagine a pack of trained huskies pulling a sled across the ice. The team is strung out one behind the other. For all but the leader, the view ahead is similar and, shall we say, graphically symbolic of their required loyalty. Only the leader is in a position to have a clear view ahead and he understands his responsibilities, with an idea also of the lateral dangers.

Perhaps it is no longer enough to have the traditional team structure of national governments as the building-block of global politics. There has to be a broader, collective constituency demanding attention for the environment, human rights, poverty reduction and cultural tolerance. There has to be an input from far-sighted and imaginative leadership.

That is why Harrovians, as potential members of the elite of the next generation, must think of themselves as global citizens just as much as national subjects, and call for – or provide – leadership. Look ahead, and sideways, at the circumstances of your future environment. Imagine what is needed to shape it, as Churchill did at the end of the Second World War.

Doers and dreamers, dream and do.

Sir Jeremy Greenstock GCMG *(The Grove 1956³) was British Ambassador to the United Nations from 1998–2003 and then the UK's Special Representative for Iraq until March 2004. Some of the above is taken from a speech delivered by Sir Jeremy at Churchill Songs 2002.*

ABOVE: *Sir Jeremy Greenstock, Guest of Honour, at Churchill Songs, 2002*

Harrow and politics

ROBIN BUTLER

D URING MY TIME AS A SCHOOLBOY AND AS A
Governor, it has not seemed to me that Harrow
is a very political school. Perhaps it never has
been. In his *A History of Harrow School* Christopher
Tyerman quotes G.M. Trevelyan as saying towards the
end of the nineteenth century 'in a school of 600 boys
I have just two people capable of talking sensibly about
politics … I might just as well talk Greek politics to the
rest'.

His comment had a special relevance to my time. My
contemporary and fellow Harrow classicist Costa Carras
had a precocious knowledge of, and passionate interest
in, not only Greek politics but British, American and
general world politics. He would have certainly qualified
as one of G.M. Trevelyan's two in 600. Yet the great
majority of us, myself included – perhaps, I am now
ashamed to confess, myself in the van – regarded this
passion as freakish. The problems of a dangerous world
– the antagonism of East and West, the development of
the nuclear bomb – left us cold in our boyhood
complacency. These matters had always been contained by
the effortless superiority of the British. When Costa Carras
was grieving desperately for the death of the Greek
statesman, Papagos, the rest of us mocked him by donning
black armbands and chanting in ironic sympathy '*papagos
apathane*' – 'Papagos is dead' – without having the slightest
knowledge of who Papagos was and what he stood for.
I have shuddered with shame at this recollection many
times and I hope that this is some consolation to Costa.

We did not even have the excuse of being remote
from great men. Churchill himself visited the School
once a year. We cheered him to the rafters for his
leadership in the Second World War of which my
generation had chaildish memories – of fathers absent
abroad, of mothers making the most of rations which
today would have been regarded as threatening starvation,
and – in my generation – of the glorious end of rationing

as our allowance would provide. But I doubt whether
many of us could have given an account of Winston
Churchill's current cares and concerns in the 1950s.

Other leading figures came regularly to the '27 Club
– invariably Conservatives. Members of the Labour Party,
although many of them were public school educated (at
places of pretentious intellectualism like Winchester),
were rarely invited. The Debating Society flourished and
I remember meetings on Saturday nights in the Old
Harrovian Room: perhaps this may seem like a mark in
our favour because I guess that Harrovians of today
would think of better things to do on Saturday evenings
than attend school debating societies. We did not have
such a wide choice of entertainments or so many exeats.
But the topics for debate were generally frivolous and,
even when they were not, speeches were not well
informed. We did not have mock elections because
nobody could have been found to make any sort of case

for the Labour Party. We did not use the word 'cool' but, if we had, we would have said that politics was not cool. Perhaps the majority of Harrovians would say that today, although my reading of *The Harrovian* suggests that there are more serious attempts to address current political issues these days.

Yet even in a Harrovian as philistine and complacent as I was, something rubbed off. Even the most ignorant of us were aware, even if only from School Songs or reading the names carved on the walls of the Fourth Form Room, that Harrow had produced two of the greatest Prime Ministers of the nineteenth century as well as the greatest of the twentieth. In my case, if I were to say what touched my otherwise frivolous soul, it was the Shaftesbury tablet. It would be an absurd exaggeration to say that the tablet had the same effect on me as the pauper's funeral had on Shaftesbury in directing his footsteps to the public service. But I stood on Church Hill and saw in my mind's eye the group of careless and irreverent pallbearers, performing a job about which they did not care about for someone who did not matter, having refreshed themselves liberally at one of the alehouses of the Hill, careless of the dignity to which the poorest of us is entitled in death. And the rhythm of the words on the tablet fixed itself in my mind and has stayed there ever since. Perhaps this was a seed which fell on the stony ground of my adolescent heart as perhaps it – or something similar – has on that of other Harrovians. It must be one of the comforts of being a schoolmaster that, contrary to all appearances, seeds are planted which bear fruit in unexpected ways, often many years later. In my case, by the time I left Harrow, the seed of public service had been planted in me.

My Harrovian past interacted with my subsequent career in Government in only tangential ways, and when it did it had its comic aspects. When I was inherited by Harold Wilson as a private secretary left behind by Ted Heath after the bitter Election of 1974, one of the things which provided the first strands of a relationship between us was that we could both sing *Forty Years On* from memory – it had also been Harold Wilson's School Song. It was of some value to me when I became private secretary to Margaret Thatcher (a Harrow parent) in 1982 that I had originally encountered Denis Thatcher as a London Society referee when he came to referee matches

on the Sixth Form Ground. He regarded a back-row forward as someone likely to be made of the right stuff even if liable to take liberties with the rules.

One moment struck me as richly comic. Shortly after John Major became Prime Minister, it fell to me to travel with him to Washington for his first meeting with President Bush, a week after John Major had declared his aspiration for a classless society. Mr Major's other principal adviser on that journey was Sir Antony Acland, then British Ambassador in Washington whose appointment as the future Provost of Eton had recently been announced. I was by then Chairman of the Governors of Harrow and it occurred to me to ask John Major whether he was concerned that the press would spot some inconsistency between his commitment to a classless society and the fact that he was flanked by the Chairman of the Governors of Harrow and the about-to-be Provost of Eton. Mr Major was shaken for a moment and then he said: 'Don't worry: the press are not smart enough to put two and two together' – and they didn't.

However – and this was the only serious interaction between my association with Harrow and my Government career – with the real prospect that Labour would be elected in the 1992 Election and with the threat to the charitable status of public schools still not entirely removed from their agenda, I concluded that the combined status of Secretary of the Cabinet and Chairman of the Harrow Governors might be embarrassing for the Government, Harrow and me. And so, a year before the 1992 Election, I retired from the Harrow Governors. In the event, the Conservatives won the 1992 Election. Even so, I think that the difficulty would have been one of appearances rather than reality.

That brings me to the final point I want to make about Harrow and politics today. Like many others I have asked myself why it is that – deplorably – for the first time since 1720, there is no Old Harrovian member of the House of Commons. Is this because of something which has happened to Harrow or because of something which has happened to politics?

In one sense it is something which has happened to politics, in that the anti-Conservative swing of 1997 removed the last of the Harrovian MPs for the House of Commons. But Harrovian MPs had for some years been

a dwindling band. Now there are two MPs who are former Harrow Beaks, but no pupils.

In a wider sense, however, I think that this says more about the current state of British public life than about the School. I suspect that Harrovians of today are neither much more nor less conscious of public affairs than they have been in the past. What has happened is that Parliamentary service as both a duty and an honour has diminished. The fashion is to treat Parliamentarians as people on the make whom we set up and then enjoy knocking down. On the basis of my knowledge, this is a huge misjudgement in the case of the vast majority of MPs. But it is the fashion and it is not surprising if the talented young people of today's generation are put off by a career which never brought much in terms of

financial reward and now brings precious little public esteem.

I believe this fashion will pass. Sadly it will probably pass when our nation faces more difficult times and the decisions taken by Government matter more for all of us. Then we will no longer be able to afford to treat our politicians as if they were Aunt Sallies in the fairground. At that time, if I am right in believing that the flame of the public service tradition still burns at Harrow, we will again see Harrovians prominent in Parliament.

Lord Butler of Brockwell KG GCB CVO (Druries 1951[3]) was Cabinet Secretary and Head of the Home Civil Service from 1988–98. He is currently Master of University College, Oxford and a Member of Her Majesty's Privy Council. He was a Governor from 1975–91.

International Links

We are a school with strong international links. Perhaps this was always true – longstanding connections with ruling families of Jordan, India, Malaysia and Thailand suggest so. Of 800 pupils at Harrow about 80 live abroad; they come from many different countries but include Hong Kong, mainland China, Malaysia, the USA, Germany and Spain.

Every year we take expeditions from the School to many parts of the world. Very recently these have included rugby tours of South Africa and Japan, cricketers going to Malta and South Africa, soccer players to China and Japan, biologists in Nepal and Namibia, climbing in Tanzania and Peru, linguists to Germany, France and Spain, musical tours of Malaysia, the Czech Republic, Italy and Hungary.

We have a successful sister school in Thailand – Harrow International. Set up as a franchise operation by Harrow Governors, the current school was built in 2003 and is one of the leading English-system schools in Asia. Two Harrow Governors inspect the school every term and we send both retired Masters and boys taking gap years to work there.

Harrow supports Mvumi School in Tanzania – a co-educational boarding school which is desperately short of funds. In 2003

Harrow pupils ran the Long Ducker race from the School to Marble Arch and back to raise over £30,000 for Mvumi.

Every July and August a thousand children come to stay at Harrow from all over the world, mostly to learn English. Through the

development of these summer holiday courses we have built up strong links with schools in many other countries, especially Japan. Many thousands of boys and girls in all parts of the globe have now had a taste of education at Harrow.

BARNABY LENON

Students at Harrow International School, Bangkok

More than
potsherds

GERALD CADOGAN

'**M**Y STRENGTH IS DRIED UP LIKE A POTSHERD', sang the psalmist. Archaeologists, however, smile in irony at his lament. Potsherds for us are like food and drink – vital evidence to tell the story of how the ancients lived, worked and traded, and where we can situate them on the time-charts of history. Besides sherds, we also need settlements and cemeteries, bones and seeds, and works of art and written texts, to form a whole picture of the past. For over two centuries a small but impressive Harrow corps of archaeologists and near-archaeologists has excavated, studied, described and deciphered such evidence. From Bengal to Yorkshire, via the Nile and the Aegean, Harrow's contribution to archaeology is a story principally of pioneers.

RIGHT:

*Sir John Gardner
Wilkinson, 'a
father of British
Egyptology'*

Pioneer number one is Sir William Jones (1746–94), nicknamed 'Oriental Jones', who after a slow start – arriving at Harrow when he was seven but staying ten years – became the prodigy of the School, and may well rank as Harrow's brightest boy ever. Born into the Georgian Enlightenment, he soon showed a phenomenal memory and, after mastering Greek and Latin, turned to Hebrew and then Arabic (or at least the script) while at Harrow. Arriving in 1783 in India to be Supreme Court judge in Calcutta, with many more languages under his belt, he now mastered Sanskrit and revealed the riches of that language – and of early India – to the West. In 1784 he founded the Asiatic Society of Bengal – and thus the discipline of Indian studies.

In 1786, in his renowned 'Third Anniversary Discourse' to the Society, Jones reported on the linguistic similarities of Sanskrit to 'Gothic' and 'Celtic', and perhaps old Persian. In short, Jones had discovered the Indo-European group of languages that stretched from Ireland to India in those days, and by now covers all the parts of the world that have been settled by Indo-European speakers. For the history of mankind, Jones's insight is on a par with Einstein's discovering relativity. And the big

question that it entailed is still far from settled: how on earth did such a widespread dispersal of cognate languages come about? Why are words still similar in languages that developed thousands of miles apart? The answer lies partly in archaeology, as it may well relate to the invention and spread of arable farming in Neolithic times or a little earlier – the greatest cultural revolution in human history – or it may reflect yet earlier movements of people or their cultures. In 1794, not yet fifty, Jones died in Calcutta, and is buried in the city's Park Street cemetery, close to Mother Teresa's orphanage. (Do not miss the chance to visit either.)

If Indian and foreigner alike revere Jones as the father of Indian studies, Harrow's next pioneer Sir John Gardner Wilkinson (1797–1875) is hailed as a father of British Egyptology and the leading writer on Egypt of the mid-nineteenth century, when the discipline was still in its infancy. From 1821 to 1833 he explored the Nile valley and seems to have been the first scholar to study el-Amarna, the short-lived capital in Middle Egypt of the so-called heretic King Akhenaten in the fourteenth century BC (shortly before Tutankhamun). His *Manners and Customs of the Ancient Egyptians* sold very well and went into several editions. In 1864 he gave his collection, with an exquisite handwritten catalogue with his colour drawings, to Harrow, where it is now in the Old Speech Room Gallery; his papers are in the Bodleian Library. Another book of travel and exploration, following a journey in 1844, is *Dalmatia and Montenegro*.

Another keen explorer of pre-Yugoslavian Yugoslavia, although he is less remembered for it than for his work at Knossos, was Sir Arthur Evans (1851–1941), the excavator of Knossos and father of Minoan, meaning Cretan Bronze Age, archaeology. He was also the begetter of the present Ashmolean Museum, and a founding editor of *The Harrovian*. At Harrow he also edited a satirical magazine, *The Pen-Viper*, which 'opened with a witty indictment of the Philathletic Club', as his half-sister Joan Evans wrote. As happens often enough with such journals, the school powers suppressed it.

Born into the Victorian Enlightment, Evans had phenomenal energy and inquisitiveness. He did not start digging at Knossos until he was 49, in 1900, although he had bought land there six years earlier on his first, exploratory visit to Crete. His achievement is still extraordinary in creating the 'Minoan' framework for prehistoric Crete, based on the stratigraphy that he and his assistant Duncan Mackenzie observed in the first few seasons of digging the huge structure at Knossos, which Evans quickly viewed as the Palace of the mythical king Minos – and the centre of the sophisticated culture of Crete in the Bronze Age (around 3100–1000 BC). Today, with over one million paying visitors, it is the second most visited ancient site in Greece, after the Athenian Acropolis. Evans and Mackenzie dug fast and made sense of it fast, and soon started conservation, which culminated in the concrete reconstructions (of impressive scholarly accuracy) that he erected in the 1920s. At the same time he was writing *The Palace of Minos at Knossos*, which incorporates his vision of a civilisation on Crete comparable to those of ancient Egypt and the Near East. As with Jones and Indo-European, so with Evans and Minoan culture, all scholars still follow today, to a greater or lesser degree, in the steps of the master.

The pioneering achievement of the present *doyen* of Minoan studies, Sinclair Hood, has been to revolutionise the quality of excavating – and understanding – the Aegean Bronze Age by introducing the rigorous methods of digging and recording as taught by Sir Mortimer Wheeler and Dame Kathleen Kenyon. Hood has excavated principally at Knossos, where he set out, perhaps with some scepticism, to test the validity of Evans's scheme and the chronological relationships that it implies – and has ended up a steady believer in Evans. He has also directed important excavations on Chios and been Director of the British School at Athens, the oldest British research institution abroad (and no more a school than the LSE or the *grandes écoles* in Paris).

The School at Athens has also played a large part in the lives of two other Harrovian archaeologists of the Aegean Bronze Age: Lord William Taylour (1904–1989) excavated at Mycenae and in Laconia under its aegis, as has Gerald Cadogan in Crete and Cyprus. It is a happy chance that four archaeologists of Minoan Crete and Mycenaean Greece have come from one school but, as Hood has written, unwise to declare it a tradition. Perhaps one day....

A quick jump to the Middle Ages of Britain reveals one more Harrovian pioneer. John Hurst (1927–2003) who died tragically last year after being attacked near his home in Leicestershire, was a pioneer of the open-area method of digging (rather than Wheeler's grid system), applying it famously to the deserted mediaeval village of Wharram Percy in Yorkshire, where digging took 40 seasons. And while he retained the strong interest in Near Eastern civilisation that he had acquired at Harrow, his main involvement was in mediaeval and later pottery. He was about to receive the Society of Antiquaries Medal just before he died (it was given posthumously) – in recognition of another creative career centred on making history, in the widest sense, from sherds, layers of earth, landscape and buildings.

Finally, Lord Byron (1788–1824) must be included here as, in a sense, a pioneer of the modern philosophy of conserving finds and monuments on the spot, so that they can be recognised in the context they deserve as part of the long processes of interaction between people and place, which are such a fascinating and vital element in the archaeological approach to history. His scathing attacks on Lord Elgin (Thomas Bruce, seventh Earl of Elgin) (1766–1841) in *The Curse of Minerva* and *Childe*

RIGHT: *Sir Arthur
Evans, excavator
of Knossos*

LEFT: *Painted and gilded cartonnage head of a mummy-case, Ptolemaic period, c. 330 BC, from the Old Speech Room Gallery Collection*

Harold's Pilgrimage are not just magnificent invective. They also show someone years ahead of his time in intuiting the lasting human value of cultural heritage in the context to which it belongs. It is ironic that he and Elgin both went to the same school.

We should also remember Constantine Leventis (1938–2002) who, like Byron, was not an archaeologist but knew and loved the subject and Hellenism, whether in Cyprus, Greece or beyond, and was a munificent and imaginative benefactor through the A.G. Leventis Foundation. In archaeology the Foundation has supported conservation and the publication of neglected finds from old excavations in Cyprus, and their display in Leventis galleries in major museums – probably even more than it has supported new excavations. Barely two decades old, the Foundation already has a magnificent record. But, although it is clearly pre-eminent, it is not alone among Harrovians' trusts for archaeology: Evans, Taylour and Hood have also been benefactors through gifts in trust.

Gerald Cadogan (The Knoll 1955³), Visiting Professor at the University of Reading, and Associate Professor at the University of Cincinnati 1974–84, has directed excavations in Crete and Cyprus and written widely on their archaeology.

Harrow and the local community

BARNABY LENON

W E AIM TO WORK CLOSELY WITH AND FOR THE local community. The Harrow Governors run the John Lyon Charity which gives £2 million every year to worthwhile projects in the boroughs between Harrow School and the middle of London – down the Harrow Road. Most of these have an educational element to them: a performance venue on the World's End Estate, new playgrounds for schools in East Finchley, grants to enable secondary schools to achieve Specialist College status, free ice-skating tuition for schoolchildren, financing work with disabled children in Westminster – these and a hundred other similar projects are supported every year by the John Lyon Charity.

Harrow works closely with local state schools. Supported by the John Lyon Charity we have built a new all-weather athletics track which is used by local schools throughout the year and is the focus for athletics coaching in the southern part of the borough. Community tennis and fishing clubs are based at Harrow and many hundreds of local residents use our swimming pool and gym.

The School administers the Harrow Club in Notting Dale, a thriving centre for adult education, sport and social life in a deprived part of London. We support a centre for Multiple Sclerosis therapy in one of our spare farm buildings (a converted cow shed).

We provide tuition in A-level Music and Latin for boys and girls from local state schools. These are subjects not provided by other schools in the borough. We offer this without charge, the students joining all the relevant classes alongside Harrovians. We are enthusiastic participants in the national Engineering Education Scheme and our boys work on applied engineering projects with local firms such as Kodak.

Every summer the School runs a highly successful course for gifted ten- to twelve-year-olds from local state schools. They live in the School as boarders (often their first time away from home) and learn new subjects (Japanese for example) as well as doing demanding projects in more established school disciplines.

THE HARROVIAN

February 2002

The Chamber Choir at Wormwood Scrubs

H.M. PRISON, WORMWOOD SCRUBS, 20 JANUARY

On Sunday the Chamber Choir travelled just 20 minutes to the Scrubs to sing the morning Mass for the prisoners, a booking made through Simon Eadon (Druries, 1965), the prison organist. I am sure it wasn't a normal sight to see two blue minibuses parked in the courtyard outside the prison entrance, but who knows what would have gone through the mind of anyone driving past the East Acton location on Sunday.

After a security check, we were taken inside the prison itself where we were greeted by 20ft-high fencing with rolls of barbed wire on top.

On entering the pink, beautiful chapel dedicated to St. Francis, the saint who found his vocation by being told to go out and exhort people away from sin, we set out for a quick rehearsal.

The Mass, due to start at 9.30am, got underway at 9.45am once the 150 or so prisoners had arrived. During the service we were reminded of the familiar whole School Service at Harrow, where some of the congregation can be noisy and a priest was needed to go and tell people to behave.

The Choir sang the Messe Sollenelle by Langlais and the world premier of a new piece by Granville Walker (brother of RHW*) – I Saw Eternity, which drew a round of applause from the very demonstrative and out-going congregation.

Afterwards we were treated to coffee with the 'lifers' and then headed on home to the Hill.

*The Director of Music at Harrow

A history of the Harrow Mission and Harrow Club

Andrew Stebbings

IN THE SPRING OF 1883 THE HEAD MASTER, DR Butler, wrote to all Old Harrovians informing them of the decision to start a School Mission in Latimer Road. The first Missioner had been appointed. William Laws was an Old Harrovian and senior curate at St Mary Abbots Church in Kensington. The Head Master wrote:

> The Masters and boys at Harrow have made themselves responsible for the salary of the Missioner for at least seven years. For other expenses of the work, such as the purchase of land and the gradual erection of the buildings required, we must depend partly on the same source, partly on societies which exist for such purposes and partly on the kind sympathy of friends including members of the Harrow Mission Association.

From the earliest days the School was deeply involved with its new Mission. There were many visitors to Latimer Road, as well as financial and administrative support. The Head Master went on:

> …a few years may perhaps prove that the strong tide of brotherly feeling which flows through successive generations of Harrow men may find one new and not uncongenial channel in ministering to the wants of the poor and the neglected and so contributing to bring together classes of our fellow countrymen who know far too little of each other.

On 12 June 1883 at a meeting of Old Harrovians in St James's Hall, Regent Street, the Harrow Mission Association was born. Dr Vaughan chaired the meeting and the speakers included Dr Butler and Lord Shaftesbury who was then 82 years old.

On Trinity Sunday 1884, the Mission Room was opened. In 1887, before a guard of honour of 90 members of the Harrow Rifle Corps, the foundation stone of the Church was laid by HRH the Duchess of Albany. The architect of both Mission and Church was Norman Shaw. A year later the Bishop of London consecrated the Church. Thus the Missioner William Laws also became the vicar of a parish that rivalled the worst of East London for poverty. William Laws wrote:

> Nothing could have been more forlorn, neglected or desolate than the conditions of this district at starting. The station of the Metropolitan Railway, which bears the name Latimer Road, was familiarly known as 'Piggery Junction' from the miserable and unwholesome establishment for the feeding of those animals which then occupied the site of our Church and Mission Room. The livelihood of the men – brick makers, costermongers, casual labourers – was always precarious while the women, the real breadwinners of the families, were mainly employed in steam laundries away from the homes and children. Rich inhabitants there were none; the moderately poor were scarce.

William Laws described the work of the Mission as spiritual, philanthropic, educational and providing entertainment. Progress was rapid. A kitchen provided penny dinners for children whose mothers worked in the laundries. The meticulously kept records show that, in its first 70 days of opening, the kitchen had served 9,507 dinners of which 1,702 were free. By 1888 Clubs for men and youths and boys were established and Laws was calling for a girls' club. From the start, sport played a prominent part in Club life and a sports field was purchased in 1887.

In 1893 a children's holiday fund was set up to enable younger members to go on fortnight holidays in Hertfordshire and Essex. This was the beginning of the camps organised by the Mission which took place annually until a property was purchased in 1985 in the Forest of Dean. In 1902 a day nursery was established, with the Princess of Wales as Patron.

By the 1920s the cracks between the Church and the Clubs were becoming apparent and were acknowledged by the Council of the Mission in 1931 when they appointed a Harrow Master as the first manager of the Clubs. In 1933 there was a gentle reproof for St Mary Abbots Church for the withdrawal of an annual grant of £40, which had for many years been used by the Relief Committee for Unemployment. By 1939 the Mission's responsibility for the Parish of Holy Trinity was ended. In his last report to the Council in 1953 Mitchell Jones (Jonah), the Club manager, stressed the changing role of the Club 70 years on:

> In 1883 the Harrow Mission was established in Latimer Road, then one of the drabbest and most squalid districts in London. Harrovians worked together to establish a centre where people could receive the necessities of life like good food and adequate clothing, and learn the happiness to be derived from recreation and social companionship. Gradually social conditions have improved. Poverty and disease have declined and the Clubs have become a centre less of relief than of community life. Though on the material side there has been a great improvement, the need for fostering human welfare in other than material ways is more marked than ever.

In 1963 approval was given for the Club to take over the old Mission Church, now no longer in use, and planning began which culminated in the opening of the new premises of The Harrow Club W10 by the Hon Angus Ogilvy in 1967.

The luxury of a huge sports hall opened up a vista of possibilities. However, the sheer vastness of the new premises threatened to destroy the intimacy of former years, while the cost of running and maintaining them became so great that the Club was fast approaching bankruptcy. Inevitably the Club decided in 1970 to sell its sports ground in North Wembley, which it had purchased in 1922. This meant that the Club suddenly found itself with large funds available to expand in whatever direction seemed best. The space in the new premises allowed for a great increase in the activities available to members, while the acquisition of first the Vicarage and then the bakery allowed for the setting up of new enterprises to help the community. The first

The Peter Beckwith Harrow Trust

In 1992 Peter Beckwith (*Elmfield 1958*[3]) set up the Peter Beckwith Harrow Trust with the object of offering up to two scholarships every year to pupils currently being educated in state schools.

The scheme is aimed at those boys who would not otherwise be in a financial position to enjoy and benefit from the advantages which a Harrow education has to offer. On scholarship day the selected candidates sit various examinations and are interviewed as well as having to demonstrate a skill, such as sport, music, drama or art at which they excel.

The successful candidates are offered two years at a preparatory school, which helps to prepare them for the five years at Harrow. Depending on financial circumstances the award can be up to full fees.

To date some 26 boys have passed through or are still part of the scheme and one of the highlights for Peter and his fellow Trustees was when one of the PBHT scholars, Luka Gakic, was made Head of School in 2002.

In 2002 Peter and his fellow Trustees decided to hand over the scholarship funds directly to Harrow School from where the scheme is now administered and which continues to allow those boys from financially disadvantaged backgrounds the opportunity to benefit from all that Harrow has to offer.

Peter Beckwith with some of his scholars

Scholarships

Our aim is to admit a proportion of our pupils regardless of their parents' income. Boarding school education is expensive – over £20,000 a year. The days are gone when a GP, for example, could afford to send four children to boarding school. But we do not want to be a school which only takes pupils from rich families.

One fifth of pupils at Harrow have their fees reduced in one way or another, mostly through scholarships. Scholarships are given for academic or musical excellence and also to boys who are outstanding at art, games, computing, acting or other subjects not examined at Common Entrance. Some of these boys have their fees further reduced by a means-tested bursary.

For the past decade we have admitted a number of boys from less well-off backgrounds whose fees have been paid in whole or part by the Peter Beckwith Harrow Trust and by John Lyon's Charity. The Peter Beckwith scheme, which has been a great success, will pay for a bright boy to attend a prep school for two years before coming on to Harrow; in 2002 a Peter Beckwith scholar became Head of School.

In more recent years Peter's brother, John Beckwith, has funded a number of sports scholarships. Recent recipients have included an Afghan refugee with a gift for cricket and a young man who ranks as one of the top rackets players in the country. We are not only attracting talented players and bringing them on: we are enabling boys to come to the School who could not otherwise afford to do so.

BARNABY LENON

Classics tour to Aphrodisias, Turkey, 1996

change had been the name. What had successively been called the Harrow Mission and the Harrow School Clubs became 'The Harrow Club W10'. The second change was that the Club membership was opened to both sexes.

But the most dramatic changes have been in the surrounding community. In the 1960s the neat Victorian terraces of Notting Dale were replaced by the tower blocks of the Silchester and Edward Woods estates. The construction of the A40 link road and Westway severed the Club completely from the White City area. In 1997, a logical boundary change moved the Club from Hammersmith and Fulham to Kensington and Chelsea. The area is now one of the most densely populated in the UK and Europe. Some 30 different nationalities occupy public housing, while gentrification has set in among the remaining older properties of W10 and the area is rapidly becoming fashionable.

As the end of the century approached it was clear that the Church building and its facilities were inadequate. The notion of a youth club is changing as the outside world presses an ever-increasing influence on the expectations of young people. Communication and access to information are central to these changes – advertising, style, fashion, television, video, the ease of travel and the rise of the influence of the sporting world and now the extended world of the Internet. These new freedoms and potentialities needed particular skills and a youth club must embrace the new world. Harrow Club and its partners recognised the need for change.

In 1996 there was a break in the succession of Harrow Masters chairing the Management Committee, with the appointment of Mary Tuck, a distinguished civil servant and local resident. Under her guidance a £2 million building appeal was launched and the comprehensive redevelopment of the buildings began, to be continued after her sudden death under the chairmanship of her husband Robin. Grant Aitken, an enthusiastic and dynamic New Zealander, was appointed manager and guided the Club through the refurbishment process. With the support of Octavia Hill Housing Trust and the De Paul Trust the old Vicarage became a hostel for homeless young people.

Throughout its history the successful evolution of Harrow Club would not have been possible without the long and dedicated work of many Old Harrovians on the Council. Over the years the commitment of Harrovians to the work of the Mission has been considerable. In 1897 the hostel was acquired to accommodate Old Harrovians willing to lend a helping hand to the manifold work of the Mission. School Monitors also played an important role in the management of the Clubs, particularly during the Great War. From the earliest days four Old Harrovian names became part of the Club's history – Pelham, Dauglish, Verney and Trotter. Henry Pelham was associated with the Mission and the Club continuously from leaving school in 1895 until his death in 1949 as Church Warden, Councillor, Treasurer, Secretary to the Council and Vice President and finally President, the first who was not a Head Master of the School. Geoffrey Dauglish was associated with the Mission from its earliest days until his death in 1937 after running the Sunday School for 35 years, being involved with the Boys Club for nearly as long and serving on the Council for 47 years. In 1909 a presentation was made to him in recognition of his attendance at the Men's Club three nights a week for 26 years.

The names of Verney and Trotter have a special significance as the sons have carried on the work of the fathers. Harry Verney started as a schoolboy on the local committee in 1898 and was a Trustee until 1955 when he handed over to his son, Lawrence. Stuart Trotter started helping in the Mission in 1907. He became manager of the Boys Club, secretary to the Council, a Council Member and Vice-President until his death in 1963. His son Hugo was already involved in the annual camps and with canoeing, serving on the Board of Management until the 1990s. Today Hugo's son, Rupert, continues the family tradition and is a member of the Board of Trustees.

Since the 1960s a succession of liaison Masters at the School continued the close connection with the Club. Roger Ellis, John Rae, Tony Davis, Michael Vallance and John Rees all gave the Club great service and appear to have derived some benefit from the experience. All of them went on to become Headmasters.

It was John Rees who inspired the birth of the Nottingdale Urban Studies Centre and the appointment of a Cambridge colleague, Chris Webb, as its first director. This created a partnership which led to the emergence of the Nottingdale Technology Centre. Both were 'firsts' in the UK. Following a visit to the Centre in 1981 by the Minister of Technology, Kenneth Baker, the Government pledged a £20 million programme to set up information technology centres throughout Britain with Nottingdale as the consultancy unit behind the programme. Although the Urban Studies Centre was closed in 1995 with much of its work becoming part of the mainstream school curriculum, the Nottingdale Technology Centre thrives.

On 23 November, 2000, HRH The Prince of Wales attended the official reopening of Harrow Club W10 as a 'community centre for the 21st century'. The School was actively involved in the event. Among those presented to HRH was Peter Theobald, an Old Harrovian and long-serving Trustee of the Harrow Mission, who had been keenly involved in the redevelopment. Since the reopening of the Club, the tradition of a Harrow Master chairing the Management Committee has been restored with the appointments of first David Elleray and more recently James Power. As I write, the tradition of Old Harrovian involvement is being further maintained with the appointment to the Club Board of Management of Edward Buxton, a local resident and the latest in the distinguished line of Harrow's voluntary servants to the community.

Squash Rackets, early history

Extract from a letter to The Times, *Jan 21, 1924. From A.G. Murray, 1st Baron Dunedin*

Sir,– There seems to be so much interest as to the early history of Squash Rackets that I feel impelled to trouble you with a letter, as I believe myself to be in a better position than any of your correspondents to throw light on the matter…

I went to Harrow in 1863; at that time the covered court did not exist. There were two regular racket courts, the Sixth Form, a huge open rectangle just below the milling ground and the Fifth Form just below it. Squash was played in the 'Corner'.* …There were two hazards for which you could intentionally play – the buttress line to the great window which returned the ball straight down, and the pipe which might send it anywhere. The 'Corner' was better for 'four' games than for singles. Squash had been played there for a very long time – *ultra memoriam* as far as I could discover. The origin of the game was undoubtedly there.

It naturally occurred to boys to utilize any space they could find in contiguity to their different Houses, taking the wall of the House as the battery wall; and most Houses (not all) had such a space. Most of them made very poor courts.

The best of these was indubitably Rendalls,[1] commonly known as Monkey's. The shape of the House formed a natural interior three sides of a square and it was full of hazards in the shape of windows, pipes, etc. The next best was at a Small House, little known and down the Hill, at that time held by Vanity Watson.[2]… After that I would put Young Vaughan's[3] … and then would come Butlers.[4]

But the point of it is that none of these House courts gave an enclosed rectangular with four walls – the present form of the court. That came about in this way. In 1864 the covered court was begun to be built. When it was finished I remember the opening match which was between Billy Dykes,[5] the amateur champion and a

A print of the School Yard in front of the Old Schools, dated 15 April 1853. The high wall on the left with the netting on top, the 'open' rackets court, was demolished in 1899

'The Corner', the birthplace of Squash, as it looks in 2004

professional from Torquay whose name I forget. The covered court being opened, the old Sixth Form court became the Fifth Form court and the old Fifth Form court was cut up into four Eton fives courts and three Rugby fives courts ... Eton fives took on fairly well ... but the Rugby courts did not, I know, have more than half a dozen games of fives played in them. They obviously invited the familiar squash, and were immediately appropriated for that purpose. From that sprang the idea of the Harrow squash court and from there it spread elsewhere ... At that time, as far as I know, squash was not played at any of the other great schools. Of course we played with the old squash hollow ball with a hole in it....

* An area in the north-west of the School Yard, bounded by the Old Schools, 'Leith's wall' and the Milling Ground wall.
1. Not the present Rendalls, but Grove Hill, closed as a Small House in 1936, now Grove Hill House and The Foss.
2. Byron House in Byron Hill Road but no longer owned by the School.
3. West Acre, burnt down in 1908 and rebuilt.
4. The Head Master's, where the two Yards still exist.
5. Rt Hon Sir William Hart Dyke, Bart., (The Grove 1851[3]), the first champion not to have learnt his Rackets in the Debtors Prison at Fleet.

An extract from a letter of response from Sir William Hart Dyke on Jan 24, 1924

Sir, – ... In 1863 I was responsible for forming a committee of Old Harrovians to collect subscriptions for building a closed racket court at Harrow School. Our efforts were so successful that we had a considerable balance over the estimate for building the court. I spent this surplus partly on fives courts and partly on what Lord Dunedin describes as Rugby fives courts. These, I can well remember, I intended for play with a racket and indiarubber ball....

Research by Dale Vargas

Squash at Harrow, 2004

One Saturday of the year

RICKY RITCHIE

I BELONG TO THAT GENERATION OF HARROVIANS WHO associate the OH Players with their first weekend at Harrow. When the admittance of 'new boys' was not restricted to the Autumn term, it was normal for those of us who entered the School in the summer to spend our first or second Saturday afternoon on the Hill watching a Shakespeare play in Speech Room – and no doubt with mixed emotions. I remember mine. I was concerned the play would not end in time for 'Bill' (a not unreasonable anxiety, given the unpredictable pace of certain OH productions). I couldn't honestly say that I was enjoying it very much; and yet I was already hoping that, before long, I would appear on the stage myself.

I now know that, for me, this 1963 afternoon performance of *King Lear* was the start of something significant. I remember vividly all the OH Productions of my school years. Those of us involved with the School Shakespeare often attended both the performances (with

RIGHT: *Will Ellis and Alice Grace in* Romeo and Juliet, *2004*

text in hand), or helped with them back-stage. The OH Players also taught me how to prompt; indeed, in prompting terms, it was the equivalent of being thrown in at the deep end. There was one matinée performance when the opening word was forgotten by the actor and I had to start the play by shouting out the word 'Tush'. Despite such accidents, however, memory lapses are, in most OH productions, surprisingly infrequent.

A packed Speech Room on a Saturday night enjoyed a special atmosphere of excitement if the play was going well, and it was, for exam reasons, well-known to the School. Even small and insignificant moments sometimes made an impression. I recall, for example, James Ramsay as Hamlet in 1981, holding up Yorick's skull and pointing it left, right and centre to ensure that all those crammed into the sides and top benches were able to see it. It brought home how an entire audience in Speech Room

might become an integral part of the production. It also illustrated how, on occasions, a Harrovian audience could imitate the groundlings of Shakespeare's time – especially when the stage allowed members of the audience to sit in the well, and place their feet on the platform. This production of *Hamlet* (the only time, so far, that the OH Players have performed this play), was also the occasion when James Morwood, a former Head of Classics, brought the proceedings to a halt as Osric, evoking more laughter in Speech Room than I can remember in any Harrow Shakespeare production.

Thus, the OH Players can boast of a number of great theatrical moments, and a number of superb performances. For instance, the actor Michael Kitchen enthused over Michael Levete's Othello in 1976 (the year when Mr Kitchen's friend, Joanna Lumley, was Desdemona, Richard Curtis was Roderigo and Kitchen himself was playing

ABOVE: *Tom Noad as Henry, Ricky Ritchie as The King of France and Mary Rochester as Katherine in Henry V, 2003*

Iago at the Young Vic); the late Michael Bates (another great actor, whose wife, Maggie, frequently acted with the OHs) expressed admiration for Jeremy Lemmon's Lear in 1972. They were not just being polite. They acknowledged that the production which they had seen – while perhaps not sustainable over a number of performances – had on a single night and in a unique setting worked in a way that only 'live' theatre can work. The 1972 *Lear* also contained Adrian Petch's Gloucester and Michael Levete's Kent. It is fitting that three of our best OH performances should have been given by these three 'giants' of the Society – Lemmon, Levete and Petch – in the first of Ronnie Watkins's two OH productions (which, uniquely, received three performances).

But not everything is this good. OH Players are sometimes accused of displaying all the worst aspects of amateur theatre – lines poorly learnt, moves bungled, and everything done for the pleasure of the cast rather than the audience. Nobody fosters this impression more than OH Players themselves, through a desire not to appear pretentious. It is not a fair impression – at least, not normally. Given a competent cast, good luck and barely adequate rehearsal time (traditionally four Sunday rehearsals starting at 10am and extending well into the evening), something worthwhile is normally achieved. But not at the expense of the actors' enjoyment.

Perhaps the worst moment of any OH production is when the hour of one o'clock approaches, and the realisation dawns that it is no longer possible to postpone the act of undressing in the dungeons of the War Memorial. Their distinctive smell and lack of amenities is another essential element of Harrow Shakespeare. But despite these (and many other) difficulties, the OH Players often 'get away with it'. This deserves an explanation. Perhaps the biggest reason is that we are, in a sense, a 'repertory' company of actors (some experienced, some not; some professional, most not) who have been brought up to believe that how to 'speak' Shakespeare is more important than how to 'act' Shakespeare. To use an analogy with opera, the music of the verse should be judged more important than the whims of the producer or the enthusiasms of the designer.

Some of the younger OH Players have greater trouble with this tradition than do the older members, partly because the Ryan Theatre has enabled more recent Harrovians to act in a much wider variety of plays than was possible when we relied exclusively upon Speech Room and the Music Schools. But despite changing fashions and tastes, it still remains true that the only reason one can even contemplate presenting a Shakespeare play on so very few rehearsals is because of the Society's tradition to allow the verse to speak for itself. It is the personal responsibility of every actor to know and understand what he is saying. And if this is accomplished, it is amazing how riveting a performance can be, even with minimum rehearsal and without any great interpretative insights.

Many professional OH actors have acted with the OH Players. Many of them are probably embarrassed to recall the style they were required to adopt – the reliance upon gesture and mime; the chastity of Harrow love-scenes; the disorganised rabble of battles. But at least they will have received a thorough grounding in the speaking of Shakespeare, and how to fill a hall without the aid of microphones. However frequently they perform Shakespeare subsequently in more modern and avant-garde productions, a Shakespeare play learnt properly at Harrow should always place an actor at an advantage over the rest of his cast.

In one of my last conversations with Herbert Harris just before he died, he said that we should not feel obliged to continue the tradition of the OH Players for his sake or for the sake of continuity. He didn't wish it to become 'a burden'. Nobody involved in amateur or professional theatre will pretend that the business of staging plays is becoming any easier. And to the extent that the study of Shakespeare at Harrow declines or becomes less central to the life of the School, the OH Players are bound to suffer. But it is not a tradition to be dropped lightly. It is not a tradition which is continued reluctantly. To ask an actor to forego Shakespeare is like asking a classical pianist to abandon Beethoven. Beethoven can be played in one's sitting room. But Shakespeare needs a theatre, a company of actors and an audience. OH Players are fortunate in having, for one Saturday of the year, all three.

Richard Ritchie (Newlands 1963²) is Director of UK Government Affairs at BP, when not acting or composing songs for revues and musicals. He is Manager of The Old Stagers, the world's oldest dramatic society.

Cup memories

FRED WOOLLEY

THE OLD HARROVIAN ASSOCIATION FOOTBALL Club (OHAFC) is one of the largest and most active OH Clubs, playing and training regularly between September and April each season and touring once a year, usually over the Easter break. In 2003 the tour was to Argentina and Brazil. The average weekend sees the Club putting out three teams. On Saturday afternoons, the 1st and 2nd XI's take on other Old Boys' teams in the Arthurian League and the Arthur Dunn Cup competitions, hosting home fixtures on the Philathletic Ground with changing facilities in the newly refurbished Richardson Cricket Pavilion and post-match teas in the Shepherd Churchill Hall. The Club is proud of the high level of hospitality offered to visiting teams. On Sundays, a Veterans XI, over 35s, plays regularly at the Bank of England Sports Ground in Roehampton. The Annual Dinner is held at the Imperial Hotel, Russell Square, with between 80 and 100 members and guests attending. Our excellent guest speakers in recent years have included the Head Master, Baron Butler of Brockwell, Rory Bremner and Gerald Harper.

OHAFC, founded in 1859, was one of the earliest Association Football clubs and several Old Harrovians were instrumental in the formation of the Football Association in 1863. The first FA Cup tournament was played in 1871/72 and it is said that Charles Alcock, then FA Secretary, had based this knock-out competition on the inter-House competition he had played in at Harrow. Alcock captained Wanderers FC to victory in the first Final at the Oval on 16 March 1872. His side contained no fewer than three other Old Harrovians and it is interesting to note that, when the FA Cup Centenary was celebrated in 1972, OHAFC was invited to represent the Wanderers, then no longer

LEFT: *Quentin Baker scoring for OHAFC against Old Carthusians at Harrow, March 2004*

in existence, by leading a parade preceding the final at Wembley Stadium.

By 1930, the original OHAFC had lapsed following the adoption of Rugby Football in 1927 as the major game at Harrow. No official soccer was played at the School for the next 50 years although the OHAFC was re-established in 1963. The Club owes much of its prosperity to 'frustrated enthusiasm' but much more to the bonds of friendship which have evolved within its membership. Quite simply, it is fun to play for OHAFC; even greater fun to play regularly. The Club has graced the playing fields of all the major football public schools, thrilling crowds, filling terraces and producing goal sprees never to be seen in the Premiership.

Even by its own illustrious standards, OHAFC is presently enjoying a boom having won the Arthurian League Premier Division in Season 2003/04. OHAFC overcame Old Boys' sides from such traditional powers in the school game as Charterhouse, Eton, Forest and Lancing. Indeed, OHAFC is the only club drawn from a historically non-footballing school ever to win the title. The Captain, Quentin Baker, and his team are to be congratulated on this very fine achievement. Going forward, OHAFC wishes to build on the excellent relations it has with the School, ensuring that it is to be the first port of call for those leavers who wish to continue playing soccer after Harrow. With 40 years of experience to call upon, the relative merits of 4-4-2, 4-3-3 and 4-5-1 are imparted at length to the less well informed in licensed premises most Saturday evenings of the season.

Fred Woolley (West Acre 1957[3]) is President of the Old Harrovian Association Football Club and was President of the Arthurian (Soccer) League from 1992–2002. He is a Chartered Accountant with PMB Holdings Ltd.

The Harrow School Archive

RITA BOSWELL GIBBS

OR THOSE WHO FIND A FASCINATION IN HISTORY, an archive holds a wealth of exciting facts and stories. Harrow School Archive contains a diverse array of tantalising snippets which can reveal an ancestor's experiences or provide excellent material for researchers, for example on educational or architectural topics.

Since the opening in 1981 of dedicated premises to hold its records, the Archive has attracted a steady stream of academic researchers, family and local historians. In addition it provides a service answering such internal questions as: 'When were the School's boarding Houses first provided with electricity?' to the researching and mounting of exhibitions, both inside and outside the School, on topics like the annual Eton and Harrow Cricket Match at Lord's.

So what types of records are held and where have they come from? We do not know where the original School Charter, granted by Elizabeth I in 1572, was kept before the first School building was built. We do know that it was pinned to the wall in the Vaughan Library for many years. Unfortunately, universal awareness of the need to consider the long-term preservation of historical documents was slow to evolve during the nineteenth century and, as a result, there has been some deterioration. We also know that the School's administrative records, such as minutes of Governors' Meetings and Account Books (dating from 1608), were at one time held in the original School building opened in 1615. A newspaper cutting of 1725 tells us that the oak chest holding these records, which was then kept in the School House and later situated in the fireplace of the Fourth Form Room, was broken into. There is no record of what was stolen. In 1887 *The Harrovian* records that the School's muniments were buried in a dungeon, the existence of which was unknown to most Harrow men, so they were to be transferred to the Vaughan Library for easier access and security. Apart from a brief spell in packing cases during

World War Two, there they remained until their removal in 1981 to the newly converted attic above the Economics School in Football Lane.

We have a good idea of what some of the School records consisted of in 1887 because the School's oldest documents had been catalogued, according to standards practised at that time, by Mr Edward Scott, a curator at the British Museum, and his results were published in *The Ancient Records of Harrow School* in 1886. These 550 documents date from the reign of Edward III and cover the period 1350–1837. They consist of records of land transactions including extracts of court rolls for the manor of Harrow Hill Rectory, grants, leases and terriers, but also include such documents as apprenticeship indentures. This collection of papers relates to the School's Founder, John Lyon, and his family; the first mention of his family appears in an extract from the Roll of a Court held at Edgware in 1370. They also record the surveyor's original

ABOVE: *Gerald du Maurier's sketch of himself and below right, the letter to his mother*

ABOVE RIGHT: *Old Sly's plan for the Old Schools, 1608*

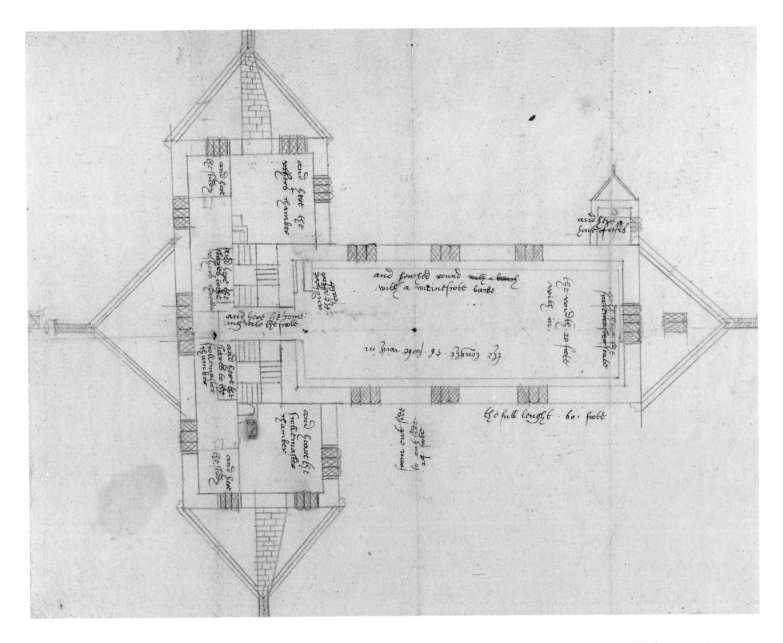

the Grove
Harrow

My Darling Mummy

I couldn't write before to Trixie, because I've had such a bad cold that I felt hopeless, and had to stop out from school, which accounted for my being 19th this fortnight, which isn't low.

I am sorry to have to tell you, but I've had another five shillings bagged, isn't it beastly? I told Bowen, and he was very sorry of course, but its no joke, I can tell you, having all your money bagged. Colonel Gouraud came on Saturday evening and gave us a lecture on the 'phonograph', & made the thing speak; I never heard any thing so frightfully perfect in my life. Edison had sent over a swell band, bottled up in it & it sounded ripping, & at the end, a little voice said, 'three cheers for the United States,' and we heard all the cheers, & cads whistling. At the end of the lecture we cheered Edison and sung the last verse of 40 years on, which were bottled up, and is going to be sent to Edison. It will probably blow him out of his room. Gouraud has given the school, a beautiful Phonograph. With best love to all I remain

your loving son
Gerald.

211

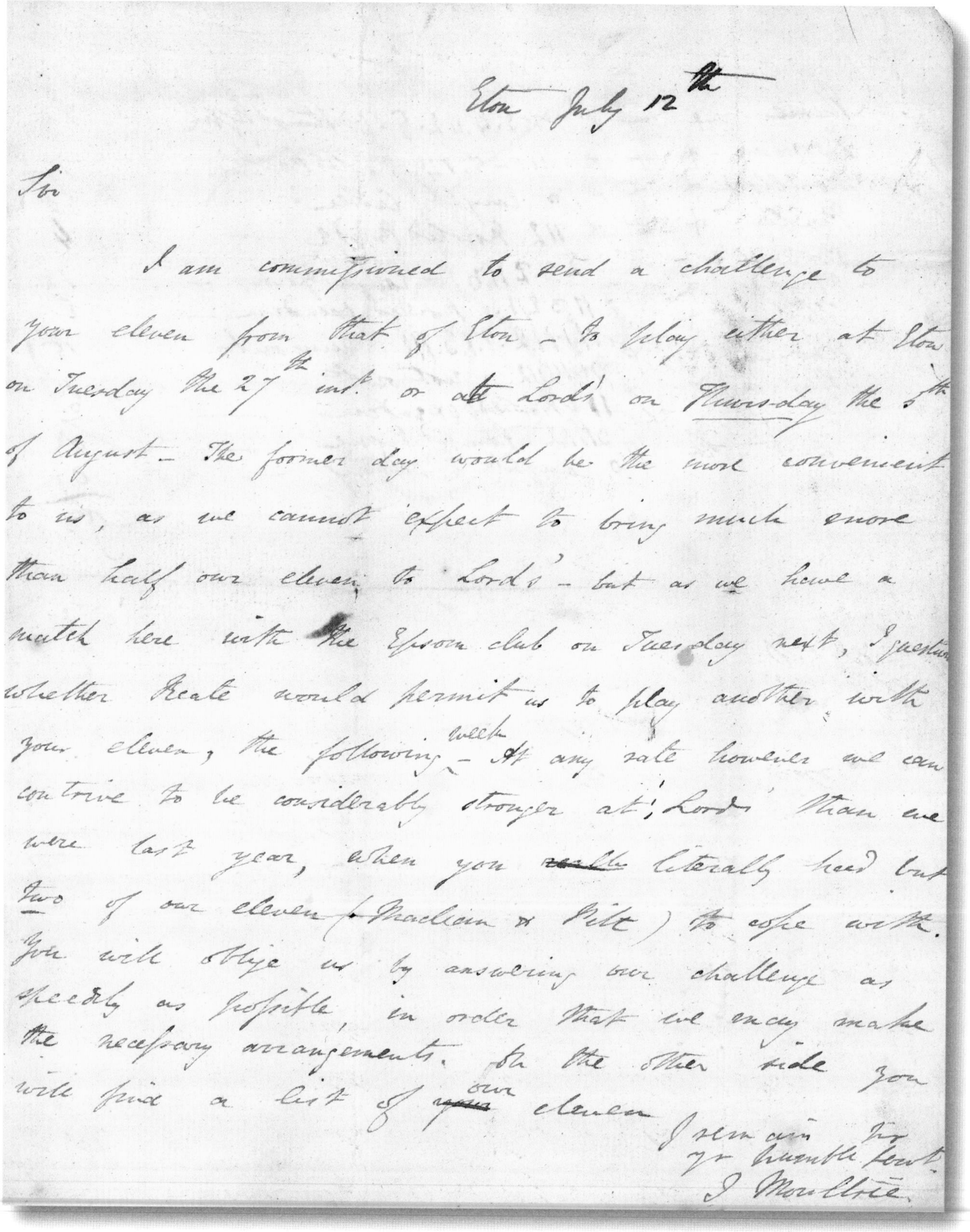

LEFT: *Challenge
letter from the
Captain of
Cricket at Eton,
1805*

Eton July 12th

Sir

I am commissioned to send a challenge to
your eleven from that of Eton — To play either at Eton
on Tuesday the 27th inst. or at Lords' on Thursday the 5th
of August — The former day would be the more convenient
to us, as we cannot expect to bring much more
than half our eleven to 'Lords' — but as we have a
match here with the Epsom club on Tuesday next, I question
whether Keate would permit us to play another with
your eleven, the following week — At any rate however we can
contrive to be considerably stronger at 'Lords' than we
were last year, when you had literally had but
two of our eleven (Maclean & Pitt) to cope with.
You will oblige us by answering our challenge as
speedily as possible, in order that we may make
the necessary arrangements. On the other side you
will find a list of our eleven
                                   I remain Sir
                                   Yr humble servt.
                                   J Moultrie

RIGHT: *This portrait of George Butler is a recent acquisition*

allowed the School to acquire a delightful oil painting of George Butler, Head Master (1805–29) sitting in his study. The background shows a set of framed miniatures on the wall which Butler had commissioned and given to the School.

In order to enrich its collection, it is essential that the School Archive is open and helpful to enquirers. Sometimes a small amount of data supplied from the records can result in the return of much more. Co-operation with other organisations can also be advantageous to both parties. The letters recently made available on-line by the Fox Talbot Museum confirm that William Fox Talbot attended Harrow, although the admission register does not mention him.

Twentieth-century records are badly affected by the growth of the disposable society, but sometimes this works to our benefit. Many people, who may have been made aware of the value of antiques through shows on the television or researching their family ancestry, now recognise the value of the items they discover in an attic or spare room. In the last few years a number of discoveries have made their way to us through this route as people are reluctant to throw away a slice of history.

The growth of technology also means that those wonderful diaries, which revealed such memories of schooldays, are no longer being kept. Since Harrow has produced many eminent Old Boys we have, thankfully, been blessed with a good selection of autobiographies, which we are keen to continue collecting.

Another result of social change has also been beneficial to the Archive. The closure of the Hills and Saunders photographic studio led to the acquisition of a vast and valuable pictorial resource. Many of the images in this book have been taken from this collection. A mixture of glass plate negatives and prints, it covers the period from 1870 to 1980. The collection provides an insight back into the nineteenth and twentieth centuries, showing activities on Harrow Hill as well as revealing its development and architecture. These include images of the School, its pupils and Masters, as well as local people who commissioned the studio to take wedding photographs, views of their homes and social events.

Over the years many volunteers have spent time organising and listing these images to improve the quality of access. There has been a steady stream of boys opting

plan of the School, titled 'a draught of a ffree schoole by old Sly', drawn in 1608.

Few original School records have survived for those years prior to the twentieth century; however, the archive has gained much from the benevolence of former pupils' relatives or descendants and has been given many historically valuable items. One gift received recently has been the chatty letters written home to his mother by Sir Gerald du Maurier while a boy in The Grove (1887–90).

Occasionally an opportunity arises to purchase a manuscript or painting of particular interest to the School. A couple of years ago a former Master drew the archivist's attention to an American website advertising the sale of a manuscript which resulted in an unexpected find. A letter written on 20 September 1803 by Spencer Perceval, concerning his son Spencer, to Joseph Drury, then Head Master, was traced to a London bookshop and purchased for a very reasonable sum. Its low value was clearly due to the fact that Perceval's importance as a Prime Minister of England had not been recognised. More recently a chance telephone call from a dealer for portrait painters

FAR LEFT: *Hills &
Saunders, the
former school
photographers*

LEFT: *The
previous site of
the Archive above
the Old Science
Schools*

BELOW: *The new
Archive at 84A
High Street*

for archives as an extra-curricular activity who have made worthwhile contributions. One such volunteer has carefully sorted and put into albums a growing collection of leavers' photographs; his dedicated work means that these can now be easily consulted. However, we have not been so lucky with pictures of Masters and staff. Surviving photographs are often not captioned, so it can a difficult exercise of deduction to identify their time and place.

The main objective for the Archive has been to build up a collection of material that illustrates all aspects of life at the School; this will continue. Since all the old administrative records were drawn together under one roof, it has encouraged the deposit of documents both from inside and outside the School. The subsequent inflow meant that the archive eventually outgrew its home in the attic and in 2003 it was relocated in smart new ground-floor premises with mobile storage racks to make the most of the space and map chests to house its various prints and plans of School buildings. It is appropriate that the new accommodation should be situated in an early nineteenth-century house, occupied from about 1834 to 1872 by Mr T. Hewlett, the School Doctor.

The School is extremely privileged to have such a wonderful collection of records. However it is very important that an archive should not be allowed to freeze in time but continues to be kept alive with a suitably

chosen selection of today's records, so that answers can be found to the questions of tomorrow's searcher. The archive motto is: 'Today's Records make Tomorrow's Archives'.

RIGHT: *Dusk on
the Hill*

*Rita Gibbs has been Harrow School Archivist since 1997. She was
previously Archivist at the Essex Record Office.*

Subscribers

M.J. Abboud
Dunbar Abston, Jr
Jack Ainslie
John Ainsworth-Taylor
John F.S. Akerman
Hugo Akerman
Akinkunle Akinkugbe
Mr & Mrs O.O. Akinkugbe
Mr & Mrs O.I. Akinkugbe
Tunku Mohamed Alauddin
Thomas Aldous
Luke Alen-Buckley
Stephen Alexander
The Hon. Brian Alexander
Mr D.I. & Mrs S.J. Allwood
Robin Alsher
M.R. Amherst Lock
K.R. Anderson
Dr John Anderson
Anthony Anderson
Mr & Mrs Mark Anderson
P.R.G. Anderson
I.H. Angus
Anthony Anson
His Hon. Judge Marcus
   Anwyl-Davies
Mr & Mrs David Archer
S.R. Armitage
C.P.E. Arratoon
G.W. Askew
Susan M. Astaire
William Babtie
Louis Bacon
Yvonne & Jeffrey Bailey
Charles Bailey
David K. Baines
M.G. Balme
Alexander Bance
C.W.N. Bankes
F.C.L. Banks
Pier F. Barattolo
Anthony & Barbara Santa Barbara
Eustace Santa Barbara
Joseph G. Barclay
Bryan Barkes
Elizabeth Barnes (née Grieg)
Mr & Mrs John Barrell
W.T. Barton
Mr & Mrs J. Barwick
Roger A. Bates
Mr & Mrs Michael E. Batten
Timothy M. Batten

Jeremy Bayliss
J.R. Beckett
P.M. Beckwith
Sir John Beckwith
The Duke of Bedford
Kenner S. Beecroft
Ian D.S. Beer
John Benn
Cyprien de Bykhovetz Benoit
Simon P. Berry
Titch Beresford
Mr. Naiyandbh Bhirombhakdi
Dr. Nidhi Bhutiani
Tarquin Black
D.L.M. Blackburn
P.B. Blackwell
T.C. Blackwell
F.J. Blake
J. Blake-Tyler
Mr & Mrs M. Blaney
Michael Blencowe
Charles Blount
Oscar A. Blustin
Alaister Boag
David Boag
Stephen Bois
Roger Boissier
Noel M. Bolingbroke-Kent
Joseph C. Bone
Dr. Srivilai Boonyakarnkul
Alan G. Boor
John Bowden
D.A. Bower
Richard Boxhall
The Hon. Reginald Boyle
Lord Brabazon of Tara
B.F.R. Bradkin
L. Bradley
M.J. Brankin-Frisby
Christopher E. Brawley
P. Brendan
A.W. Brierley
P.N.D. Broadhead
H.W. Brodie
Sebastian Bromley
Mrs Anne M. Brooke
Dr Amanda Brown
Mrs Susan Brown
Sir Rupert Buchanan-Jardine
J.W. Buckley
Alan Buckmaster
Laurence & Caron Burgess

Mrs Neville Burston
Axel M. Busch-Christensen
Daniel Busk
Lord Butler of Brockwell
Edward Button
J.W.H. Buxton
D.J. Caldecott-Smith
Donald Cameron of Lochiel
John D. Campbell
Ian Campbell
James A. Campbell
C.A.A.F. Campbell
Mrs Angela Cannon
A.R.P. Carden
P.M.A. Carden
Sir Kenneth Carlisle
Rev. Mark Carter
James Carter-Johnson
Lt Col & Mrs Paul Cartwright
Nick Cartwright
T.P.K. Carver
C.N.A. Castleman
Richard & Carolyn Cater
Albemarle J. Cator
Dr & Mrs Roger W. Cattermole
Dr Mark Cecil
Peter Cellier
George Challenor
J.G.W. Chalmers
Mike & Susan Chamberlain
Dominic Chambers
A.C.K. Chan
Mrs Loula Chandris
Zehao Chang
Andrew Yves Charbin
Anthony Cheng
Miti Chinvaravatana
Richard Choi
A. Chung
Nicholas Church
J.S. Churchill
John E. Clive
M.H. Cockell
Oliver G.L. Cohen
Mr & Mrs Peter Cohen
Mr & Mrs A. Collett
John D. Collins
Rob Collins
Richard C. Compton
John Cook
Peter J. Cook
Gary Cooke

Sally Cooper
James T.R. Cooper
John Means Cooper
The Earl of Cork & Orrery
Mrs Jenifer Ida Cotton-Buller
E. Cottrell
B.A. Covey
J.A. Coxon
Timothy Cragg
Harriet Crawley
Peter Creegen
Sir Ian Critchett
Dr Jonathan Crowston
E.A.C. Crump
William Crutchley
Shaun Dakin
Robert M. Davies
E. Michael R. Davies
Tom Davison
Christopher Dawson
J.E. de Broë-Ferguson
Dr Sophie des Clers
Jonathan de Jager
David de Pass
Richard F. de Robeck
Edmund de Rothschild
Leopold de Rothschild
T.R. de Zoete
Simon Deborchgrave D'Altena
Nicholas Defty
Nigel Defty
Daniel R. Shashoua
J.C.R. Dennis
Archie Dennis
Darby Dennis
George Dennis
Peter K. Dennis
M.J.L. Denny
James Dewdney-Herbert
Farhad Diba
Andrew Dick
Robert Dick
Alastair B. Dick-Cleland
R.H. Dickinson
Alistair Dickson
J. David Dixon
Dr James Dodd
Peter Doherty
C.P.C. Donald
G.E. Donald
R. Douglas-Miller
Michael Dover

Stephan R. Drake
Ardeshir B.K. Dubash
Jonathan Dudley
S.E.H. Duggan
Fergus Dunipace
Mr & Mrs C.N. Dunn
Alexander Durgan
K.J. Durward
Peter T. Dutton
A.J. Eady
E.C. Ecroyd
Mrs M.J. Edey
Charles Edwardes-Ker
Mildred Joy Eiloart
The Eitel Family
Charles H.W. Elgood
Evy Elliott
Roderick M. Engert
Caroline Ernest-Jones
Robert Etchells
J.W.Y. Eu
H.G. Faber
Robert Fairer-Smith
R.A. Farquharson
H.J.P. Farr
Tim Farr
Major G.S. Farrant
Dr I.W. Farrell
J.G.W. Feggetter
Erik N. Feldman
Alex Ferdi
A. St J. Ferrari
Benjamin James Figgures-Wilson
Nigel L. Firth
Barrington Fisher
Robert Fleming
A.K.H. Fletcher
H.R. Florin
J.M.H. Ford
N.J. Forman Hardy
David & Caroline Fortune
Arthur Fosh
D. Jemison Foster
Neil W.D. Foster
Richard Foster
W.F.E. Foster
E.J.F. Foster
Donald Fowler-Watt
Philip H. Fox
Donald Francke
Jamie Friend
Nicholas Fry
Simon Alexander Fujiwara
James Furlonger
J. Gajland
Norman T.G. Galbraith
W.J.H. Galgey
Sarah Gall
David Andrew Gallagher
Andrew Gallagher
Rupert G.A. Garnett
Simon Garrett
His Hon. Judge Gaskell

Dr George B. Gasson
Michael Gates Fleming
Marina Gates Fleming
R.A. Gates
E.J.H. Geffen
Alec M. Georgala
Martin B. Georgala
James Gibbons
Mr & Mrs J.L. Gibbons
J.P.J. Glover
Simon Gluckstein
Robert J.H. Glynn
James Goddard
Peter & Lani Goodliffe
I.R.L. Gordon
Basil Gotto
Mrs J.M. Gowrie-Smith
Michael Graham-Jones
I.G.W. Grant
Colin Michael Guilford
Allan Gray
A.C. Gray
Kristian A. Gray
J.N. Green
David L. Green
Charles Gregson
Dr R.E. Gregson
E.A. Creighton Griffiths
Evan Shelby Griswold
David Q. Gurney
Carol Gurney
D.F. Gwynne
Mr & Mrs S.D. Gwyther
Jungho Ha
James Haggas
Paul J. Haigney
Alan Hakim
Capt. Andrew G. Haldane
M.W. Hall
Mr & Mrs G.J.L. Hall
Dr A.M. Hall-Smith
Anne Hall-Williams
G.J. Hambro
Dr David V. Hamilton
HRH Crown Prince Hamzah Al
   Hussein
Michael Hargreave
Timothy Hargreave
Michael & Judith Harper
George Harper
Simon Harrap
Peter Harrild
John R. Harris
Alastair Harrison
E. Harrison
Martin Harrison
Andrew Richard Harrison
Luke Hartley
Edward Hasell McCosh
David Haskoll
Howard Hastings
Mr & Mrs S.J. Haycock
John Hay-Edie

Toby J.W. Head
Algernon Heber-Percy
David Heimann
Michael Henderson
Cecil Q. Henriques
Lord Herbert
Christopher Hermon-Taylor
Archie Herries
Tim Hersey
Tim Hewitt
Oliver Hicks
Alexander Hicks
Eugene Higgins
Henry Highley
Sam Highley
John Hignett
Roderic Hill
O.R. Hilton-Johnson
Guy R.A. Hindley
Janak & Mona Hirdaramani
Alex Hodgson
David W. Holdsworth
A.D.R. Holland
Dr J.E. Holland
J.N.C. Hollins-Gibson
B.H.J. Holloway
Dr C. McKinnon Holmes
Anouchka Holmes
Mrs R.A.A. Holt
Michael Hosking
D.G. Howes
Gurth Hoyer Millar
Guy W.C. Huber
John Hudson-Davies
Alexander Hughes
L.B.C.C. Humphreys-Davies
P.D. Hunter
B. Hurl
Guy Hurley
Giles P.D. Hurley
Raymond Hurst
Mr & Mrs Robin Hutchins
Jonathan W.M. Hwang
Cynthia Ingraham
Tim Ingram
Edward S. Iskandar
Seraphine V. Iskandar
Israni Family
Walter Ivens
Michael Jackson
Rupert Jacobs
Byram N. Jeejeebhoy
Dr O.H. Jefferis
Niels Jensen
Ms Cao Gui Jie
Tom E. Johnson
Adam C. Johnston
C.E. Jones
Elizabeth Jones
Frederick W. Kalborg
Dr Patrick J. Kaye
Lt Col J.R.D. Kaye
R.J.M. Keatley

J.M.S. Keen
A. Graham Keighley
C.A.H. Kemp
James Kennerley
Ben Kilpatrick
James Kininmonth
Brad Kirkland
Jonathan Kitchen
Sergey Kiyashko
Mr & Mrs Kiyashko
Laurence Knight
Christopher A. Knowles-Fitton
Ms. S Krywald-Sanders
Jason Kuok
Lai Cheuk Kwan Arthur
Ian Kwok
Francis Kyle
John Lade Inskipp
John F.S. Laing
James Lambert
Christopher R. Lambourne
Dr F.R. & Mrs A. Lamont
H.A. & C. Lamotte
Stuart Lancely
John Lander
Hugh Lang
Peter Latilla-Campbell
Mr & Mrs S.K. Lawrence
A.T. Lawson-Cruttenden
Edward M. Lawton
J.F. Leaf
Mr & Mrs John Leat
Mrs John Lecky
Tae Jik Lee
Matthew Harold Leggett
Peter-Carlo Lehrell
Paul D. Leigh
J.P. Lemmon
Capt. & Mrs N.S. Lemos
Major Joseph E. Lesser
A.P. Leventis
H.K. Leventis
M.J.W. Levien
The London Library
Carole Lindgren
Christopher W.M. Lipka
Mrs Rupert Litherland
Marcus Littlejohns
William Littlejohns
Mrs Rhidian Llewellyn
Alexander Lloyd-Jones
Chulayuth Lochotinan
C.L.J. Lock-Necrews
J. Lotery
Gordon Loughridge
Alastair Lowe
Guy Luck
Brook Lyons
G.E.W. MacFarlane
Colin I.C. MacGregor
Frederick I.A. MacGregor
D.W.T. MacKenzie
Guy Edward MacKenzie

Alec C.G. Mackie
C.G. Mackie
Duncan Macpherson
Dr Jane MacRae
Farida & Zafar Malik
Suzi & David Malin-Hyams
C. de L. Mann
Jonathan Marks
Christopher Marsden-Smedley
N.G. Marshall
W.T. Martin
Manuel J. Martins
Edward M.N. Martins
William Massey
P.T.E. Massey
C.D. Massiah
A.M. Master
P.H. Master
P. Mastima
Sir Carol Mather
Daniel Mather
Adrian May
R.C. Maydon
Wing Cdr. H. Maynard Mitchell
N.A.H. Maytum
J.R.M. McBeath
Michael McClelland
Charles W.B. McClure
Felix C. McClure
Thomas D. McClure
Luke W. McClure
Colin McCorquodale
Oliver McEvoy
James A.C. McGowan
Ben J.E. McLean
James A.J. McLean
Colin W.D. McLean
John McMullen
Fergus J. McMullen
Charles Meaden
Mr & Mrs Robert Mears
John D. Mee
Elizabeth Mee
Nilesh P. Mehta
Alexander Melnikoff
His Hon. James Mendl
Alastair L.D. Meneely
Mr & Mrs T. Messel
R.E. Micklem
T.W. Micklem
C.R. Miller
James Miller (1948²)
James Miller (1975³)
John Miller
T.W. Miller-Jones
Lord Millett
J. Milligan-Manby
George E. Milligen
J.R.F. Mills
Mr E. & Mrs N. Minne
James Minoprio
Hugo Minoprio
Stephen Minoprio

Richard D. Minoprio
F.C. Minoprio
John Minoprio
F.P. Mitchell
Paul Mitchell
William E. Mocatta
C. Patrick Molony
Keith Moores
John K.S. Morgan
Kenneth F. Morgan
Hamish M. Morrison
Graham Morrison
Richard Morrissey
Philipp Mosimann
Nicholas Moss
Andrew Moss
John Gordon Mucklow
Sean Mullaney
Kevin Mullaney
Mrs P.J. Murphy
D. Mark Narayn
R.H.B. Neame
J.B. Neame
A.R.B. Neame
Richard D.S. Neave
Marcia Neely
Amos J. Nelson
Sir Paul Newall
S. Niarchos
W.J. Nicholson
Frank Nicholson
Sir Paul Nicholson
W.F.P. Noad
Alfred Nock
Mrs M. Noble
Philip Noble
Dr Remington Norman
J.E.T. North
Stephen E. Norton
Mr & Mrs F.W. Notenboom
Oliver D. Nutt
Mr & Mrs Edward Obiora
Prince Nicholas Obolensky
Christopher & Nneka Okeke
Terence & Charles de Pentheny
   O'Kelly
His Hon. Judge Openshaw
A.E. Oppenheimer
Arnaut Orford
Jonathan Orme
Sir Simon & Lady Orr-Ewing
Mr & Mrs Robert A. Osborn
Charles Osborne
Selwyn Moresby Owen
S.G. Pampanini
Mr & Mrs Richard Parkinson
Sir John Parsons
R.W. Parsonson
Prof. & Mrs Lissouba Pascal
D.F.E. Paske
Dr & Mrs H.S. Patel
Robert Paterson
John Patrick

Major J.H.H. Peile
James Pembroke
Robin Pender
Mrs Serena Percival
Stuart L. Perry
Mr & Mrs J. Pexton
R.L. Phillips
David B. Phillips
R.H.C. Phillips
Dennis Pinkstone
S. Pleydell-Bouverie
Nicholas W. Porritt
Sir Jonathan Portal
Cdr & Mrs R.A. Preece
James E. Prentice
Richard Prideaux-Brune
John C.L. Prior
Andrew J.L. Prior
Edward C.L. Prior
David Proger
T.G. Proger
Elke Gräfin Pückler
James Purcell
A.C. Quilter
Guy Quilter
Peter H. Radcliffe
Dr John Rae
Datin S.A.B.A. Rahim
Prakarn Raiva
I.S.M. Rea
Alistair R.W. Read
Jason Read
Pat Read
Peter Readman
Charlie Reid
Hubert Reid
Simon D. Reid
Charles Reynard
Mr & Mrs Paul Reynolds
Ryan D.W. Reynolds
Mr & Mrs R.J.G. Richards
Dominic H. Ricketts
Mrs Jane Riddell
G.J.F.T. Rippingall
Richard Ritchie
Michael H. Robinson
Alexander Roche
Michael G. Rodopoulos
Dr Torben M. Roepstorff
R.B.B. Ropner
J.G. Ropner
J.C. Ropner
Bruce Ropner
Vicomte Roland de Rosiere
David J. Ross
W. M. Ross-Wilson
James A.E. Rous
Richard W.J. Rous
B.H. Rowles
Peter Royle
Godfrey C. Royle
Christopher Rui Chieh Chang
Waleed Saigol

Muwaffag Salti
S.C. Sampson
Susie Sanders
John L. Sanderson
V.L. Sankey
Constantin Peter Schmitz
Mr & Mrs Thomas Schoch
Prof. F.D. Schofield
Alexander Schouvaloff
Mark C. Schueppert
Mark W. Scicluna
Mrs Caroline Scott
Jamie Scott
Dr & Mrs D.G. Scotter
William Scully
Nigel Seale
Richard L. Seaman
Peter H. Seed
M.P. Seed
C.J. Seligman
H.C. Seligman
W.H. Seligman
Nigel Seligman
D.G. Seliquiau
Sebastian J. Serrell-Watts
C.P. Sewell
Roy Graham Seymour
J.R. Shannon
R.S.D. Sharp
Tony & Anne Shellim
Robert E. Sheridan III
Robert Sherlock
Richard Shirley-Smith
Azad Shivdasani
Maroi Shoji
Mrs J. Short
Ben Siah Cy
Peter R. Siddons
Geoffrey R. Simmonds
Sarah & Robert Simpson
Stuart & Paula Sinclair
D.A. Sinclair Scott
Forbes Singer
Narttaya Sirimongkolkasem
E.M. Skinner
Fred Slater
Sam Slater
H.J.C. Smethurst
Alexander J.B. Smith
James Smith
Brian Smouha
Nicholas B. Snow
Anthony Speelman
Mr & Mrs M.A. Spencer
Oliver Spindler
Fred Spratt
The Hon. Michael Spring Rice
James E. Stafford Allen
Richard J. Stanes
J.M. Stayt
Jonathan Stedall
Michael J.A. Stephens
T.N. Stephens

T.C. Stephenson
Mrs Stephenson
Mark Stewart
N.G. Stogdon
The Ven. T.V. Stoney
Stephen Stout-Kerr
D.C. Straker
Hugo Stratford-Hall
Barton Stratford-Hall
Brian Straton-Ferrier
Patrick Streeter
J.A. Streeter
John Y.R. Strover
Colin Stroyan
R.A.R. Stroyan
M.J. Stuart-Grumbar
Peter D. Sullivan
John B. Sunley
John R. Swain
W.L.G. Swan
C.A.S. Swan
Sebastian Swarbreck
Anthony Swinburne-Johnson
Maj. Gen. Sir John Swinton
Tai Ying Loong
HRH Prince Talal bin Muhammad
Nigel E.C. Talbot-Ponsonby
Nicholas & Jane Taylor
M.J.E. Taylor
Julian Taylor
Lt Col D.R. Tetley
Garry F.D. Tetley
Richard R. Thayer
Geoffrey Theobald
A.C. Theobald
H.J. Theobald
O.H. Theobald
Mr & Mrs S.C. Thomas
Myles Thompson
Nimble Thompson

J.P.B. Thompson
S.S.M.B. Thomson
E.J. Thornton
Christian Thwaites
C.S. Tolman
Oliver James Michael Tomalin
M.H. Tomalin
Mr & Mrs Robert M. Tomlin
Leo Tong
Princess Nathalia Sophia
    Toumanova
Ian Tower
Dow Travers
A. Travis
Miss Caroline Treffgarne
Guy Tregoning
Oliver Tregoning
Hugh Trevor-Jones
Peter Trinder
P.H. Trollope
Bertie Troughton
Jonathan Trower
J.O.R. Tupper
James W.H. Turner
C.H.E. Tyson
His Hon. Judge J.E. Van Der Werff
J.D.C. Vargas
J.J.S. Veisblat
Edward Versen
A. Villas-Boas
Dr & Mrs G. Visick
Vichai Viturawong
Dr Patrick Vivian
Simon Vivian
Mrs C.D. Voelcker
Levin-Friedrich von Bismarck
Dominik A. von Bohlen und
    Halbach
Hugh & Netta Wace
P.D. Wachman

Frederick Wade
F.J.D. Wakeham
Richard M. Walden
Hugh Richard Walduck
Nicholas Stanley R.D. Walduck
Stephen Walduck
T.H. Walduck
M.C. Walford
Dr D.M.C. Walker
Sir Timothy Walker
R.J.B. Walker
J.B.A. Wallace
Ian H. Wallace
Timothy R. Ward
Julien Ward
Oliver Ward
M.C.B. Ward
C.B.M. Ward
F.P.N. Ward
C. Roger P. Ward
C.V.D. Wardell
Mrs Michael Warren
Peter Warren
Alexander Watson
S.C.H. Watson
P.H. Watson
Ewan Wauchope
Major P.E. Webb
Robert Weeber
W.A. Weir
James Wellwood
J.S. Wellwood
Alexander Welman
Timothy W. West
Mr & Mrs Graham J. West
M.E. Weston-Dictus
David P. Wheeler
Major J.F.T. Wheen
Dr & Mrs Ian R. White
Mrs Gretchen White

Dr. Jeffrey White
Sir George White
W.E. Whitehouse-Vaux
Henry V. White-Smith
Ian L. White-Thomson
Gillian Whitmee
Laurence Whyatt
Alan Wightman
Charlie Wilce
Karim Wilkins
E.W.B. Williams
R. Gerald Williamson
A.D. Willis
Andrew G. Wilson
Major Richard Wilson
Thomas D. Wilson
Sir David Wilson
K.G. Wingfield Digby
A.S.R. de W. Winlaw
R.T.G. Winter
C.G.M. Wishart
Marcus Wisskirchen
Roland & Diana Habdank
    Wojewodzki
Mr & Mrs Bruce Wong
Hiram Wong
C.J.B. Wood
Capt. B.A.V. Wooley
T.D.C. Woolland
Fred Woolley
William Worsley
W.G. Wright
N.J.S. Wyatt
James Wyman
Kim K. Wynes
Rhydain Wynn-Williams
Trevor C.H. Yang
M.A. Yannaghas
Marc-Antoine Zora

Index of names

Picture acknowledgements

Julian Andrews 56-58
Peter Beckwith 199
Tim Bentinck 171, 173
Roddy Bloomfield 119–122
James Fife 99
Fox Talbot Competition 114
Sir Jeremy Greenstock 187
Mark Greenstock 165–167
Pen Hadow 174–175
Harrow School Archive
    endpapers, 11, 12, 13, 18, 22, 23,

26, 27, 30, 36, 42, 53, 60, 61, 74, 79,
85, 87, 88, 89, 92, 94, 104, 105,
117, 124, 127, 142, 143, 160, 169,
170, 171, 172, 175, 183, 184, 206,
210–214
Patick Kaye 2, 215
Hugh Lang 105
Jeremy Lemmon 68–71
Michael Levien 116, 118, 126
Patrick Lichfield 3, 6, 8, 29, 130–131
Stephen Minoprio 77

Xin Pang 16, 45, 65, 107, 144
Chris Phillips/The Old Speech
    Room Gallery 43, 47–51, 84, 137,
    155–158, 196
Chris Phillips/Frank Nicholson 115
Hugh Saxton 150–151
Geoffrey Shakerley 10, 21, 24, 25,
    32, 37, 44, 57
Richard Shirley-Smith 112–114
Jonathan Stedall 134
John Stenhouse 135, 145–146

David Stogdon 59, 91, 125
Martin Tyrell/Ryan Theatre
    176–178
Dale Vargas 17, 31, 33–35, 41, 66,
    106, 123, 125, 180, 182, 202, 209
Tom Wickson 85, 90

Other pictures are from the Harrow
Collection